Theatre and Change
in
South Africa

Contemporary Theatre Studies

A series of books edited by Franc Chamberlain, Nene College, UK

Please see back of this book for the other titles in the Contemporary Theatre
Studies series.

Theatre and Change
in
South Africa

edited

by

Geoffrey V. Davis

Rheinisch-Westfälische Technische Hochschule, Aachen, Germany

and

Anne Fuchs

Université de Nice–Sophia Antipolis, Nice, France

in collaboration with the
Institut de Recherches Interéthniques et Interculturelles
(IDERIC)
de l'Université de Nice–Sophia Antipolis

ho
ap

harwood academic publishers
Australia • China • France • Germany • India • Japan • Luxembourg
Malaysia • The Netherlands • Russia • Singapore • Switzerland
Thailand • United Kingdom • United States

Emmaplein 5
1075 AW Amsterdam
The Netherlands

Cover drawing: *Preparing for the Day* by W. Kentridge.

British Library Cataloguing in Publication Data

Davis, Geoffrey V.
    Theatre and Change in South Africa. –
    (Contemporary Theatre Studies, ISSN
    1049-6513; Vol. 12)
    I. Title II. Fuchs, Anne III. Series
    792.0968

    ISBN 3-7186-5650-7 (hardback)
    ISBN 3-7186-5651-5 (softback)

For Michel

and
in memory of Barney Simon (1932–1995)
to whom South African theatre owes so much

CONTENTS

INTRODUCTION TO THE SERIES

Contemporary Theatre Studies is a book series of special interest to everyone involved in theatre. It consists of monographs on influential figures, studies of movements and ideas in theatre, as well as primary material consisting of theatre-related documents, performing editions of plays in English, and English translations of plays from various vital theatre traditions worldwide.

Franc Chamberlain

LIST OF PLATES

ACKNOWLEDGEMENTS

A project such as this cannot be completed without the editors incurring many debts of gratitude. First and foremost, we have to thank our contributors, some of whom function as theatre practitioners in the most difficult – and often violent – of circumstances, and yet found the time to give interviews and prepare articles for us.

Our thanks go to Malcolm Purkey and Pippa Stein, our hosts in Johannesburg, who together with their neighbours William and Anne Kentridge, proved the most hospitable of friends and resourceful of informants.

To Stephen Gray go our thanks for many kindnesses, not least his introductions to a seemingly inexhaustible circle of friends in the arts.

Many people gave us the benefit of their experience, among them Andries Oliphant and Matthew Krouse of COSAW, Barney Simon of the Market Theatre and Phillip Stein of Vita Awards.

Funding from the University of Nice made possible Anne Fuchs's journey to South Africa and Geoffrey Davis's appointment to the English Department, which greatly facilitated cooperation on this project.

Geoffrey Davis acknowledges the generosity of St. Edmund Hall, Oxford, which provided a most congenial working environment during the final phase of preparations.

We are particularly grateful to the Editor of *The Weekly Mail* and *The Guardian* for granting us permission to reprint articles relating to Matthew Krouse's work which appear in the Appendix.

To Michel Fuchs, Corinna Wohlfarth and Rüdiger Schreyer go our admiration for their successful battling with computer technology on our behalf; and to our publishers, our thanks for their commitment to this project.

Geoffrey V. Davis and Anne Fuchs

INTRODUCTION

I. HISTORY OF THE PROJECT

The initiative for this collaborative volume we owe to an idea of Jacques Alvarez-Péreyre, one of the pioneers of South African studies in France.

Two events may be said to have played a formative role in the evolution of this project. In 1989 the Evangelische Akademie of Bad Boll in Southern Germany organised a symposium on South African drama, which was attended by the editors as well as by Chris Balme, Mark Fleishman, Matsemela Manaka and Malcolm Purkey. Subsequently, the editors organised a special session devoted to developments in contemporary South African theatre at the Modern Languages Association Convention held in Chicago in 1990. Malcolm Purkey and the editors presented papers on the work of the Market Theatre and on Junction Avenue Theatre's *Tooth and Nail*, while Matsemela Manaka spoke about his own work for the theatre. This preliminary view of the field served to focus our ideas and led us to formulate our concept of a book which would be devoted primarily to theatre practitioners, writers, directors, actors and cultural activists, rather than critics.

After several earlier separate visits to South Africa, we undertook a research trip together in the autumn of 1992 to gather material, carry out interviews and enlist further prospective contributors. Our desire to visit the Grahamstown Festival, which annually provides a useful overview of the state of theatre arts in South Africa, was unfortunately thwarted by the fact that it falls within the European university summer term. We were, however, extremely fortunate to find ourselves confronted in Johannesburg with a rich array of theatrical and cultural events. The range of theatrical fare on offer was astonishing. There may very well be a crisis in theatre in South Africa as elsewhere, but it did not seem to lie in the quality of the productions.

Athol Fugard's *Playland* was on at the Market Theatre, superbly acted by John Kani and Sean Taylor; Barney Simon had brought the Chilean playwright Ariel Dorfman's *Death and the Maiden* to South Africa; William Kentridge had devised a memorable version of

Büchner's *Woyzeck*, renamed *Woyzeck on the Highveld*, using puppets and animation; Paul Slabolepszy had two shows on at the Laager, *Mooi Street Moves* and *The Return of Elvis du Pisanie*, while Pieter-Dirk Uys had revived his long-running *An Evening with Evita Bezuidenhout*. This book, we hope, reflects something of the excitement of that period of theatrical activity which we were fortunate enough to experience.

II. MAJOR THEMES

Between them our contributors have an extraordinary wealth of experience in the theatre. They include playwrights and actors, visual artists and poets, directors and administrators, theatre critics and academics in the fields of theatre studies and sociology. Some have combined several of these functions in the course of their careers. A number of them have worked together in theatre companies whose productions have proved of seminal importance for the future direction of South African theatre, prime among them Workshop '71, the Market Theatre Company and Junction Avenue Theatre Company. Many have gained experience of theatre practice overseas while working for higher degrees, touring shows, directing performances, lecturing or living in exile. Two bring the perspective of the returned exile to bear on the question of change in contemporary theatre.

Other circumstances — personal, political, ideological — and other editors — particularly those with the immediacy of experience gained from living continuously inside the country — would have produced a different book, perhaps even a radically different one, by a different set of contributors. Yet we believe that the contributions assembled in these pages record an exciting and stimulating, if perhaps inevitably partial view of the state of theatre at a particular historical juncture.[1]

The issues addressed, the experiences recounted and often reassessed, the solutions proposed, the degree of theatrical innovation and experimental exuberance evinced, and not least the sheer determination to survive combine to give the reader a sense both of the real and present difficulties theatre is facing and of its possible future orientations at one of the most complex moments of political transition in the history of South African society.

Theatre in South Africa, it has been said, has long been ahead of political events, has pioneered social change. Will it rise, then, to the

---

[1] Our cut-off date was effectively early 1993.

considerable challenges posed by the rapid political transformation we are currently witnessing? It is to this fundamental question that the contributors to the present volume — in their various ways — seek to offer an answer.

It is clear that political change on such a scale will engender, indeed already is engendering change in many aspects of theatre. As the now "irreversible" move towards a hopefully democratic, non-racial, post-apartheid society gathers pace, the nature of the required changes will become more apparent. These will affect the themes playwrights write about, the formal aesthetics they adopt and the theories evolved about their work in like measure. Past achievements will have to be re-evaluated as new priorities are established. New forms of theatrical organisation will have to be put in place more appropriate to altered political circumstances.

Our contributors, it will be seen, are caught up in an active process of reflection and reappraisal. They are redefining their aims, artistic and political, searching for new and vital theatrical forms commensurate to the challenges posed. The series of difficult, self-critical questions raised by Malcolm Purkey, for instance, in the light of his own experience working on Junction Avenue's highly experimental project *Tooth and Nail* are in fact those all our contributors have to face: can theatre continue to maintain its autonomy and to exercise its critical role? Can one rethink form and find new content? Can a concept of post-protest literature be developed? Can theatre involve itself in the process of societal transformation? How might theatre contribute to a post-apartheid society?

Such questions are being posed in the context of a re-assessment of what has constituted South African theatre hitherto over the decades of apartheid during which all manner of constraints — apartheid legislation, bannings, censorship, media restrictions — hampered theatrical work. Now that many of these have fallen away and new possibilities are opening up, which will be subject no doubt to restrictions of a different, presumably financial order, many of our authors are asking what the essential contribution of the theatre companies has been to date. Robert McLaren, fresh from the experience of returning to South Africa after fifteen years, looks back over the history of Workshop '71, identifying its lasting significance in its early espousal of values and practices which have become fundamental to any notion of a democratic, non-racial society. Barney Simon reviews the Market Theatre's struggle to survive in terms of the extraordinary stimulation to theatre offered by South African society, of the "reference to life" apparent in all its efforts. His political commitment to a multi-racial society and his celebration of the "dignity" of work inform many of the papers collected here. Malcolm Purkey writes of the history of Junction Avenue, analysing the Company's workshop process, its commitment to "issue-driven" theatre and drawing the lessons from the "partial success" of its most recent project *Tooth and Nail*. Ari Sitas summarizes the genesis and growing influence of the Workers' Theatre which has emerged from the social and industrial struggles in Natal, attributing its increasing influence to its stubborn overcoming of the almost insurmountable odds represented by social deprivation, unemployment, exploitation, even the deaths of its members at the hands of vigilantes. Anthony Akerman contributes an informative autobiographical piece on the experience of directing and writing South African plays as an exile in Holland. Matthew Krouse offers an often hilarious account of the fate of his irreverent cabaret show *Famous Dead Man* at the hands of the censors.

The process of change in South African society will require theatre to address new themes and evolve new forms. That new forms of social participation are already being developed is instanced by Doreen Mazibuko's project in compiling and directing a play to educate black audiences in the practice of voting during the run-up to the first non-racial election in 1994. Hers is of course not the only such project. The Handspring Puppet Theatre Company, for example, is currently exploring possibilities of theatre-in-education as a means of bringing training in science to disadvantaged school children.

The process of social transformation poses acutely the question of theatrical form, which has of course long preoccupied progressive theatre makers. Purkey's *Tooth and Nail* project has already been mentioned. But there have been other experiments worthy of note. William Kentridge expounds here the formal and theoretical thinking informing his transposition of Büchner's *Woyzeck* to the highveld, adducing his sense of the landscape around Johannesburg, the use of puppets and video animation, the development of localised characters and the genesis of the musical score. Mark Fleishman, too, seeks to imaginatively transcend the limitations of the written word through advanced formal experimentation, evinced in his attention to the role of the physical image.

In South Africa formal experimentation can of course draw on a wide range of hitherto often neglected African cultural sources. Peter Horn, himself a poet, points to the potentialities inherent in the figure of the traditional praise-singer, whose role is currently being reactivated in the context of working-class and trade-union culture, while

Maishe Maponya emphasises the importance of custom and ritual in African performance styles.

What type of theatre will in the event prove most productive in the future of course remains a matter for conjecture. In a magisterial survey of the whole range of South African theatre, Zakes Mda predicts, in spite of a certain scepticism regarding the recent projects of such as Manaka and Mazibuko, that it is with Organic Workers' Theatre and Theatre for Development, forms that would ensure democratic participation, that the future of South African theatre lies.

Three of the papers included here address questions of theory, which may also be seen to be exercising the minds and informing the projects of the practitioners. Brian Crow and Chris Balme examine performance practice in several of the plays which have brought South African theatre to the attention of international audiences. Crow takes the example of the early workshopped productions of Athol Fugard, John Kani and Winston Ntshona to analyse the nature of the unusual collaboration of white and black, playwright and actors within apartheid structures, distinguishing the dimensions of theatricality, both psychological and social, involved in that process, and thereby implying the question as to how such collaborations might be constituted in a post-apartheid society. Balme subjects the performance aesthetics of the highly successful plays of Mbongeni Ngema and Percy Mtwa to rigorous analysis in an effort to define how they function on stage, questioning whether "this tried and proven theatrical idiom" will be preserved in future or abandoned in favour of new forms of expression. In spite of the overseas success of *Sarafina*, it would seem that the latter is more likely and in the opinion of contributor Jerry Mofokeng, who looks at the way such plays project and distort South African experience overseas, it is certainly more desirable. Martin Orkin, who here joins the debate over what actually constitutes the "popular" in township theatre, is similarly of the opinion that such theatre has now exhausted what he terms its "original contestatory impetus" and should give way to new forms of theatre foregrounding "present struggle" in which ideological positions and oppositional stances will be less idealised, more diverse and, in the light of social development, more complex.

Social change has led, not least in the arts, to the breaking-up of apartheid structures and to a rapid movement towards the setting-up of new democratic organisations to replace them. It is true that this process has encountered many obstacles and that the birth of new structures has been and is being accompanied by much resistance as those who have for so long determined the course of the arts in South

Africa see their fiefdoms under well-organised and intensifying attacks. The final contributions to this book are most revealing on the
struggle to establish new representative organisations. ANC member
Carol Steinberg and theatre critic Arnold Blumer look at how political
change has begun to undermine the position of the traditionally white-
dominated regional Performing Arts Councils and analyse the options
open to them if they are to survive meaningfully in the post-apartheid
period. (Interested readers will no doubt have been following the very
rapid sequence of transformations which have taken place in the short
space of time since these articles were written). Finally Ramolao
Makhene, in an absorbing interview surveying the whole course of his
varied and influential career as actor and activist, stresses the importance of creating new organisational structures not just within the
theatres themselves, their managements and administrations, but for
and on behalf of theatre workers too. His account constitutes a unique
inside view of the formation of PAWE — the Performing Arts Workers
Equity — and of its initial successes amid the complexities of changing
theatre structures, the ending of the cultural boycott and the re-order-
ing of funding priorities on the part of donors.

Much of what now happens in theatre, as in the wider South
African social formation, will depend on a general willingness to resolve a myriad of political problems equitably. That this is not at
present entirely the case is revealed by the on-going violence racking
the country. This affects everyone in South Africa, including theatre
workers. Ari Sitas's reference to the deaths of members of workers'
theatre groups in Natal is only one instance. There are many more.
Fatima Dike here provides a moving gloss on the title of her play *So
What's New?* to recount the effects of the violence that now surrounds
her in her daily life in a township. Our interview with Barney Simon
abounds with the evidence of violence: the case of his housekeeper
accused of being a witch, her house burnt down; the decline in audience figures due to a fear of violence even in the centres of the cities;
the violent circumstances in which performances are mounted in war-
torn townships like Sebokeng.

That theatre life continues at all in such conditions is a source
of wonder.

III. OTHER ASPECTS

The very richness of the ever-changing theatre scene precluded asking
each and every South African practitioner to contribute to this volume,

but there are nevertheless some aspects of the theatre and some practitioners that we and any specialist reader would have enjoyed hearing
about. In the latter category must be placed one of the great father-
figures of South African theatre, Gibson Kente. Kente, whose township
morality musicals inspired other black South African playwrights and
directors, not only trained generations of actors and singers including
Mbongeni Ngema, Percy Mtwa and Gcina Mhlophe but, one might
almost say, really introduced urban black South African audiences to
the very concept of popular theatre, or at least to theatre which both
entertains and has relevance to their own lives in the townships. We
have recently learned that Kente has made a return to one of the
formative influences on his own work, Dorkay House, where in the
late fifties and early sixties he had taken part in the classes and productions organised by Union Artists; he very soon left to further an
independent career in the townships. But 1992 saw Kente back at
Dorkay House, advising, teaching, becoming the mentor to the new
generation of urban black theatre enthusiasts. What will come of this
is yet to be seen, but most certainly it is an important aspect of South
African theatre which has yet to be fully told.

   Another aspect to be noted both in the townships and the rural
areas is the ground swell of training and experimentation taking place;
the old Bapedi hall in Meadowlands is still functioning as a training
centre and will soon be renovated to produce more urban black talent;
Akakani in the Northern Transvaal is a centre which uses drama for
development, creating and teaching through the methods of Augusto
Boal. We should have liked to know more. Historically, too, the work
of Zakes Mda with the Maratholi Travelling Theatre was of great
importance, but this has been well-documented by Zakes himself in his
recent book.[2] How much should this volume, indeed, concern itself
with the past? Workshop '71, Fugard and the *Woza Albert!* tradition can
be seen as seminal influences on the way theatre is changing today; the
later work of the practitioners involved we have by and large excluded
to make place for new and fresh contributions to the theatre scene. We
do however regret the absence of analysis of the work of Matsemela
Manaka who was originally one of the moving spirits of this publication. Here another element intervened: township violence, family deaths,
financial problems, all prevented Matsemela from finding the time to
be interviewed or write about his own work. In particular it would

---

[2] Zakes Mda, *When People Play People*, (Johannesburg: Witwatersrand University Press and London: Zed Books, 1993).

have been interesting to have his views on the future of South African theatre, his many experimental plays would have well qualified him to talk of the changing scene. *Ekhaya – Coming Home* in its various versions was one of the first plays about the exiles returning to South Africa; this physical but also cultural return was translated into the very performance practice with, originally, exiled actors taking rôles and music by exiles being introduced.

Then there is the paradoxically thriving Natal theatre scene with its important component of Indian theatre which ranges from the rising Ismael Mahomed to Saira Essa and Charles Pillai not forgetting Ronnie and Kessie Govender and Essop Khan. The new face on the scene was Ismael Mahomed whose vivacious satirical discussion of the traditional values of Indian family life in South Africa in his play *Purdah* caused quite a stir. But Mahomed does not confine himself to the Indian scene alone and his double bill of *Boere Orkes* and *Potjiekos* in 1993 at the Windybrow Theatre in Johannesburg explored more particularly the Afrikaner soul but also the general changing situation in South Africa. Apart from Natal's Indian playwrights and the Natal Workers' Theatre Movement which produced such plays as *The Long March* and *Bambatha's Children*, the region has been well known in the past for the controversies surrounding the Natal Playhouse, home to Natal's Performing Arts Council (Napac). The ebullient Nicholas Ellenbogen eventually left the organisation to set up his own brand of "Theatre for Africa", much lauded by British royals and a recurrent triumph on the Grahamstown Fringe. With his departure (although not directly connected with it) Napac's finances slid into permanent crisis with Durban Council finally refusing to foot the bill until an evaluation committee had reported on its shortcomings. Hoping to save its orchestra and dance company through local community involvement this Performing Arts Council will have to agree to fundamental restructuring not only of its performing organisations, but of its very board of directors. Maybe its dramatic fall will, as Humphrey Tyler suggested in an article in the *Weekly Mail* in June 1993, show the way to the restructuring of the other Arts Councils whose situation is discussed in this volume.[3]

---

[3] By 1995 Napac had embarked on restructuring, with a new board of directors — notably including Mbongeni Ngema — and had been renamed *The Playhouse*.

IV. SOUTH AFRICAN THEATRE IN 1993

The Grahamstown Festival as usual took the temperature of South African theatre. On the whole it confirmed the position of those who had already shown their capacity for adapting to change way back in the 1980's, figures such as Paul Slabolepszy, Pieter-Dirk Uys, Andrew Buckland and Reza de Wet who all showed at the Standard Bank National Arts Festival of 1993 that they had not abandoned a pioneering spirit. Paul Slabolepszy was present with the well-tried, soul-searching delusions of the poor white Afrikaner in *The Return of Elvis du Pisanie*. There was nothing revolutionary about this crazed and mind-blasting reworking of Barney Simon's *Hey Listen* from the 1970's however much the audience roared its approval of Slabolepszy's own virtuoso performance. More geared to change, although desperately short of new theatrical ploys, was his other 1992 production: *Mooi Street Moves*. What was new was the portrayal of the black character/white character encounter which can be found in so many of Slabolepszy's other plays (and indeed in those of Fugard), but which has the setting and the tables turned. Here the setting is new urban multi-racial Hillbrow and the black character, so often in the past asserting a mere moral superiority, displays in this instance the superior ease of one who is in charge of his own physical environment.

At the time of writing Pieter-Dirk Uys, following his own (or P. W. Botha's) precept of "Adapt or di(y)e" tries, while retaining his performances in drag as the basis of his one-man-shows, to deal with the new situation through what Robert Greig calls the "split self" of the insider and the outsider.[4] Evita Bezuidenhout remains very much the staunch insider in contrast with her worldly-wise sister, Bambi Kellerman, who returns to South Africa after her marriage with an ex-Nazi.

If P.-D. Uys has found a vehicle for his ambiguous attitude to life, sex and South Africa, Andrew Buckland continues his perpetual search for new theatrical form. From his 1986 *Pas de Deux*, through the *Ugly Noonoo* and *Between the Teeth*, to his 1993 *Bloodstream* and the postmodernist *Manifesto II*, the young author-actor-director has continually experimented with theatrical space, movement and language. It would seem that (although Junction Avenue's *Tooth and Nail* is a comparable

---

[4] Robert Greig, "Time to say boo to the bogey," in *Weekly Mail*, July 16th 1993, p. 37.

attempt) no one has so far explored theatrical form in South Africa with such sheer technical brilliance allied to meaningful topicality for those who can read the signs.

South Africa's multiple theatre scene is indeed outmatched by its multiple audience potential: learning to read the signs in theatre can be a vertical progression but it is more often a horizontal challenge. Reza de Wet's plays, often clothed in Afrikaner myth and magic realism such as 1992's *Mirakel* and 1993's *Mis*, can only be understood by an Afrikaans-speaking audience, whether it be for the language or the peculiarly Afrikaner ethos; this does not mean that her plays are not connected to change.

However, appealing to all audiences, and this often through the universal appeal of music, seems to have been a major preoccupation in 1993 Grahamstown. Three white culture-brokers directed, helped direct, or composed musical plays which critic Robert Greig accused of being 'Golden Bough' theatre,[5] something to do with political correctness, with audience and producers throwing overboard Eurocentric baggage and crossing over aesthetically to make the right kind of identifications. Be this as it may, what one may ask is the alternative to being politically correct? Perhaps what Greig objects to most are the fables with problems resolved by magic and Africans treated in "noble savage terms". That Hilary Blecher, who had previously adapted and directed *Poppie Nongena* at the Market, should return to South Africa to direct *Daughter of Nebo* with outstanding artists such as Arthur Molepo, musicians Victor Ntoni and Rashid Lanie, designer Sarah Roberts and choreographer Nomsa Manaka, only adds to her credentials as a progressive director. The credentials of Phyllis Klotz, joint Director with Smal Ndaba of *Ubuntu Bomhlaba* are those of a dedicated community arts worker from her associations and contribution to *You Strike the Woman, You Strike the Rock* through her subsequent contributions to the Sibikwa Community Theatre Project. And if *The Daughter of Nebo* and Capab's *Orphans Of Qumbu* were initially based on ideas imposed from without the Black community, *Ubuntu Bomhlaba* originated very much from within. *Orphans of Qumbu*, a western-style opera composed by Michael Williams was part of Capab's Outreach programme and used Black community singers from the Grahamstown township which to some extent answered criticisms of all former Festivals which had failed to address the needs and expectations of the

---

[5] ibid

Black population of Grahamstown. Another musical at the Festival which Greig did not put in the 'Golden Bough' category as it dealt with United States and South African civil rights issues today rather than the issues in traditional communities was also the work of a returning exile, Duma Ndlovu, and the king-pin of the South African musical, Mbongeni Ngema. Change this time came from a less South African-centred vision than that of Ngema's previous works.

V. WHICH THEATRE FOR WHAT AUDIENCE?

That the South African theatre scene in general is looking more towards the world outside is undeniable. Exiles are returning with skills learned overseas, an institution such as the Grahamstown Festival awaits with some trepidation the influx of foreign productions which might well overshadow indigenous work. But other companies are eager to learn and to experiment with new ideas: Malcolm Purkey recounts having been influenced by foreign theatre forms; both Matsemela Manaka's Soyikwa Theatre Company and Smal Ndaba's and Phyllis Klotz's Sibikwa Theatre Company have looked to the rest of Africa for new musical instruments and forms. It would seem that both looking for, and coming to terms with, performance arts from elsewhere (although we can be relatively optimistic about South African theatre holding its own with the rest of world theatre) is another facet of what Greig termed the 'Golden Bough' syndrome: in both instances, theatre is already trying to go beyond the issue of apartheid.

Essentially in the case of theatre (as in that of literature generally) if one sets aside the move away from purely oppositional work and a greater concern with the individual approach, the one great problem more specific to South Africa is that of multiform audiences. Language, class and race have divided the country for so long under the apartheid regime, that the legitimacy of cultural diversity is sometimes seen as retrograde and not politically correct. What seems certain, surveying the scene as a whole, is that new democratic structures, whether they concern Performing Arts Councils, Festivals, workers' rights or private institutions such as the Market Theatre, must be, and are being, created, so that free range may be given to diversity and that audiences may make their choices unhampered by imposed financial or political factors. This of course would be utopian, but Barney Simon's *Theatresports* in 1993 is an interesting example of the deep reflection surrounding these issues. This performance, given both at the Grahamstown Festival and regularly at the Market Laboratory consisted of a cast of experienced actors playing scenes suggested to them on the spot by the audience. This "method" has obvious connections with both workshopping and development theatre, treating themes from the everyday life of actors and audience but it is also perhaps educating an audience to ask for what they want from the theatre, a consideration sometimes ignored by critics.

Geoffrey V. Davis and Anne Fuchs, Colomars, 1993.

Editors' Note

The name "Wits" appears in interviews several times throughout this book. "Wits" is the familiar abbreviation for the University of Witwatersrand, Johannesburg.

'A TRULY LIVING MOMENT': ACTING AND THE *STATEMENTS* PLAYS

BRIAN CROW

If the playwright and the actor have any serious and significant function in the new South Africa, it will be to explore the forms, actual and potential, of South African social reality. This will be done, as it is in all 'serious' drama everywhere, by the presentation of absorbing characters involved in actions with implications which are recognisable as more or less generally significant for that society. But it will also be done, as elsewhere, not so much through the selection and treatment of specific issues and themes, but by means of something which is inherent in the medium of theatrical performance itself, which is the exploration and disclosing in organized theatricality of the forms and structures of everyday theatricality.

A drama may be 'about' an identifiable subject with one or more thematic implications — say, the formative but troubled relations between a young white boy and his mother's black servant; but in ways which are not so easy to articulate, which are not 'about' anything in directly apprehensible terms, it may also disclose the 'feel', the texture of being and relationship for characters who, like ordinary people in real life, have no choice but to play roles, to be expressive to each other on certain terms and not on others, in certain modes and not in others which are at least theoretically possible. We are thus offered, as performers and as audiences, a certain kind of knowledge — a knowledge more practical and sensuous than cognitive — about the roles available for playing in that society, the conditions underpinning them, and the terms on which social actors may be mutually expressive.

This is where the actor becomes so crucially important and so much more than the interpreter of a script which is already finished,

which already 'means' as much as it can mean. For even if what the
actor brings to a performance is usually based on a script, and could
not happen without careful attention to it, there is created in performance a dimension of 'meaning' which communicates to the audience
— beyond the explicitness of subject and theme — a view of the terms
on which people, at this time and in this place, may be mutually
expressive, what roles it is possible or impossible for them to perform.
It was something like this, surely, that Athol Fugard was getting at
when he wrote in his notebook that "[o]nly a fraction of my truth is
in the words", the rest being in what he calls the "Carnal Reality of the
actor in space and time."[1]

One of the effects, as well as purposes, of the apartheid system
was to prevent the full realization of that reciprocal recognition which
is the basis of civilized society, and through which every individual
acquires the sense of identity and of self-worth that Fanon called "the
certainty of oneself." By its very nature that system denied, in the name
of so-called 'separate development', the common humanity which
must be the basis of the open-ended potential for mutual expressiveness. So the scenarios and roles possible in the theatre of everyday
South African life under apartheid were extremely limited, rarely es-
caping externally 'overdetermined' forms of interaction and the modes
of expressiveness associated with them. Thus, the white 'madam' and
her black maid may interact daily but the faces — or masks — which
they present to each other are narrowly determined by prevailing
notions of what is considered acceptable in that relationship. In just the
same way, the possibilities for expressiveness between white and black
men at work are limited by the boss-'boy' relationship which structures the scenarios, roles and dialogue generally considered acceptable
for them to engage in. Marx's assertion that it is impossible to grasp
the characteristics of intellectual production without understanding
material production in its specific historical form could equally well
have been made of social theatricality, which is always profoundly
affected by the social division of labour and its associated attitudes.

If apartheid and other systems, which for economic or ideological reasons (most commonly both) deny the possibilities of full reciprocal recognition and impose rigorous constraints on mutual expressiveness — which thus become dominated by external imperatives and

---

[1] *Notebooks 1960/1977*, ed. Mary Benson (London: Faber and Faber, 1983),
p. 171.

in certain societies by racial stereotypes — this is not to say that there is a corresponding poverty of response behind the masks. As Fanon and others have shown, the rigidity of self-presentation *vis-à-vis* the 'other', and the sometimes extreme narrowing-down of social interactions and their expressive possibilities, in reality conceal turbulent depths of affect, in which desire, dependence and hatred of the self as well as of others are swirling currents.

At its best, during the apartheid years, South African theatre not only identified and protested against the political and social evils of the system but explored both the constraints on social interaction and expressiveness, and their psychological consequences. It did this in a variety of forms, styles and genres, and for audiences white, non-white and, sometimes, both. But within all this diversity it is striking how central the performer has been in the making, as well as the ultimate performance, of this theatre. In some of its finest achievements during the apartheid period, South African theatre has been peculiarly an actor's theatre, and this, I suggest, has contributed in no small way to its achievement. One of the particular genres of this actor-centred theatre — and one of the most characteristic artistic products of the apartheid years — has been the South African workshop play. Here, the collaboration between actor and director-author, and between white and black, has produced a distinctive dramaturgy and a special kind of theatrical experience which has thrilled audiences well beyond South Africa, as well as producing some remarkable explorations of South African social theatricality.

The British actor Simon Callow, criticising the dominance which the contemporary director has won in the theatre and what he sees as its baneful consequences, has suggested that "the director has interposed himself between actor and writer, claiming that they cannot speak each other's language" and that 'acting' itself has become a pejorative term, "used to delineate something as impure, an accretion and a product of the actor's egomania." The upshot, according; to Callow, is that

> [t]he crucial element in the act of theatre, the actor's delight
> in the opportunities afforded him by the writer, has been
> abolished, outlawed by a breed of directors who have little
> experience and no comprehension of the rich and vital pro-
> cesses of acting".[2]

[2] Simon Callow, *Being an Actor* (London: Penguin Books, 1985), p. 218.

Salvation, he argues, lies in the writer and the actor being restored to each other, "without the self-elected intervention of the director, claiming a unique position interpreting the one to the other."

Important though it is, this is not the place to argue the merits or otherwise of Callow's thesis. Its interest for us lies in its perception of the creativity of the collaborative relationship between the actor and the writer. In ways which are, regrettably, far from common in contemporary theatre, some of the South African workshop plays demonstrate in quite remarkable fashion both "the actor's delight in the opportunities afforded him by the writer" and "the rich and vital processes of acting" And in some, the functions of actor and writer have even overlapped.

The earliest, and to my mind still the best, of the workshop plays were the product of a collaboration between the white writer, actor and director Athol Fugard and a number of actors with whom he regularly worked and enjoyed close relationships, notably the white South African actress Yvonne Bryceland and the two black actors, John Kani and Winston Ntshona. In embarking on this collaborative phase in his career, Fugard was in fact only taking one step further his established practice of making plays with the active participation of the actors who would eventually perform them. Not only did the early Sophiatown pieces, *No-Good Friday* (1958) and *Nongogo* (1959) develop out of Fugard's acquaintance with young black actors and artists like Zakes Mokae and Lewis Nkosi, but he had already used various techniques of improvisation and devising with them in the creation of the play texts. Having, on his own admission, become 'blocked' after his writing of *Boesman and Lena* (1969), Fugard began workshopping an idea presented to him by Kani and Ntshona which was to become the first of the *Statements* plays, *Sizwe Bansi is Dead*.

The workshopping process, as described in Fugard's *Notebooks*, involved the two actors doing an improvisation, using only a table and chair in which they played black waiters serving a bar full of arrogant whites in a local hotel. The improvisation over, Kani and Ntshona analysed the feelings which the exercise had simulated, which they found had included resentment at their subordination but also a sense of dependence. Fugard notes that Kani in particular was provoked into asking questions about the discrepancy which the improvisation had highlighted between the mask which blacks, in such a situation, are forced to wear, and the face that lies behind the mask. This and other methods used by Fugard and his actors in these workshopping sessions were evidently designed not only to represent the observably realistic behaviour of South Africans but also to disclose what normally remains concealed, or at least unanalysed — the deepest subjective responses to social relationships and interactions, what Fugard elsewhere (writing of Sartre's sense of anguish and its relevance to *Waiting For Godot*) calls an "appointment with self" (p. 102).

In this and other workshop plays Fugard's way of working with his actors was designed to provoke them into making their personal journeys into the psychic recesses where the subjective residue of their social experience is waiting to be explored and incorporated into their performances. This accords with his insistence, reiterated in his *Notebooks*, that what happens to the actors — the significance of their awareness within the moment as they perform — is at least as important as the audience's experience in witnessing the play. In Fugard's existentialist perspective the self, society and Being itself are all intrinsically theatricalist phenomena, properly explored by the 'holy' actor (Fugard was at this time deeply influenced by his knowledge of Grotowski) prepared to remove his or her own masks in the course of descending into experience which is normally unconscious or repressed. The effect of what Fugard has called "a truly living moment in theatre" is to return an audience to an enhanced experience of being that is normally unavailable to it in everyday life. To make it available, it has to be first experienced by the actor, who must be prepared to do the painful work of self-exposure so as to extend his own and the audience's consciousness. For "[w]ithout consciousness", as Fugard reminds us in the *Notebooks*, "we become victims instead of actors — even if it is still only a question of acting victims. And in this make-believe of our lives the audience is self" (p. 107).

If the *Statements* plays have offered audiences truly living moments in the theatre — which I believe they have — it is because in their making and performance the actors and writer have collaborated to disclose self in ways which have wider implications, opening up to scrutiny the patterns of role-playing and interaction in apartheid society itself. In doing so, they reveal both the oppressive constriction and rigidity of apartheid-determined relationships and modes of expressiveness and — the actors using their own art and persons as emblems and epitomes — the potential for versatility in the construction and presentation of self, which may thereby be a means of survival and even of resistance in such an intensely oppressive society.

In the opening monologue of *Sizwe Bansi* Kani played a character, Styles, who in his rôle as proprietor of the township photographic studio sees himself as witness of the township's collective life and the recorder in film of its aspirations and dreams. Kani/Styles rôle-plays a variety of characters: himself previously as a car-worker at the Ford plant and at home, and not as a photographer; 'Baas' Bradley, his boss at Ford's; the man who's just got standard six; the members of the large family who come in for a group portrait and so on. Much of the substance of Styles's speech is to do with the oppressive — and in the case of Mr Ford's visit to his plant — quite ludicrous constraints and rigours of black life, and the struggle to achieve an element of personal freedom from such imprisonment within a regime controlled by others. But, while the *content* speaks of a gruelling rigidity of role and interaction enforced by white masters, the *performance* actually enacts a protean versatility in imaginative apprehension and the playing of rôle.

In contrast with the effortlessly rôle-playing Styles Sizwe Bansi is virtually devoid of histrionic creativity, unable even to image his 'dream' for his wife back home. But with a good deal of help from Styles, Sizwe is soon able to project the images of self he wishes to have recorded. If these are the first steps towards greater expressive versatility a much greater challenge, ironically, awaits this most timid of 'actors'; for he must face the challenge of 'dying' as himself and assuming the identity of the dead man he and Buntu find in the alley outside Sky's place. The tension between Styles's rôle-playing versatility and the rigorous constraints evident from his commentary on black life is not thematized as the conflict between the fixed expectations of established identity (however constrained and impoverished these may be) and the repugnant but potentially liberating (or at least ameliorating) possibility of new identity. Buntu, whose idea it is, argues the merits of swapping photos from Sizwe's invalid passbook into the dead man's valid one against Sizwe's objection that he cannot live as another man's ghost:

> When the white man looked at you at the Labour Bureau what did he see? A man with dignity or a bloody passbook with an N.I. number? Isn't that a ghost? When the white man sees you walk down the street and calls out, 'Hey, John! Come here' . . . to you, Sizwe Bansi . . . isn't that a ghost? Or when his little child calls you 'Boy' . . . you a man, circumcised with a wife and four children . . . isn't that a ghost? Stop fooling

yourself. All I'm saying is be a real ghost, if that is what they
want, what they've turned us into. Spook them into hell, man!
(p. 38)[3]

    Though he is appalled by what he is doing, Sizwe feels the force
of Buntu's argument, especially when he resorts to rôle-play to image
for this reluctant actor the new 'Robert' in the line on pay-day at Feltex,
or walking into Sales House to buy a new suit, or becoming a respected
member of his local church. Sizwe rehearses his N.I. number and
assumes his new name; and the play concludes on the optimistic image
of Sizwe in Styles's studio striding through the City of the Future as
Mr Robert Zwelinzima, man about town. However limited it may still
be in Sizwe's case, 'acting' — the capacity to be knowingly protean in
appearance, and to exploit the expressive possibilities of theatrical
performance — has triumphed over both the rigidity of the oppressive
system of apartheid and the natural inhibitions of the human actor.
    In their next workshop production, *The Island*, Fugard and his
actor-collaborators again not only explored further this new kind of
theatre but the energies of theatricality itself as a positive weapon in
the struggle against apartheid. In this case, the denial of reciprocal
recognition of blacks by whites is presented in its most extreme form
and context — imprisonment on Robben Island, where men are sent
"to be lost between life and death". For their gaoler Hodoshe the
prisoners are merely objects of sadistic pleasure, their lives constrained
into a straitjacket of absurdly meaningless but exhausting labour.
But as they recognise, when they recall the day's horrors in their cell,
there is a certain shrewd logic to Hodoshe's apparently primitive
brutality:

> JOHN. This morning when he said: 'You two! The beach!' . . .
> I thought, Okay, so it's my turn to empty the sea into a hole. He
> likes that one. But when he pointed to the wheelbarrows, and
> I saw his idea . . . ! [*Shaking his head*] I laughed at first. Then I
> wasn't laughing. Then I hated you. You looked so stupid, *broer*!
> WINSTON. That's what he wanted.
> JOHN. It was going to last forever, man! Because of *you*. And
> for *you*, because of *me*. *Moer*! He's cleverer than I thought. (p. 49)

---

[3] References to this and the other '*Statements*' plays are to the texts published
in *Statements: Three Plays* (Oxford and New York: Oxford University Press,
1974).

Their gaoler did not have to read Fanon to discover that one of the most terrible of all punishments is to pervert the process of reciprocal recognition, so that what should be a bond of solidarity is turned into a relationship of hateful antagonism. Painful as they were, the rigours and absurdities characteristic of black subordination of which Styles spoke at the beginning of *Sizwe Bansi is Dead* seem almost trivial compared with the extreme oppression of the constraints imposed on John and Winston in *The Island*.

And yet, even here, the capacity to exercise the expressive freedoms associated with theatre has not been destroyed. It's apparent, for instance, in the prisoners' improvisation as they imagine their 'phone conversation with the 'boys' at Sky's place . But it takes a much more sustained, explicitly theatrical form in their (or at least John's) determination to perform an improvised version of *Antigone* at the prison concert. Through this John and Winston not only help themselves to survive mentally, and to win an opportunity for expressiveness normally denied them, but also to make a statement of resistance against the system which oppresses them.

What that system seeks — and may ultimately achieve through the prison regime on Robben Island — is the annihilation of the identities of those who resist it. The image of such extinction of personality is another prisoner discussed by John and Winston called old Harry:

> When you go to the quarry tomorrow, take a good look at old Harry. Look into his eyes, John. Look at his hands. They've changed him. They've turned him into stone. Watch him work with that chisel and hammer. Twenty perfect blocks of stone every day. Nobody else can do it like him. He loves stone. That's why they're nice to him. He's forgotten himself. He's forgotten everything . . . why he's here, where he comes from. (p. 71).

This is the end of the line: a man completely reified, devoid of expressiveness, incapable even of self-recognition. And it is, as Winston recognizes, his own ultimate destination. The point is made all the more painfully and poignantly by having John discover that his sentence has been commuted on appeal, and that he will be released in three months. But even if Winston faces the prospect of the eventual and permanent extinction of his selfhood the playing of a rôle at least allows him to make his statement, to assert amidst the despair and horror the reason and meaning of his incarceration, and — like Antigone

— to go to his "living death" because he has honoured "those things to which honour belongs" (p. 77).

As in their previous production Winston Ntshona played the character who lacks natural versatility in rôle-playing while John Kani, as in his rôles of Styles and Buntu, played the character who embraces and celebrates the possibilities of theatricality. "Look, Winston, try to understand, man . . . this is Theatre." Winston's difficulties with it include learning the plot of *Antigone* and being pressured into doing something which he thinks is merely child's play. Worst of all, he hates being laughed at by John when he first puts on his character's crudely made wig and false breasts, which only exacerbates the main problem — that he does not want to play a woman. John, however makes the point that even if the audience laughs because it knows it is Winston beneath all this "rubbish" it will not always do so:

> There'll come a time when they'll stop laughing, and that will be the time when our Antigone hits them with her words. (p. 61)

The final scene of *The Island* validates John's insight, demonstrating how theatre can overcome even the most grotesque inadequacies and obstacles to 'hit' us with the truths it speaks. If theatricality cannot do for Winston what it may, if he is lucky, do for Sizwe/Robert — that is, give him an identity with which he can at least survive in the apartheid system — it can provide the means, however recalcitrant he has been about performing, by which he can honour his personal commitment to the cause which has put him on Robben Island.

Statements after an Arrest under the Immorality Act, which was first performed in 1974, a year after *The Island* and two years after *Sizwe Bansi*, is a play for which Fugard claims sole authorship. But even if it was not devised in the same 'workshop' fashion as its predecessors, and did not feature Kani and Ntshona, it has a familial resemblance to them in being the product of Fugard's collaboration with an actress, Yvonne Bryceland with whom he had worked closely during the '60s and '70s and who had played a major rôle in his evolution as a theatre artist — and in continuing his exploration, albeit in a different key, of the themes of identity, reciprocal recognition and personal expressiveness under apartheid.

In *Statements after an Arrest* a white woman, Frieda Joubert, and a 'coloured' man, Errol Philander, accord each other the reciprocal recognition, the acknowledgment of each other's individual identities, which Fanon thought to be indispensable to civilized society and the South African government decreed to be immoral and illegal. Sitting in a dimly lit room in her house, naked after lovemaking, their conversation — laced though it is with the tensions of racial and social difference, the guilt of adultery and the fear of discovery — reveals an intensity of personal connection and a potential for mutual expressiveness that negate the ideological fixities of apartheid. At the same time, Frieda does not wish to be seen in full light by her lover, reacting strongly to him lighting a match to do so. Seeing, in Fugard's existentialist thought, is an essential element in the process by which persons define themselves, as one watches others watching oneself and so, circumscribed by gazes, seeing oneself. And here, the gaze is inevitably imbued with political as well as sexual significance, Philander wanting to be seen for the full human person he knows himself to be, Frieda avoiding, in her fear, the full implications of seeing and being seen.

When they are raided by the police not just their illicit relationship but the identities, the sense of selfhood, they have established for each other through that relationship are destroyed. In a sequence of camera flashes evoking their subjective responses to the trauma of exposure Frieda jabbers a 'confession' while the intelligent, sensitive Philander disintegrates before us, his "performance", as a stage direction indicates, degenerating, "into a grotesque parody of the servile, cringing 'Coloured'" (p. 99). But with each sequence of flashes the two characters, though still 'confessing', speak from a more private, more deeply introspective part of themselves. Frieda speaks of the pain of losing him, not only as her lover but, more profoundly and terribly, as an element of her own being:

> I don't want to see myself. But I know that will also happen. I must be my hands again, my eyes, my ears . . . all of me but now without you. All of me that found you must now lose you . . . . In every corner of being myself there is a little of you left and now I must start to lose it. (p. 105)

For Philander there is a sense of physical dismemberment, of the loss of head, body, limbs and hands, until he is left with only "the emptiness" which is his self. And for the audience there is the contradiction of the deep subjectivity of Frieda's and Philander's monologues, with their implications of rich reciprocity and mutual expressiveness, set against the flat, expressionless formality of the police evidence.

If the photography of Styles's studio in *Sizwe Bansi is Dead* records the dreams and aspirations of its clients, the photographs of *Statements* serve to destroy them. The pessimism of its depiction of the destruction of reciprocal recognition between the races is only relieved by its implied conviction that such relationship is nevertheless possible. For Frieda and Philander there are not even the deeply qualified victories achieved by Sizwe and Winston in the earlier plays. But even if its mood is more sombre than the two preceding plays, and its tragic implications about the prospects for reciprocal recognition and truly human relationship under apartheid even bleaker, *Statements* nevertheless shares with its companion-pieces an intense commitment to the actor and to acting, to their capacity for disclosing the deepest recesses of the self in its confrontation with others and with social institutions and practices.

The 'drama' of the struggle against apartheid in South Africa reached its happy climax with the celebration of the advent of majority rule. But if Mandela's South Africa has now, at least for the time being, yielded its major role on the world stage the drama within South Africa continues, even if in less obviously 'dramatic' terms. What the future may hold for its peoples is still deeply uncertain; but what is definite is that a multiplicity of scenarios is now developing in every aspect of South African life, with the social and political actors vying for control of — or at least a satisfactory part in — the script. If the largest determinant of what will happen is inevitably the economy, in a country with the history of South Africa there is a more than usually complex and decisive interplay between economic, political and cultural forces. And at the cultural level — including the artistic culture — there is, suddenly, an altogether new agenda embracing challenges the outcomes of which will be crucial, ultimately, for all South Africans.

In these new circumstances the hitherto fundamental rôle of serious literature and theatre in documenting and protesting against apartheid is now bound to change. What theatre and other artists will make of post-apartheid realities remains to be seen, and it will be fascinating to observe the directions in which South African theatre will go in the next few years. Fugard himself, in a recent interview, has suggested that in the completely new situation that has come about with the ending of apartheid theatre artists, like others, will have to negotiate a far more complex and ambiguous ethical and political landscape. It may be that the workshop play with its distinguished history of black-white artistic cooperation and other types of theatre which proceed from the close and sympathetic collaboration of writer, director and actor, will have an especially important part to play in representing the new forms of social interaction, the new modes of mutual expressiveness which are bound gradually to develop in South Africa.

"THE MANY INDIVIDUAL WILLS." FROM *CROSSROADS* TO *SURVIVAL*: THE WORK OF EXPERIMENTAL THEATRE WORKSHOP '71.

Robert McLaren

> South African is a term which applies to something which doesn't exist at the moment. When we can really talk about things being South African according to that definition we will have a country where the majority in everything is black but the rest of the population which makes up that South Africa will also have its own important part.
>
> Finally, the culture will fundamentally have a black impetus, will look black like our theatre looks black, but will actually be the result of fertile interaction between people who are not only black. I mean our theatre looks black in many ways but it's not black obviously, not exclusively black — you can only say it is South African because I have a part in it and I am not black.[1]

In early 1992 I worked with students at the University of the Witwatersrand on a production of *Samora Continua*, a play produced by Zambuko/Izibuko, our theatre group here in Zimbabwe.[2] It was a time of attenuated continuities and long-awaited resumptions — as the Frontline[3] crumbles and the apartheid beast slouched to Codesa to be reborn.

---

[1] Shirley Pendlebury, "Jailbird's Eyeview: and interview with the cast of *Survival*", in *Snarl*, (Summer 1976) Johannesburg. p. 3

[2] For an account of the history and work of Zambuko/Izibuko see "Theatre on the Frontline: the Political Theatre of Zambuko/Izibuko," in *TDR* (*The Drama Review*), 36, 1 (1992), pp. 92–114.

I have felt, at times with despondency, at others with detachment, that Zambuko/Izibuko is Workshop '71's reincarnation in another world. Flesh and blood as it is, it had always seemed to be the South African's group's ghost, primitively enacting more sophisticated rituals underwater. I remember — as others remembered Ben Jonson — the quickfire wit, the creative forge of Mthoba, Sibanda, Maredi, Moloi, that could make an evening's improvisation crackle with a static that nothing since in my life in theatre has equalled.[4]

At the level of making the play, all since has seemed pedestrian. At the level of performing it, our Zimbabwean theatre groups at their most dynamic appear sleepwalkers alongside Ngema, Mtwa, Makhene, Sibanda.[5] Yet at the level of ideology, trapped below ground in the shafts and tunnels of apartheid isolation and misinformation, it is the South Africans who suggest miners — over-confident but ignorant — as they crawl now, at last, into the light, the sun that bakes the Zambezi, that sparkles on the Rovuma, that lights up the Samoras, the Netos, the Cabrals they must now gaze on with blinking eyes.

My return to South Africa after 15 years exile to work on *Samora Continua* revealed that the South Africa I spoke of back in 1976 is not yet. The Performing Arts Administration at the University is still, apparently unashamedly, all white. Yet in *Samora Continua* eleven white South African students participated with eleven of their black colleagues in a piece of African theatre in which they had to speak, sing

---

[3]The term "Frontline" and hence "Frontline States" refers to those states on the frontline in the war against the *apartheid* system. These countries included Mozambique, Zimbabwe, Zambia, Tanzania and Angola.

[4]James Mthoba, Seth Sibanda, Dan Selaelo Maredi and Gertrude Moloi were all brilliant improvisers. Mthoba remained in South Africa and has had a fine career in acting and teaching, in particular doing pioneering work in the field of theatre with and for the blind. Sibanda remained in the United States along with Maredi. He is active in theatre there. Maredi was active in the United States and after the unbanning of the ANC returned to South Africa to continue his career as playwright and director in South Africa. Gertrude Moloi disappeared from the stage after the dissolution of ZZZIP!.

[5]Mbongeni Ngema and Percy Mtwa were actors with Gibson Kente, subsequently devised and acted in the successful *Woza Albert!* and then split up, Mtwa to do *Bopha!* and Ngema to become famous with the hit musical *Sarafina*. After the collapse of Workshop '71 Dan Ramolao Makhene went on to develop a career in acting. He also worked with trades union and community projects and is now chairman of the Performing Arts Workers Equity (PAWE).

and dance Shona, Njanja, Ronga and Zulu. Though the ghost of Stanislavsky and the ghost of his ghost, Lee Strasberg, breathed a restraining frost over their acting, they got it in the end and my old image moved into tighter focus — a South African theatre with "a black impetus" but "the result of fertile interaction between people who are not only black."

Having a drink with Mthoba, in a Pimville shebeen more recently, our talk reminded me of what made creative work in Workshop '71 so special. Life around us was full of paradox — wit in oppression, suffering, resistance and transcendence. People like Mthoba had the ability to pluck it out of the air, savour it and then inject it, sparkling into our work. Take this:

> [Dan laughs and points to his (Lefty as played by Mthoba) teeth, which are pretty ragged]
> Dan: Wat makeer met jou tande?
> Lefty: Jy ken die ouens.
> (What's up with your teeth? You know what the guys are like)[6]

Yes, Dan, the gangster chief, knew what the guys were like. He had broken a few teeth himself in his time. An observation about broken teeth is picked up and with a shrug and a laugh, transformed effortlessly into a profoundly suggestive perception of urban black life.

I have never since, with the exception of the actress, Thandi Montsiwa (More), with whom I worked in London on *Prey No More*, participated in a process of playmaking where so much wealth and inspiration came from the actors. Perhaps that is why when I write a lot of the material myself in the playmaking process — as I have been forced to do at times in Zambuko/Izibuko — I have seen it as a sign of failure. I only wrote because Mthoba, Maredi and the others were not there.

Now Maredi is back in 'the TJ' — Johannesburg — to rejoin Mthoba. Mabohe Ramowela was on stage again for the first time since 1976 in Maredi's *Kgathala, The Man* and in a play being directed at the time by Bess Finney. Makhene is there, so is Sephuma. Siphiwe Khumalo runs the stage at the Wits Theatre. Themba Ntinga returned briefly from the United States. Sibanda is acting in the States. I remain in

---

[6]*Crossroads* (unpublished Ms).

Zimbabwe. Recently there was a meeting to discuss reviving Workshop '71. Some felt it was possible. Others felt a brand new association was better, leaving Workshop '71 to rest in peace in its honoured historical niche. Meanwhile a critic reviewing our production of *Samora Continua,* called it 'Workshop '92'.

Opportune moment to write of it perhaps. The temptation is to tell its stories, not its story — Workshop '71 was more than a theatre organization. It was a way of life. The anecdotes that tie us together are rooted in the social fabric of Johannesburg in the 1970s. The temptation to tell its *story* is less seductive. A chronicle would provide valuable "background information," be important for the archives but let, perhaps, an outsider do that, not an "angry old man"[7] looking back on history. An analysis, with all the ice of its sibilants, would also be good — no doubt. But what I want to do is talk about it in a way that only *now* I can do. It was only yesterday that the security police tried to bribe a close friend of mine to lure me back to South Africa, if only in transit, in order to lay hands on me. Those threats, those people continue to exist in the changing South Africa, as the activities of the Third Force and the assassination of activists attest. But things have changed enough for me to write this article.

When the Institute of Race Relations brought Bess Finney,[8] Mshengu (Robert McLaren), Dan Maredi and James Mthoba together, it produced a cocktail — not the Molotov type that, it is reported, Mutwa in 1976 accused us in Workshop '71 of teaching young Sowetans to make and throw. Rather the cocktail that characterized Workshop '71 at its founding and substantially through most of its existence was made up of four elements: liberal philanthropy, a political agenda, a dream of livelihood and an intense interest in theatre as an art.

Liberal philanthropy

Founded at the Institute of Race Relations with the frank and avowed aim of achieving "contact" and conducting its first and at various times subsequent workshops and performances at the Institute's premises at Auden House, Braamfontein, Workshop '71 was at the start a liberal initiative. Bess Finney was working at the Institute and it was to her

---

[7] This is a phrase used by Raeford Daniel in an article in *The Weekly Mail,* March 27–April 2 (1992), p 31.

[8] Bess Finney, well-known Johannesburg stage and television actress and drama teacher.

credit that as Workshop '71 began at an early stage to challenge and move away from the basic premises of liberal multiracialism — benevolent "contact" within the parameters of white domination — she travelled with it.

Crucial to this development was language. Because I could speak Zulu and Xhosa and had already spent a short time in Lesotho trying to improve my Sotho, I was able to suggest that, in both our theatre work and discussion, participants of the workshop should feel free to use any of South Africa's major languages. Maredi was a virtuoso in *Tsotsitaal*. Mabotlhe Ramowela no longer had to negotiate the rough edges of English and relaxed into Sotho. Mthoba moved freely from one language to the other. Others, who had been voiceless, found a voice — and the dynamic, the balance of power, in the workshop shifted. Whereas previously discussion had been dominated by well-meaning but not necessarily knowledgable English-speakers from the Northern Suburbs, now the full richness and originality of life in Alexandra and Soweto became available to the workshop. It was the sad reality of white South African liberalism that one by one the white members began to drop out. Even in the liberation movements, whites who have worked side by side with their black comrades for decades in struggle, cannot string a sentence together in a black South African language and can even resent it when their inadequacy is exposed by shifting the mode of communication from their own language to those of the majority of their countrymen.

By the time we came to perform *Crossroads* for the first time, of the whites only Finney, Shirley Weinberg, Shirley Pendlebury and myself remained. It is true others left for other reasons than language. This will be touched on later.

Cassim Bakharia, classified "Indian" in the glossary of apartheid, and Crane Soudien, classified "Coloured", also remained. This is where *Tsotsitaal* came to play a unifying role — Lenasia and Bosmont could join Alex and Soweto in speaking it.

Of course, the decision on language had consequences which went far beyond discussion — into the work itself. If Workshop '71 pioneered anything it was the freedom to use language on stage as it is spoken in the community. The linguistic map of Workshop '71's plays charts the intricate interactions of the Johannesburg area's different ethnic groups and races. That this facility to move from language to language could embrace wider areas than the Witwatersrand was proved by the cast of *ZZZIP!*, who were able, often extempore, to translate the script during performance into a dominantly Zulu register in Natal, Xhosa in the Eastern Cape and Sotho in Lesotho and Pretoria.

Crossroads reflected all the major languages but in a context in which none dominated, with the possible exception of *Tsotsitaal*, which was to be expected in a play that was partly based on the life of Lefty Mthembu, king of gangsters and therefore 'tsotsi superior.' For the actors themselves it gave them the freedom to create and portray their lives authentically in workshops and finally in the finished products. Language was the lifeline that connected the editor's work to what I referred to earlier as "the paradox — the wit in oppression, suffering, resistance and transcendance" of their world.

Two factors led to the move away from the liberal patronage of the Institute. The first lay within the Institute and white South African liberalism itself and the second with the inevitable reaction against it — Black Consciousness. Many theatre groups in those days began work in a church hall or some such liberal venue only to find eventually the milk of white benevolence turn sour as the basic contradiction within the liberal make-up expressed itself — a desire to be good and do right by others, especially the less privileged, and a basic inability to tolerate behaviour outside the 'accepted' parameters of its own culture.

In the racist consciousness, the dirt of others is dirtier, the noises louder, the ignorance more overwhelming, the odours more insufferable than one's own. I remember my neighbour in the old block of flats in central Johannesburg where I lived for the duration of my work in Workshop '71, who periodically called the police when I had black visitors. On one occasion I emerged to find him brandishing a saw and threatening to cut off the head of one of my best friends. On another, when I challenged him on his assertion that my visitors had been making a lot of noise, he said that even when 'they' talk softly, 'it's their voices' — he just could not stand 'their voices.'

Workshop '71 moved out. Paradoxically despite its estrangement from the citadel of liberal philanthropy, another thing Workshop '71 pioneered was the re-instatement of racially mixed theatre audiences and casts, banned since the early 1960's, through the introduction of a system of invitations with donations at the door for performances of *Crossroads*, Mutwa's *uNosilimela* and a two-hander acted by Bess Finney and myself entitled *Lerato, Whiteman's Version*.[9]

---

[9] "*Lerato*" (Sotho) means "love". *Lerato, Whiteman's Version* was a programme of extracts from European theatre on the theme of love.

The tremors of the Black Consciousness upheaval hit Workshop '71 on many fronts. As a 'multiracial' activity, we were particularly vulnerable. As a white trespasser in an area the black petit-bourgeois intellectual regarded as his domain, I too was a particular target. The call was for blacks to withdraw from contacts with whites. Those who persisted were labelled 'non-white' or more precisely 'guinea-pigs,' 'schizophrenics.'[10] Paradoxically, I and one or two others in Workshop '71, the foremost of whom was Mango Tshabangu, appreciated the importance and validity of the Black Consciousness call. This was reflected in the pages of *S'ketsh* magazine which we jointly edited.

One night some young men from Lenasia, who had begun to be regular attenders of the Workshop, came up to me and asked if I had read the People's Experimental Theatre (PET) Newsletter, which called on blacks to cease collaborating with whites. They said they felt this was correct and they were going to withdraw. A little while later Shirley Pendlebury, who was the only remaining white in the *Crossroads* cast, also approached me, asking whether I thought she should withdraw. Such was the spirit of the time and our own active acquiescence in it, that I said "Yes" and she withdrew.

When Maredi, Sibanda, Lucas Radebe, Seilaneng Khomongwe and others left Workshop '71 to take part in the play, *Mboni*, directed by Lynn Hooker, those who remained, including myself, Tshabangu and Mthoba, decided to turn our backs on the success with mixed audiences in town which our first play, *Crossroads*, had achieved, and concentrate on performances to solely black audiences.

The play that resulted was *ZZZIP!*, in which there was virtually no English and not a great deal of *Tsotsitaal*. The dialogue was now mostly Zulu and Sotho and the cast was completely, for the want of a better term, black African.

uNosilimela, which followed and was performed simultaneously with *ZZZIP!*, was to a large extent shaped by its author's concern that his statements reach white as well as black audiences and consequently it was performed both in town and in the townships. *ZZZIP!*, on the other hand, failed disastrously to communicate to mixed audiences in town. In fact it was literally designed to fail there. On only two occasions was the play ever performed in such circumstances. In East London and during the Workshop '71 Theatre Festival in 1975 in the

---

[10] These were phrases used to describe those black actors who took part in *Crossroads*. See *People's Experimental Newsletter*, 1 (1973).

Box Theatre, University of the Witwatersrand.[11]

Mthoba's initiative to found Izigqi within Workshop '71 both revived the old and introduced the new. Its *Visions of the Night* was a return to the experimental workshop material of *Crossroads* but its production of Douglas Turner-Ward's *Happy Ending* was designed to go beyond the halls and theatres which had up to then circumscribed Workshop '71's work and reach out to the deaf, even the blind, to ordinary people in their homes.

With the establishment of Workshop '71 Theatre Company as a professional group, productions like *uHlanga, the Reed* and *Survival* were performed before mixed audiences in towns — the latter being commissioned by the Space Theatre, Cape Town — and to black audiences in the townships. The reason for this, as I put it in the 1976 interview, was ultimately that "as a professional group we've got to get audiences and this is one of the reasons why we have to perform in town as well." Clearly the admission here is a grudging one though it was in the same interview that the concept of South Africanness referred to earlier was expressed. When the interviewer asked: 'Do *you* think of *Survival* as black theatre?' Ntinga replied:

> You know there's nothing that makes me so sick as black, white, this that! NO, it's African theatre. If black means African, South African, *then* it's black theatre.

The 1976 Uprisings brought about a situation of intense confrontation. It was now almost impossible for me as a white to move about Soweto as I had before. *Survival* opened in Soweto without me because the cast adjudged it unsafe for me to be there. I remember visiting a teacher friend of mine in Orlando East. Some youths came down the street towards me. From an exaggerated distance I hastened to greet them in colloquial Zulu to demonstrate an image of myself and personalise our encounter. I knew that the penalty for failing to do this could be death. This was from one who for six years had been confronted by police, gangsters, *tsotsis* and aggressors in many different and difficult situations in Soweto at all times of day and night. It was significant that when *Crossroads* was revived in 1976 the cast found it

---

[11] After the embarassing experience in East London, the cast decided simply to bypass a performance at the white Rhodes University in Grahamstown and proceed straight to Port Elizabeth for performances in the black "township" of New Brighton.

impossible to perform the 1972 ending, consisting of songs which the audience joined in. Instead the 1976 version ended with a hymn to freedom and then exit. The liberal philanthropy of its inception passed through the isolationist assertion of Black Consciousness to the futuristic glimpse of a new South Africanness — only to be hacked apart by the bitter hatred and killings of 1976. It took a mass movement for non-racial democracy in the 1980's to revive the lost visions of South Africanness so confidently expressed by the actors of *Survival* when they spoke of a South African culture but one which "will fundamentally have a black impetus."

The political agenda

Once, after the police had hauled us off the road to Soweto into Booysens police station on suspicion of being up to no good, I was visited in my flat by the Security Police. They displayed impressive erudition, describing to me how in numerous revolutionary situations, including the Chinese, theatre had been used effectively as a propaganda medium and an organizational and agitational weapon. As they left, one of them said, as a passing shot: "we are not interested in the Immorality Act."

I and my friend, Rob Amato[12], had often discussed theatre in the context of the struggle in South Africa during our years together at Oxford. These were the days of '68. I had moved from a South African liberal position to support for the Labour Party, participating in anti-Vietnam War demonstrations at Grosvenor Square and partial identification with the hippy and King's Road counter-culture. Oxford, however, had done little for my understanding of political and cultural struggle. I had done a B. Phil in English Literature from 1500 to 1660 and started a D. Phil on the Theatre of Cruelty. At that time it was my discovery of Artaud and the Theatre of the Absurd that engaged my enthusiasm.

It was therefore surprising that I conceived of popular theatre as a potentially revolutionary medium in South Africa and hardly

---

[12] Robert Arnato, playwright and director. He funded the publication of the theatre magazine, *S'ketsh*. He was instrumental in founding the Imita Players in East London and the Sechaba Players in Cape Town, who staged *The Sacrifice of Kreli* by Fatima Dike — Stephen Gray (ed.), *Theatre One* (Ad. Donker, 1978) — and played an important part in the making of Matsemela Manaka's *Egoli* (Soyikwa-Ravan, no date).

surprising that I did so in a state of ignorance and isolation. I had done little to study the history of political resistance in my country and nothing to join up with those nationalist and anti-apartheid organizations that were active in Britain at the time. I returned to South Africa in 1969 with plans to involve myself in popular theatre and a blueprint to use theatre as both a cover and an organizational opportunity to conscientize and prepare the ground for mass political resistance. I do not remember the details now but I do remember outlining them to a representative of the Rowntree Trust in an effort to secure a financial commitment to *S'ketsh* magazine, who described them as 'classically Maoist' — Maoist possibly, in many aspects except the fundamental and essential one, namely that such activity was useless unless integrated into a mass political programme and formulated and put into practice in co-operation with others within an organizational structure.

Thus, behind my own work in Workshop '71 there was at the inception a political agenda, bizarre and naive as it might now sound. It was an agenda that called for a theatre programme that bypassed the 'élite' and aimed at the popular masses, in which the play acted as a hub for organizational and conscientization work involving written literature of different kinds. In order for it to succeed it was important to avoid all the activities traditionally associated with political protest. This meant that even the play, while facilitating a political process, should not in itself be overtly political — in content for example. This accounts for my refusal to get involved in demonstrations or any political organizations in the period I was working with Workshop '71. Instead I got a permit from the Johannesburg Non-European Affairs Department to enter Soweto, on the pretext that I was from Oxford and working on a research topic on popular entertainment, and a job at the University where I hoped to be paid for doing virtually nothing. I then looked about for opportunities to put my popular theatre / political conscientization plan into operation.

Was it a measure of our ineffectiveness that the Special Branch knew all the theory of Focoist cultural strategy but failed to arrest me for its practice? Or was it just easier to get me on an immorality charge?

As an exploratory activity I accepted an invitation from Bess Finney to participate in a drama workshop at a church in Rosebank involving Anglican youth from Soweto and the white Northern Suburbs. The theme was, inevitably again, "contact" — as expressed in the Simon and Garfunkel lyric, "Bridge Over Troubled Water."

Our group's presentation depicted, among other images, a black preacher translating the sermon of his white colleague into Xhosa. The white priest preached the liberal message of love and tolerance, which his interpreter transformed into a revolutionary denunciation of oppression and a call to resist. The atmosphere in the audience was extraordinary. The white members could sense from the reaction of their black friends that something was going on. They became nervous and began to ask questions. Whites in their luxurious church in Rosebank were used to having all the answers. An occasion such as this was for them an opportunity to share, yes, though for how brief a period, to condescend, to patronise — not to ask their black brothers in Christ questions. The drama subverted the traditional relations of power and privilege in the audience.

The Anglican drama workshop opened up two opportunities for me — one at the Institute of Race Relations, the other in Soweto itself. In collaboration with June Mahlalepula Chabaku, a social worker based in Soweto, I launched a drama workshop at Naledi Hall, attended by a number of those I had met at the Rosebank workshop. For over a year we laboured on a script in Zulu and Sotho about Naledi life, meeting and rehearsing every Sunday until the usual difficulties of unpaid, voluntary work on rest days in the ghetto overcame us.

The work at the Institute produced Workshop '71's first play, *Crossroads*. It was a considerable success but, according to my blue print, with the wrong people and in the wrong areas. For popular black audiences its experimental, ensemble, 'poor theatre' style was alienating. As Felicia Mabuza, at that time taking part in the Phoenix Players musical, *Phiri*, wrote in her review:

> I feel strongly a band should be used because the songs do not jell (sic) well without a rhythm section, the voices are too amateurish to carry it off alone.

A common reaction from township audiences to the play was: "Shame, when you have got more money, you will get instruments and proper costumes." We had to face it. Gibson Kente[13] had set the stand-

---

[13] Since the early 1960s the most popular playwright in South Africa, with productions such as *Sikalo*, *Lifa*, *How Long*, *Mama and the Load* and many others. For thousands of South Africans his plays have been their introduction to the stage. His only published play is *Too Late* (in *South African People's Plays*, Heinemann, 1981).

ards and Peter Brook, Grotowski and the Living Theatre, along with traditional story-telling and mime, were no competition.

At this point the demands of the political agenda called for a turnaway from multiracial audiences, from the dream of livelihood and artistic experimentation, in the direction of a work sited fully in the popular culture and its theatre traditions, popular enough and accessible enough to attract a mass audience. *ZZZIP!* was the result — a musical comedy, for 50c.

ZZZIP! took its plot from Ben Jonson's *The Silent Woman*, just as Phoenix Players' *Phiri* was based on his *Volpone*. The difference was that the latter, like its predecessor at Dorkay House *King Kong*, was a big budget jazz opera, based in the culture of the Soweto élite and featuring a tycoon as its central character and money as its central theme. The former was a low budget Soweto soul and *mbhaqanga* musical based in the grassroots culture of Soweto youth and ordinary workers and, though similarly featuring a rich man and the battle for his inheritance as the central theme, involving a host of altogether less reputable characters. The idea was that *ZZZIP!* would go one better than Kente and Dorkay House and bring the musical register of popular theatre right up to date. For the youth and ordinary people in Soweto at that time the "*akulalwa*" all-night soul gigs and the music of the Movers and Mahlathini were all the rage.

ZZZIP! was popular and, but for one or two promotional blunders, it could have been far more popular than it was. Nevertheless it turned out to be a mistake. The blueprint involved by-passing the élite. However, their approval or disapproval proved to be important. *ZZZIP!* lost Workshop '71 the nascent respect of the black intellectuals and artists, which the far more serious content of *Crossroads* had begun to command. This allied to its apparent commerciality suggested that our main motive was financial. When the low admission prices were cited in our defence, the answer was simply that we were operating a cheap commercial operation on the same basis as the OK Bazaars. We also failed to recognize that commercial as Kente's productions were, they were grounded in the religious, moral and, ultimately, with plays like *How Long* and *Too Late*, in the political mores of his community. *ZZZIP!* not only seemed to have no message whatsoever, but worse, it seemed to be actually immoral, given the extremely frank talk and behaviour of the Returned Soldiers (divorced women) and the central device of passing off a young boy as 'the Silent Woman.'

After *Crossroads* had seemed to pioneer the re-birth of political satire and protest in the theatre, *ZZZIP!* aborted it. As for the modalities of the political strategy itself, all our energies went into promoting the entrance of our wooden horse into the citadel and we hardly began organising the infrastructure for conscientization and agitation it called for.

By the time we started work on *uNosilimela*, the original strategy had apparently begun to fade. I say apparently because it is difficult to recall what at different stages in our work I had precisely in mind. The agenda was a secret one. I discussed it with no-one and I certainly did not write about it. The closest I came to that was a camouflaged reference in an article I wrote for *Ch'Indaba* (the successor to *Transition*):

> a theatre that by-passed the un-conscientized élite, and would involve all sorts of side-effects for the mass audience. Scripts would be sold at performances to encourage reading as a habit — in all languages. Discussions after the performance would focus on technical matters, for those wanting to make their own plays, and the play's potential implications. Performances would not be confined to public halls in urban areas but would take place outdoors, in private houses or yards, schools, factories and especially in outlying areas ....[14]

From *uNosilimela* on, it would therefore appear that the covert plan to use popular theatre for mass political organization came to be submerged in the actual political significance of the plays' statements themselves. *uNosilimela*, while in itself an essentially conservative play, was seen at the time to make important statements about African art, culture and religion, in keeping with the assertions of the Black Consciousness movement. *uHlanga* extended this view of African history but now linked it to more aggressive racial politics (Eldridge Cleaver) and a far more militant vision of African revolution (Cabral). *Survival* and *Small Boy* turned their backs entirely on African romanticism and dissected the anatomy of *apartheid* prisons — the reality of concrete and steel and the image of a whole society that is experienced and perceived by millions who live in it, as a prison. *Survival* takes up the image of revolution but this time in the much more specific context of the South African revolution as symbolized in the four prisoners' hunger strike. The naked hatred, rage and determination to die rather than live on enslaved prefigured the revolt of the youth that followed

[14] *Ch'Indaba*, 2 (1976), pp. 38–43.

shortly after in Soweto and then all over the country, a revolt the play got caught up in itself when police invaded a performance in Soweto and closed it down.

A dream of livelihood

The political agenda assumed that whatever the theatre, profits would not be its aim. Just as I was later to experience again in Zambuko/ Izibuko, political theatre can be most comfortably waged by those who already have adequate incomes. It can also be made by extremely dedicated cadres, who, though poor, see their work in theatre as an important part of their struggle to transform society. In the main however, it is difficult for those without an adequate livelihood to perform political theatre without any consideration of gain. It also happens that some embrace the political ideology of the group in order to exploit its financial potential — especially the case in South Africa.

It was an obviously legitimate expectation on the part of many of those who came from Soweto and Alexandra to attend the weekly workshops and rehearsals and subsequently to participate in performances of *Crossroads*, that ultimately they would earn something for their pains. An aspect of the dialectic in Workshop '71 was the contradiction between the dream of livelihood and the hidden political agenda. From this contradiction others flowed: to perform to lucrative mixed audiences in town or to persevere in the sub-economic search for the popular audience; to go or not to go on overseas tours; to be a performing or a training body; to bribe or not to bribe the press, etc.

The actors who performed in *Crossroads* were excited by the large audiences and the money they paid, by the attention they received, by the Germans who filmed it for television. The success of *Crossroads* enabled Workshop '71 to purchase lighting equipment and a Ford Transit van. This the actors accepted but in the hope that ultimately they too would reap the benefits. It was the frustration of this hope that precipitated the withdrawal of Maredi, Sibanda, Sephuma, Radebe and others, first to join Lynn Hooker in *Mboni* and then Makwedini Mtsaka in *Meko*.[15] Sibanda then went on to play a lead role in Kente's *How Long*, as did Sephuma in *I Believe*.

The consequence of this was a change in the workshop's policy. Payment for the actors was introduced in *ZZZIP!* and *uNosilimela*. At

---

[15]*Meko* was an earlier version of the play later published under the title of *Not His Pride* (Ravan, 1978).

first payment was contingent on covering expenses but as this meant that often there was little to divide amongst the actors, a basic minimum was agreed on. Fortunately the enjoyment the actors got out of acting the two plays made up for the poor payment they received. The staging of *uNosilimela* was an essential part of its ideological statement but the erection of the audience seating it demanded was an expensive, tiring and time-consuming task. It was only worth erecting it for a run of at least four or five performances. Runs of this kind were quite new in Soweto so that very few people would turn up for weekday performances and the better attended weekend houses could hardly cover total costs.

It was only when Workshop '71 decided to form a professional company that the contradictions concerning livelihood were for a time resolved. The reasons for the formation of such a company will be discussed in the next section. The experiences of the earlier plays made it clear that in order for a professional company to succeed, costs had to be small. It was decided for this and other reasons to be discussed later that a one-man play, featuring Mthoba, be the first production of the new company. This was *uHlanga*. The play was sufficiently successful to pay the actor and the technical team, including Siphiwe Khumalo, who had acted in *uNosilimela*, a basic salary and prepare the ground for the next production for which nominal rehearsal fees would be paid. Maredi and Sibanda were recalled. Themba Ntinga, who had acted in *ZZZIP!* and had been given a full-time job working for Workshop '71, came in and a fourth, Fana Kekana, was recruited.

Fortunately, *Survival* proved to be a financial success, especially on its return to Johannesburg from Cape Town and East London. It was possible to employ another workshop member, Seilaneng Khomongwe, for front-of-house. Siphiwe Khumalo was on lights. The company operated as a co-operative. All takings were banked and statements then presented to the group, which decided in the light of circumstances what to do with the money, e.g. whether to pay itself bonuses, in addition to basic wages, or to save for future productions, buy equipment etc.

But the *Crossroads* myth was long in dying. Workshop '71 had all along cherished nostalgic dreams of reviving it. A revival would also bring other members of Workshop '71 into the family, the new professional company we had established. These considerations overrode the obvious economic dangers of a large cast.

At the Space Theatre the *Crossroads* revival did well, as it did in East London on its way up to Johannesburg. At the Market Theatre it was a financial failure and many of Workshop '71's assets had to be sold off to cover the actors' wages, including the PA system and musical instruments purchased for *ZZZIP!*.

Perhaps the play had become a little dated. However, I believe one of the main reasons for its failure was my own undemocratic decision to play it semi-arena instead of endstage, as it had been done in its first performances and subsequently at the Space and the Window Theatres. *Crossroads* needed a compact audience situation in order to achieve its sense of communality of experience and the semi-arena at the Market's upstairs theatre did not give this.

But by then *uHlanga* and *Survival* were due to leave the country. I had always opposed the chimera of overseas tours, seeing our first responsibility as reaching the popular audience at home. I did not believe either that European and North American audiences were likely to relate to our material.

However, just as it was possible to challenge my dedication to free political theatre by pointing out that I already had an adequate income, so it was possible to point out that I had already been to Europe and North America — if New York City and Vermont can be called North America. Maredi, Sibanda, Mthoba and company had never travelled abroad. So it was agreed that *uHlanga* would go to the Royal Court Theatre, London, and that *Survival*, with Sephuma as understudy, would undertake a tour of the United States under the auspices of a professor from a Californian university. But the profit derived, especially from the latter, was to be sent home to enable Workshop '71 to recoup its fortunes and continue its programmes. As it happened, though Mthoba and Sephuma returned to South Africa, Maredi, Sibanda, Ntinga, Kekana and myself remained away. No profits were ever sent home — and that was the end of Workshop '71.

An intense interest in theatre

The experimental nature of some of our work, particularly in the early days, was difficult for some to take. A detachment of white liberals, whose aesthetics were as conservative as their international politics, left after one or two workshops, loudly proclaiming that theatre was made by learning scripts and enacting them on stage, not by pretending to be frogs and flowers.

One later exercise nearly lost us the entire Alex contingent. This consisted of the actors smelling their own shoe and then placing it with all the others in a pile in the center. With eyes closed they then had to identify their own shoe by sniffing shoes until they came to it.

Obviously some of the ideas were over the top, but much of the work in the early workshops was brilliantly innovative.

In actor training workshops only the experienced actor who is already acting in plays, will be satisfied to go on for long without the desire to do a play becoming overwhelming. I had selected some passages from the mediaeval morality play, *Everyman*, for acting work and when at a meeting of the workshop it was decided that we now do a play, it was suggested we develop and adapt *Everyman*. The inadequacy of the Christian morality it expressed in the real world of Soweto, had already struck us. Maredi and the others brought stories of the gang war between the Msomis and Lefty Mthembu's *Spoilers* in Alex and Mthoba and others talked of *Crossroads* in White City, Jabavu, one of the most dangerous parts of Soweto.

The first performance of the play was meant to be at an English workshop at the University of the North. However, the University authorities refused to allow a play with a multiracial cast to perform on its campus. Another venue, the dining room of a nearby school, was hastily arranged and there it was performed to an excited audience. As has happened so often in my experience, theatre that is conjured up in a school dining room, a hostel laundry, a technical college workshop, a disused hall, far surpasses in atmosphere and magic performances in venues especially designed for performance.

For South Africa the workshop techniques of *Crossroads*, the ensemble nature of the performance, its barefoot style, its sparse use of simple representational props and costumes, were a revelation. The official opening of the play at Auden House was preceded by a demonstration workshop in which the actors shared with the audience the exercises and explorations which characterised the process that had produced the play.

The decision to perform a play at all had already caused problems for Workshop '71 and plans to take it to venues in the black townships compounded them. A number of theatre actors from various theatre groups had been attending the workshops, Sam Mhangwane's Sea Pearls, to name but one. For them Workshop '71 was a training ground — neutral territory, so to speak, where actors from different groups could come together, learn and share skills, and criticise each others' plays. Once Workshop '71 became itself a theatre group, performing to the same audiences as they were, these relations changed. It was no longer neutral territory. It was competition.

Though Workshop '71 continued its training role and organ-ized regular workshop performances of other plays, its original neutral status was lost and its ability to be directly useful to many theatre groups was diminished.

Whether to be a performing group or a training workshop came to be one of the recurrent dilemmas in its history. During the period when both *ZZZIP!* and *uNosilimela* were on the road there was little time for training workshops. In their aftermath though there was a move away from performance back to training. In the Winter 1975 issue of *S'ketsh* it was reported:

> *Crossroads* and *ZZZIP!* are no more and Credo Mutwa's *uNosilimela* is under new management. This is in accordance with the Workshop's decision to give up public perform-ances and concentrate on its activities as a part-time theatre school.

There followed a programme of workshops: Modern Dance with Les Carelse, Movement with Roberta Durrant, Directing with myself and Acting with Mthoba. In subsequent years, even outside South Africa, in Lusaka, in Tanzania, I have met people who claim to have been members of Workshop '71. I did not remember them be-cause they did not participate in any of the productions, but literally hundreds of young actors, playwrights and directors attended Work-shop '71's training sessions to take whatever they could pick up back to their groups and into the community.

After *Crossroads*, came *ZZZIP!*, an exercise in musical farce and knockabout. It produced exceptional performances from Mthoba, Makhene and Gertrude Moloi, and a fine sense of ensemble in the cast itself. However, it was an experiment in quite a different direction from *Crossroads*, as was the staging of Credo Mutwa's epic, *uNosilimela*. In conception *uNosilimela* was an extraordinary piece. Because of the imaginary recreation of traditional African staging featuring a number of acting areas, the action was able to swing, unbroken, from one fantastical episode to the next, from myth into symbol into reality, from the past into the future and back again to the present, from the land of the spirits to earth, from drama, to music and dance and then to narrative.

The play was derived not only from African traditions of stag-ing but from orature itself. In rehearsal and performance it remained just that, oral. We never worked from a complete written script. Mutwa carried the whole play in his head.

It was at this time that Mthoba established Izigqi. I remember having discussions with him over beer, *boerewors* and *pap* at his home in Mofolo, in which he spoke of his interest in making theatre for the blind and the deaf. I had met Lloyd Richards of the National Theatre of the Deaf in New York. We spoke of how we should really be making a theatre free of the press, the need for publicity, budgets, equipment, props etc., just a small group that would perform informally anywhere and get to the people themselves, where they live, where they work, where they study, rather than try and get them out into the uncertain Soweto night to see a play in a dreary municipal hall. Mthoba had not been involved in *uNosilimela* and he also wanted to pursue his interest in experimental theatre, a process we had started with *Crossroads*. The result was Izigqi. He was joined by some of the more committed members of the *ZZZIP!* cast — Ntinga, Makhene, Ntombikayise Khumalo — and Shirley Pendlebury of *Crossroads*.

Izigqi put together a programme of movement and dialogue they called *Visions of the Night*, the Douglas Turner-Ward play, *Happy Ending*, and Strindberg's *Miss Julie* and began performing, "before invited audiences, free of charge and especially in places where theatre seldom or never goes. Such as hostels small country institutions, hospitals, homes for the aged, the blind, the deaf and the dumb." The scripted plays were not as successful as their group-improvised piece and it was from that line of work that Mthoba's next experiment, *uHlanga, The Reed*, derived.

With *ZZZIP!, uNosilimela* and Izigqi's work all in performance, Workshop '71 was able to stage a festival at the Box Theatre, University of the Witwatersrand, over 10 days featuring these plays together with a revival of *Crossroads*. This was the culmination of a phase in the development of Workshop '71. It was clear that a new direction was needed. *uNosilimela* illustrated part of the problem. Here was a play of great originality and significance yet, in performance, though many admired it, it just did not have the impact it should have. The reason was clear. Its conception and staging were not adequately realised in performance because of the weakness and lack of rehearsal, training and experience of many of the performers.

Unlike those who acted in other groups such as Phoenix Players, Imita Players and Serpent Players, those who took part in Workshop '71's activities and productions were seldom of the educated or professional intermediate classes. By and large they were unemployed youth and low-paid workers — drivers, domestics, typists etc. Maredi was a tailor, Mthoba a number of things, including stores clerk and

Putco bus inspector. Ramowela was an untrained teacher, Makhene a library assistant. Sibanda, Ntinga and Tshabangu were usually unemployed. The actors recruited by Mutwa for *uNosilimela* were of particularly humble backgrounds, being mostly uneducated, unemployed township youth. For such actors to produce the kind of performance *uNosilimela* needed, a long and intensive period of training and rehearsal would have been required. However, Workshop '71 was an amateur organization, rehearsing at night and on Sundays and unable to pay rehearsal fees. Given this and the difficult circumstances of the actors' lives — one cast member was stabbed to death at a party, others were injured or imprisoned at different times — it was quite impossible to hold adequate rehearsals. Even performances presented problems. A number of our actors actually lost their jobs when their employers discovered that they were acting. Sana Mashinini of *uNosilimela*, for example, was fired from her job at Uncle Charlie's Roadhouse when her boss saw her photo in the newspaper. "You are now famous," he said. "You don't need this job anymore."

We knew that our work was original and significant in conception but that until our performance of it was good enough to bring this out, we would not realise the potential of our plays. It is here that the dream of livelihood and the intense interest in theatre as an art came together. We decided to form a professional company, which went on to produce *uHlanga, Small Boy* and *Survival*.

There was an element of bravura in our choice of plays. As *ZZZIP!* was obviously a response to *Phiri*, so *uHlanga* tried to take *Sizwe Banzi* one step further, while *Survival* was partly derived from our feelings about Barney Simon's production of the Canadian prison play, *Fortune and Men's Eyes* by John Herbert.[16] In Workshop '71 we had strong beliefs in certain things and when we saw others in the theatre failing — in our perception, of course — to see what we saw, we made an aesthetic and ideological statement in the form of a play.

With *Phiri* it was the élite, out-of-date cultural choices which we tried to improve on in *ZZZIP!*. We admired *Sizwe Bansi Is Dead*. For many the play showed the way forward into an experimental theatre of political comment, at a time when Workshop '71's *ZZZIP!* seemed to be turning its back on what it itself had pioneered with *Crossroads*.

---

[16] Barney Simon, writer and director. See Anne Fuchs, *Playing the Market* (Harwood, 1990).

However we felt that ideologically speaking, like *The Blood Knot* before it, it was flawed.[17]

In addition to responding to the ideological content, there was the fact that the play was a two-hander. What can be achieved then by one actor, we asked ourselves? Mthoba and I set out to find out.

In addition the interest in African Theatre that *uNosilimela* had inspired made a festival in Lagos, Nigeria, a tantalizing prospect. These influences combined to produce *uHlanga*. Just as the starting point in the making of *Sizwe Bansi* had been a photograph, so in *uHlanga* it was the body of the actor himself. Mthoba was a thin man and the opening idea of a skeleton taking on flesh and coming to life was derived from this. The rest of the play, while an exploration of African history, was also an exploration of transformation — transformation of the actor and his body and of the stick he carried and an exploration of the possibilities of *dialogue* available to an actor alone on stage.

As for Simon's production of John Herbert's *Fortune and Men's Eyes*, we asked: "Why do North American plays about North American prisons when we in South Africa are the world's leaders in the field?" We decided to do a *South African* play about *South African* prisons. We discovered that three of the play's four actors had first-hand experience of South African prisons. This introduced the play's basic idea, namely that of "the prison within/prison without." If *apartheid* South Africa was itself a prison state, then the society was "the prison without" and real prisons were "the prison within." The play developed this idea and was particularly concerned to explore how, for black South Africans, being black in the prison state was already an imposed state of inhumanity, an involuntary involvement in a system that led to the constant likelihood of passage from the prison without into the prison within and back again. The power of the actors' own improvisations produced four personal reports in contrasting styles whose combined statement, culminating in a hunger strike which was symbolic of total political revolt, was intended not only to indict the apartheid system but also to defy it.

---

[17] See Lewis Nkosi on *The Blood Knot* in *South Africa: Information and Analysis*, 63 (May, 1968), pp. 1–8, R. Kavanagh on *No-Good Friday* in *Theatre and Cultural Struggle in South Africa* (Zed, 1985), also "Political Theatre in South Africa and the Work of Athol Fugard," in *Theatre Research International*, 7, 3 (Oxford, 1982). For *Sizwe Bansi* (sic) *Is Dead* itself, see R.K., "*Sizwe Bansi* (sic) is alive and struggling for freedom," in *The African Communist*, 58 (1974), pp. 122–8.

    The processes of making *uHlanga* and *Survival* involved inten-
sive experimentation, not only with the material used but in particular
with ways of presenting the material. One scene in *Survival*, which was
eventually cut out anyway, that of the '*umthondo esandleni'* humiliation
imposed on black men in many different situations in apartheid life,[18]
was tried in a variety of styles — slow motion, backwards, in mirror
images, in mime — in an effort to project its horror without repeating
the humiliation imposed in real life by imposing it on the actors.

    One particularly powerful session of experimentation produced
a whole new play, *Small Boy*. Each of the four actors was given a
photograph cut out of a magazine. Having made life stories for the
photographs they were placed together in a prison cell — in an exercise
similar to Harold Pinter's early playwriting technique.[19] The resulting
interaction, involving power relations in the cell and a young boy the
old lag forced to share his blankets, was so skillfully shaped and dis-
turbingly portrayed that it was acted as a lunchtime companion piece
to evening performances of *Survival*. *Survival* itself became extremely
successful, particularly in its final run at the Box Theatre, Johannesburg. It must have been the first play of its kind in South Africa to run
for six consecutive weeks at one venue.

    As a conduit for liberal philanthropy, Workshop '71 could be
said to have bitten the hand that slapped its bottom. As a medium for
conscientization and political mobilization of the masses, Workshop
'71 was a spit in the wind. As a dream of livelihood — with the
exception of the professional company's shortlived adventure —
Workshop '71 was, during the time of its existence, fool's gold. As a
laboratory of theatrical experimentation it promised, despite its successes, more than it ultimately delivered.

---

[18] The phrase literally means "penis in hand" and was, or perhaps still is, used
for inspecting workers coming from the countryside for venereal disease. It
is related to the "tausa dance" in which the worker or prisoner strips naked
and does a dance step designed to reveal parts where forbidden or stolen
objects might be hidden. There is — or should be — a debate about the
depiction onstage of such practices. Workshop '71 either did not depict them
or did so in an artistically representational way. The actors and director of
Asinamali had no such qualms.

[19] As in *The Dumbwaiter*, for instance, in which two well-conceived characters
are placed in a room. The play's plot and dialogue develop from their interaction.

But as Engels put it: "The many individual wills active in history for the most part produce results quite other than those intended — often quite the opposite." Though our labours did not produce the results we hoped for, the results we *did* produce were in themselves extraordinary, considering that Workshop '71 had to function in the hostile environment of apartheid South Africa, that it only lasted six years and that it had access to virtually no funding whatsoever.

Workshop '71 pioneered performances by black and non-racial casts to non-racial audiences. At its workshop training sessions many theatre artists were exposed to theatre, to particular concepts of theatre, to theatre skills and possibilities.

Some of the leading directors, playwrights, actors and technicians in Johannesburg theatre today were once Workshop '71 members. If the Workshop itself was not able to provide a livelihood at the time, it provided many of its members with the skills and experience with which to make a living in the theatre subsequently. Workshop '71 opened up the theatre to the people's languages, suggested democratic ways of making plays and running companies and eventually came to embody in its aesthetic and in its practice the ideal of a non-racial democratic South Africa in which the majority rules and the culture of the majority comes into its own. Perhaps when all is said and done, the actual results of Workshop '71's work were more substantial and in the long run more valuable than those its founders struggled variously to achieve.

Productions by Workshop '71

1972 — *Crossroads*, staged in various venues in the Transvaal. Lesotho, Cape Town and East London, extracts published in *S'ketsh Magazine* (Summer, 1972).

1973 — *The Song of the Lusitanian Bogey* by Peter Weiss, Johannesburg.

1973 — *ZZZIP!*, staged on the Witwatersrand and in Pietermaritzburg, Durban, East London and Port Elizabeth.

1974 — *Miss Julie* by Strindberg, *Happy Ending* by Douglas Turner-Ward and *Visions of the Night*, all by Izigqi. Staged in the Johannesburg area.

1975 — *uHlanga – the Reed*, staged in Johannesburg, Cape Town, East London and at the Royal Court Theatre Upstairs, London.

1976 — *Survival*, staged in Johannesburg, the Western Cape, East London and at various venues in the United States, published in *South African People's Plays* (London: Heinemann, 1981).

1976 — *Small Boy*, short play performed in tandem with *Survival*.

WHOSE POPULAR THEATRE AND PERFORMANCE?

MARTIN ORKIN

I

Contestatory theatre practice and theatre criticism in the post-1976 period inevitably both reflect and interact with the developing crises in the apartheid social order. To a large extent such work not only still operated, perforce, within the ambit of apartheid hegemony but was also, in certain respects, determined by it. Within a state that abused ethnicity to exploit difference, the search for responses, accordingly, sometimes evidenced simple counter-reaction: the construction of, or discovery of, *unitary* versions of the "nation," "national culture," the "people" — "proper" creative and critical endeavours or voices that would represent a "truly" united majority or "national" non-apartheid position. Moreover, the often single-minded high moral tone with which new positions were asserted or sought, sometimes suggested, it may be argued, a mirror image of apartheid dogmatism.

In the study of theatre, the term "popular" implies some form of mass-based or majority-situated legitimation or support. There has been no lack of endeavour in theatre and performance to attempt to communicate or claim a "popular" voice for particular dramatic enterprises. But of course, all hinges on how the word "popular" is understood and how it is measured. I will argue that it is doubtful whether such an authentic "majority" voice may ever be easily established for South African theatre and performance, particularly in the decade and a half following the 1976 uprising. Ian Steadman's preference for describing "developments in oppositional work as part of an 'adversary tradition' which has seldom achieved popular status" (Steadman: 1990b, 209) is a more useful point of departure for any discussion of drama emanating from the subordinate classes.

In South Africa the attempt to discover or construct a version of "popular" theatre has entailed, in the criticism of the past decade and a half, an inevitable and necessary focus on "class" and "race". But critics have also identified some of the difficulties involved in such a project. In an article published in 1987, which develops earlier positions, Kelwyn Sole, arguing for the importance of an awareness of class, recognises nevertheless that "classes are constantly in the process of formation, change, reproduction and deformation into other, sometimes contradictory forms of identity and consciousness," and that they are, as well, often "the bearers of other forms of (non-class) identity" (Sole: 1987, 81). Proletarianisation, he notes for example, has not necessarily interfered with the "feeling of racial identity among black people" particularly because of "the historical way in which capitalism came to South Africa" (83). Moreover, "life in the townships, in the rural areas and in the workplace assist this diversity by giving a variety of possible identifications — class, ethnic, racial, sexual, regional" (83). Sole uses such and other points to argue against blanket ideas of populism but, at the same time, he recognises the value of "populism" in helping to avoid use of an exclusively class-dominated discourse:

> The emphasis on popular culture does have some advantages. Identities and ideologies in South Africa today are not always reducible to class terms, although they are shot through with class determination: populist discourse gives regional, ethnic, racial, sexual and other issues an autonomy which has been underemphasized elsewhere . . . these identities are not merely an effect of class struggle — they are interpellations (such as the "people"), identities and cultural usages (such as choir singing and self-help societies) which cut across class divisions in black society and which cannot be reduced to these divisions, although they are constantly reabsorbed and mobilised in the struggle between groups and classes. (88–9)

Ari Sitas, one of the pioneering facilitators of working class theatre in Natal, like Sole working from a class-based analytic position, also argues, from within his immediate context, against simplification. Addressing the problem of ethnicity in Natal, he observes: "there is no one appropriation of 'Zulu-ness': nor is there," he also argues only "one culture of resistance: there are many" (Sitas: 1990, 35). And Ian Steadman, who also draws on materialist discourse but argues for the use of the term "black theatre" to avoid, in discussions of "popular" drama, "trivialising the race issue" (Steadman: 1987, 2), nevertheless emphasises the need to avoid simplification or trivialisation of other kinds. Drawing on Mouffe he asseverates:

I prefer to view the creative practitioners of South African theatre as being inscribed in a multiplicity of social relations ranging from relations of production to relations of race, sex, vicinity, language and religion. Unlike some commentators, I argue that the practitioners of the theatre have many subject positions. The playwrights I study might well be inscribed in relations of production as workers or petit-bourgeois intellec-tuals, but they are also either male or female, white or black, Zulu or English (Steadman: 1990b, 211)

II

Given these reservations and sensitivities, these critics, drawing in one or other way on materialist discourse, nevertheless choose to fore-ground, as I have observed, "race" and "class" as particularly germane to the study of theatre. Not only demanded by the nature of apartheid society, as well as by the kind of materialist discourses within which they work, this was perhaps in the seventies and eighties a necessary counter-hegemonic activity in a literary world which was still, in the study of drama, often dominated by tenaciously conservative critical practices. These tended to privilege a very narrow focus upon kinds of interiority which might be found in South African versions of the practice of new criticism and the teachings of Leavis.

Thus, addressing the impulse to lay claim to the creation of a "popular" or "national" theatre, Sole's main project in his article is to argue that in South Africa "the dominant populist discourse hides the paucity of black literary expression with knowledge of, or by, black workers: a paucity which is easily forgotten in the prevalent rhetoric about 'popular' or 'mass based' literature" (Sole: 1987, 96). Accord-ingly, one of his conclusions is that "any attempt to conceive of an oppositional 'national culture' will have to . . . include working class expression as a major constituent" (91).

Sitas's main concerns in his article are also primarily material-ist. He explores and emphasises the multiple ways in which subject positions within classes are established, or may be modified or affected by a variety of factors. But, as I noted earlier, while they privilege the importance of class, both these writers identify and grapple with the problems raised by race and ethnicity. By contrast Steadman, while recognising the importance of an awareness of class, prefers to stress, as I also noted, the need to recognise the effects of racism in the working of the apartheid state. Thus, participating in or reflecting the desire which writers and artists manifested increasingly in the eighties

to validate cultural activity and present it as "work" that contributed
to the liberation struggle, Steadman identifies Matsemela Manaka as
"on the one hand . . . an artist and theatre practitioner trying to create
innovative performance" and on the other as "a concerned and committed black cultural worker expressing a vision of South African
society" (Steadman: 1986, 9–10). Against certain of Sole's strictures
about tendencies in Black Consciousness writings, he examines less
critically its attempts to construct a mythical past as a unified or
organic African history at the same time as working for a unified image
of the oppressed at the present time — as Manaka has it in *Pula*, "we
are fragments of a common segment cemented by the blood of a
common struggle" (cited in Steadman: 1986, 8).

While they place different kinds of stress upon the factors of
"race" and "class" then, these critics clearly imply or consider such
factors to be the most significant concerns in the study of "popular"
theatre and performance. There is no need to contest the obvious
validity of such a focus. What we may pursue, however, is the extent
to which we are willing to accept that the discourses from which these
concerns come should be the decisive arbiter of what may be considered part of an imagined authentic "popular" theatre. It is not the use
of such discourses — if anything, discourses which were invaluable
and vital to the anti-hegemonic struggle in the post-1976 period — that
need to be questioned, but the possibly tempting tendency to apply
them in inflexible ways (no different from the state's application of
apartheid discourse) that should perhaps be guarded against. For
instance, despite the concern which these critics evidence, when we
examine theatre emerging from the oppressed classes it is difficult to
avoid at some point recognition of the powerful presence in the plays
themselves of a strong predilection for religious discourse. Yet these
critics show little interest in this, although another critic, who also
draws upon materialist modes of thought, Bhekizizwe Peterson, by
contrast does make slightly more than passing reference (albeit still
only very briefly) to the fact that "a significant proportion of black
theatre emphasises religion . . . the enunciation of Christianity in *Woza
Albert!* is similar to that advanced by the adherents of contextual
theology and black theology. Both were influential social currents in
the seventies and within the Black Consciousness movement" (Peterson:
1990, 241, 243–4).

Apart from the very pertinent example of *Woza Albert!* and
apart from the well known instance of aspects of Gibson Kente's plays,
the phenomenon is easily discoverable elsewhere. We may note briefly

here that in criticism of Manaka's *Egoli*, for example, much energy has been expended on discussions of the construction of a mythical pre-colonial black past, on the one hand, and the attempt to unmask conditions of production in the mines on the other. But little attention has been paid, for example to implications in the song sung by the miners, postulating the possibility of a religious form of redemption for the workers:

> Thina sibanjelwe amahala We have been caught for nothing
> Singenzanga lutho We have committed no sin
> Tixo Somandla God Almighty we ask from you
> Sibuza kuwe, senzeni na? What have we done?
>
> Kule lizwe lenhlupeko In this country of poverty
> Sikhulule somandla Set us free. Almighty
> Nguwena kuphela Owaziyo You are the only one who knows
>
> Ukuthi iqiniso liyaphilisa That the truth heals
> Sicela kuwe, Somandla We ask from you Almighty
> Suza izitha Chase away our enemies,
> Siza iSizwe, Esimnyama Help the black nation. (*Egoli*, 19–20)

Maponya's play *Gangsters* presents the martyred figure of the poet Rasechaba on a cross, and the symbol is used on stage throughout the performance. The first act of *Sarafina!* climaxes in a funeral scene in which the preacher delivers a contestatory and religious sermon:

> Children of God. Bantwana baka Thixo. God has given and the police, they have taken. Children of God, what has happened to these children is not the unusual. For the nation is in the grave. The nation is blowing in the wind. Crossroads have been bulldozed and many have been left homeless in Cape Town. Voices that speak to us have either been sent to Robben Island or executed at Pretoria Central Prison. America and Britain have sold too many guns to the South African Government to kill our children.
> [He bows and says his last Amen]
> (cited from playtext very kindly lent to me by the playwright)

This is followed by a prayer for divine aid sung by the whole cast on stage.

Reference to such discourse is too frequent in too many post-1976 plays to suggest merely echoes of old assimilationist traditions. What is to be made then of this aspect of "popular" theatre and performance? Does it indicate that, against the strongly favoured materialist discourse drawn upon by many theatre critics, and against related discourses flowing through subordinate class and group liberatory struggle, religious discourse also has its own power and currency amongst the "masses"? And if so, should it properly be largely erased in accounts of what are deemed to be the authentic "popular" concerns?

Manaka, Maponya, and to an extent Ngema often, too, pursue markedly essentialist and idealist presentations of the subject in their plays (Manaka has described several of his most recent works with the phrase "search for self"). Yet although Sole notes the concern with humanism and the privileging of the artist in Black Consciousness theatre, he does so in predominantly proscriptive mood. Few critics have been interested in pursuing and interrogating this privileging of an essentialist form of interiority either, in terms of what it may have to suggest to us, more extensively, about "popular" culture and current preoccupations of theatre practitioners coming from the oppressed classes.

Such objections, we may reiterate, hinge upon the meaning that may be attached to the word "popular". It is true that from within the perspectives of materialist discourses we may argue that religious, essentialist and idealist preoccupations are instances of interpellation, or false consciousness, or reflect the class positions of the theatre practitioners involved. But this is, arguably, to insist on a mode of asserting or defining the "popular" (according to a particular discourse exclusively) in a way, as I have already suggested, at least analogous to the restrictive practices of apartheid hegemony. When Steadman cites, as another means of understanding the term "popular", "the ways in which members of a majority oppressed group use literature and performance to conscientise audiences in relation to a broad vision of structural change in society" (Steadman 1990b, 208–9), what those structural changes are will of course, again, be determined by the discourse on which the formulation depends. To privilege any such version of change and to argue that concerns in theatre not complementary to them are not "popular" may perpetuate in new forms, accordingly, the well known pre-1990 South African habits of censorship and erasure.

III

But can conceptions of the "popular" to any extent be based instead, then, on a study of what is fashionable or preferred by oppressed-class audiences? Here too there are problems: to what extent, in the post-1976 period (as indeed before) has theatre been performed in spaces of easy access to oppressed-class audiences, and how were the various audiences that witnessed performances during this period constituted? As is well known, there are still no proper theatre buildings in the townships of South Africa. Community or church halls and other temporary spaces have been used for the performance of plays; practitioners have often in consequence been more vulnerable to censorship and/or police interference. The telling absence of any proper theatres in the townships remains even at the time of writing — Bhekizizwe Peterson (Peterson: 1990, 233), in early 1990, is able to mention only the Funda Experimental Centre just outside Soweto as an example of a township space currently available for theatre and relatively free of government interference. Commenting on the work of the Durban Workers Cultural Local Ari Sitas some years earlier foregrounded as "imperative" the need "to situate the physical *spaces* of cultural reproduction amongst South Africa's workers" (Sitas: 1986, 89).

Very little information on or work about the constitution and size of most oppressed-class theatre audiences, furthermore, exists. The largest township audiences ever, still appear to have been those that watched the relatively conservative Gibson Kente's plays in the late sixties and early seventies (followed by the impressive drawing power to the Market Theatre, of Mbongeni Ngema's *Sarafina!* in the late 1980s — a play sometimes maligned by radicals for its "commercial" bias as well as for its presentation of women). The size of audiences watching Black Consciousness plays in the early seventies in the brief period during which they were allowed to be performed before government action suppressed them, or performances by other workshop theatre groups, for example, is unknown or unrecorded but likely to have been relatively small. And after 1976, as is well known, theatre activity in the townships diminished drastically not only because of increasing militant struggle in the townships but also, most especially, because of continuing police and army presence.

From the perspectives of Black Consciousness and materialism Kente's moderate position in the context of his large audiences provides a problem for radical constructions of "popular" theatre. And, as I remarked, the work of dramatists drawing on Black Consciousness in the post-1976 period such as Maponya and Manaka — frequently cited by Steadman, in discussions of "popular" theatre — has not won nearly the same kind of township following. In view of the continuing lack of established township theatre space, most evidence of audience

composition and size in township performances of work by such dramatists, by other workshop groups or by the Reverend Julius Mqina —
also noted by Steadman in discussions of popular theatre — remains
so far simply not available.

Especially since 1977 when theatre apartheid was in some
important senses officially dispensed with (amongst other continuing
modes of oppression, subsidies are still non-existent for example, for
oppressed-class or contestatory theatre groups), theatre spaces in the
cities were, of course, available for use by oppressed-class theatre
practitioners. South African contestatory theatre has been, accordingly, in the post-1976 period able to find some kind of home in venues
such as the Market Theatre Complex in Johannesburg, the People's
Space Theatre (in the late seventies) in Cape Town and the Baxter
Theatre. But, in the argument of most commentators, audience composition in such spaces, more easily conjectured or measured, is made
up of, probably, liberal-minded or dissident members of the ruling
middle classes, together with those township people able to afford the
price of tickets and a journey into the city. Again, these are usually
described by commentators as likely to be predominantly members of
the township middle- or petit-bourgeois classes only. It is true that a
measure of theatricality has entered the political sphere: the use of
ritual poetry, oral performance even enacted scenes at political meetings, at rallies and at funerals. But we do not yet know enough about
such events to make reliable generalisations. While this is, most certainly, a compellingly interesting development in the South African
theatre practice, it remains for the most part at present in effect
marginalised, a transitory, and, beyond the moment of its happening,
largely uncharted activity.

Yet other considerations complicate the problem of attaching
significance to audience size, in the endeavour to establish the "popular". As Steadman notes, "the notion of box-office appeal . . . is inex-
tricably tied to marketing strategies based on access to media and
capital" (Steadman: 1990b, 209). Accordingly, it is sometimes argued
that the "popular" should be distinguished from what the "people"
may ("misguidedly") prefer. Separation of the "popular" from the
"people's" view or a "people's" culture, also entails definition of the
latter as "produced by and addressed to the oppressed people in any
society, often domesticating them in a conservative way, and preclud-
ing any real interrogation of the structural causes of their oppression"
(209). But, again, from within materialist perspectives, this procedure
may arguably itself evidence or entail the practice of vanguardism and

élitism. It is difficult to avoid the conclusion that we cannot take anything for granted in claims made about audience support for what may be proposed as authentic "popular" theatre.

IV

Any attempt to argue for or discover an authentic "popular" theatre is undermined also by the fact that theatre practice in South Africa has always to some extent involved practitioners from different classes and groups. Certainly, in the emergence, performance, and sometimes publication of contestatory theatre, emanating from or involved with members of the oppressed classes and groups, there has usually been at some stage dissident ruling class involvement. Steadman bases his discussion of what he defines as "community theatre" for example, on only two projects in both of which "the initiative came not from the communities themselves, but from cultural agents: educated social workers and theatre practitioners who entered the communities as outsiders and attempted to use the experiences of community members in order to educate them" (Steadman: 1990a, 311–2). It is worth noting here that the one project was to form the subject of an academic thesis; the author of the article describing the other project was also an academic who has since emigrated from South Africa. It is well known too that the "worker" theatre movement in Natal similarly resulted, in the first instance, from the intervention of non-working class agents with academic backgrounds.

Nevertheless, for certain critics, constructions or versions of a pure non-diluted "popular" theatre and performance are at least implied as ideals against which actual theatre practice may be measured. Indeed, even at the level of literary / dramatic influence, Ian Steadman can identify, in a discussion of "popular" theatre, fear of the contamination of just such an hypothesised pure "popular consciousness." He wonders whether the fact that Manaka draws on European theorists like Artaud and Grotowski may isolate him from "popular consciousness" (Steadman: 1986, 17). The myth of an organic, unified or single consciousness becomes here the ideal goal towards which the equally putative "popular" theatre needs to strive.

Perhaps the best example of this may be found in aspects of Sole's work. As I noted earlier, he argues that only theatre with "knowledge of or by black workers" will legitimate claims to a "national" theatre, and sees the involvement of non-working class elements as something that helps to prevent such mythic authenticity from coming into being. For him, Black Consciousness was launched by those "out-side of the focus of the means of production and distribution, the students . . . [and] seems to have begun as, and up until now largely remained an ideology particularly attractive to the radical middle class" (Sole: 1987, 48). Consequently, "while the literature which has grown up around the Black Consciousness ideology can be seen to be radical, innovative and assertive, and while black writers and perform-ers have become caught up with the role of being 'poets of the people,' there remains a gap between writer/performer and his or her commu-nity which tends to be obscured by prevalent rhetoric about the litera-ture" (62). This gap produces "hiatuses and silences" so that, "a great deal of black literature that has been written down in this country has been produced by a relatively better educated, more articulate class of black people with definite political priorities and preoccupations's" (46) and these "better educated more articulate" practitioners, "some-times but not always, represent the views of the black lower classes they claim to speak for" (46).

    The result, in terms of his preferred discourse, he warns, may be obfuscatory: "If it is not seen that social and class struggles over access to economic and political power are the major dynamic of social change, that these struggles are not synonymous with racial struggles, and that black artists and intellectuals are not necessarily at one with a vaguely defined 'black people,' the resulting ideology and literature will lend itself most easily to appropriation by an aspirant black bour-geoisie which may seek power and wealth for itself at the expense of the 'ordinary black people'" which it claims to represent (58–9). He offers a precise articulation of what he considers the prerequisite for "authentic" representation of the working class: "the observation that the working class is important because it is one of the two major contending classes in capitalist society with access to the means of production, and the only one structurally in a position to alter the relations of production" (87).

    This kind of criticism demands of a "national" theatre not only transmission of this particular version of materialist discourse, but as well, requires that it come from, particularly, "authentic" working class practitioners. The "gap" which Sole detects between practitioners and community, is perceived negatively. But how indeed, we may wonder, can the "gap" between the dramatist or writer and her or his community which Sole worries about ever be completely avoided, once the move into articulation via theatre is taken and practitioners of theatre begin, through such preferred or chosen narratives, to perform their work? Even in "worker" theatre, Sole acknowledges that translating the direct experience of work and means of working class expression into theatre does contradict and alter some of the expectations and preconceptions of audience and actors. And the moment the worker play is produced beyond its original trade union meeting the "gap" between practitioners and their original community and purposes is likely to increase. Again, "worker" plays have also been performed after their first trade union meetings out of the trade union context, for example at university halls and on overseas tours. Sole observes that "the separation of working class performers and writers from an organic relationship with the culture which bred them is . . . the norm" (79), but one wonders what alternative he has in mind or whether any such alternative has ever been possible. It is difficult to conceive of a dramatic situation where such a "gap" would ever be absent, to provide an uncomplicated and spontaneous form of "worker" theatre.

Moreover, as I noted earlier, cultural agents who are not working class have been the primary facilitators for the emergence of "worker" theatre and although the growth of this theatre is impressive in the Natal area, it has yet to demonstrate convincing spontaneous growth beyond their ambience. We still know most about the emergence and growth of worker theatre only through the writings and descriptions of the two (non-working class) facilitators most actively involved in the project and unlikely therefore in their reportage to be non-partisan (see, for example, Sitas: 1986; von Kotze: 1988). These observations in no way detract from the remarkable nature of the phenomenon and its growth — but they are ones that underline a possibly quixotic streak in urges to construct or imagine a purely working-class theatre with no non-working class involvement, which may then be used as the springboard to criticise a variety of non-"worker" theatrical projects.

V

The idealisation of particular versions of the "popular" or the "national" in terms of which aspects of contemporary theatre may then be interrogated, is also in other ways problematic. When Sole notes that Black Consciousness theatre is written by "better educated, more articulate" members of the community it is difficult to conceive of his implied preferred alternative — the less educated, less articulate theatre practitioner? In the first great age of theatre in English, the Elizabethan and Jacobean period, most plays, sometimes subversive in thrust, were also produced by similarly "better educated and more articulate" members of the social order. We may wonder, then, what kind of mythic dramatist is being constructed by this kind of postulate, against which contemporary writers are being positioned (and to a degree at least, graded).

Again, Sole goes on to argue that "better educated and more articulate" writers have particular "political priorities and preoccupations." But if we agree that the class or group position of the artist or theatre practitioner is significant, the inevitable gap between such practitioners and the community from which they come will render not only Black Consciousness dramatists liable to related observations. It is difficult to imagine how any dramatist, or for that matter any drama critic or scholar can evade being grouped with an articulate and educated stratum — in many cases too, positioned, probably, in a petit-bourgeois if not middle class context. While it may be reasonably argued that Sole's distinctions are not to be treated as absolute but point helpfully to relative degrees of knowledge and involvement, the implicit mirage of a practitioner organically at one with her or his (working class) community's consciousness and experience, often encourages a strongly censorious notation of "failures" and lapses in work which does not conform to particular ideological discursive formations.

Theatre practitioners, by virtue of what they do — the nomenclature of "cultural worker" notwithstanding — may seem, from this perspective, doomed always to be to some extent at least separated from the community experience in which "ordinary" people are involved. Consequently, in terms of this reasoning, a certain, inevitable, marginality in all theatrical endeavour, and indeed, in the practice of dramatic criticism, which also comes from critics occupying positions outside those occupied by the "less educated" and "less articulate" must needs follow. And for the critic and scholar too, any claims to awareness of the authentic "popular" theatre would presumably need to be qualified by the position she or he occupies (always outside the "ordinary" experience of the working classes and groups), her or his desired links with one or other version of the liberation struggle, and her or his explicit or implied discursive constructions of an "organically whole" alternative.

There are complexities to be considered even in the matter of language. Sole's criticism of the development of Black Consciousness theory, that its ideas, communicated in English are sometimes inaccessible because "many lower class people do not have the tools (reading and English language skills)" (Sole: 1987, 54) to respond to published work, applies of course as much to his own writing as it does to Black Consciousness writers, or to any other critical or theatrical work published — and, to a degree also, performed — in English. Much of the contestatory drama (and drama criticism) that has appeared in South Africa, and certainly that which has subsequently been published in one or other way is predominantly in English. Although Mphahlele has argued that English has been appropriated by the oppressed classes as a tool of liberation, Njabulo Ndebele stresses that it must still be treated with caution (see Mphahlele, 1984; Ndebele, 1987). But the important fact that English is, although one of the official languages of apartheid in present-day South Africa, still spoken by a minority of the South African peoples as their first or home language, renders all work performed in it, certainly in terms of audience-based criteria for the determination of the "popular", part of a minority activity.

VI

Problems in constructing mythically "perfect", "whole" and "uncontaminated" alternatives to what we find in current theatre and performance, as well as some aspects of the project to define or insist on versions of a "popular" or "national" form of theatre and performance may be set against the rather different treatment given to the concept of "popular culture" by the noted drama historian Walter Cohen. Drawing on Peter Burke, he describes popular culture as "perhaps best defined initially in a negative way as unofficial culture, the culture of the non-élite, the 'subordinate classes' as Gramsci called them" (Cohen: 1985, 18). Yet Cohen also argues that "a purely popular theatre cannot exist in a class society" and he notes how Renaissance theatre consisted of a mixture of popular and élite elements in the immediate institutional context:

> Most of the actors in the public theatres came from the lower classes. Though often of comparably humble origin, many of the playwrights managed to acquire a university education or its equivalent. The theatres themselves . . . drew on both popular and aristocratic stage traditions: similarly they operated under royal license, patronage, and censorship while appealing to a large clientele in the pursuit of profit. Although the plays attracted virtually all urban social strata, the lower classes probably dominated the audience numerically. (19)

In consequence, Cohen identifies a "structured complexity of ruling-class power and popular opposition" and argues that "in Renaissance England and Spain, a relatively unified national culture rendered unthinkable any absolute demarcation between popular and learned traditions, while obscuring basic inequities and genuine class conflict" (29). Thus, argues Cohen, "to adapt various contemporary formulations, a demystification of ideology and ideological state apparatuses must balance enthusiasm for the creative, the autonomy and the utopian thrust of popular culture" (29).

And he maintains therefore that in theatre and society alike, only a "*combination* of learned and popular culture made it possible to dismantle ruling-class views and replace them with new perspectives of greater scope, power and social justice" (29, my emphasis).

In South Africa the operation of apartheid hegemony has ensured a powerful process of penetration into the subordinate classes in a variety of ways that may make Cohen's particular focus on intersecting complexities especially helpful. We may recall here Steadman's emphasis in 1986 that there are continual oscillations within the hegemonic system, stressing the flux of cultural relations and arguing that popular culture is defined in a continuing dialectical relationship with the cultural forms of the dominant group, class or culture (Steadman: 1986, 2).

It is true that theatre practitioners do at least in part negotiate with the processes of transformation within the social order. In any attempts at intervention what discourses may be preferred by the practitioners themselves, in the theatrical presentation of such transformations, or attempts to contribute to them, will always entail for each practitioner a particular choice. But in the critical study of contestatory theatre and performance, the tendency at times evident in even the finest criticism of the past decade and a half, to insist on only certain strategies and certain concerns in the name of sometimes idealised non-complex alternatives, should now be more determinedly resisted. Drama, as we may recall, itself based on conflict, and, essentially dialogic, always reflects or identifies or participates in different versions of struggle inevitably involving a variety of opposed or contradictory discourses.

Moreover, against insistent critical concerns to "forge" and "build" a "national" culture it may be, in addition, argued, that the culture of the "new" South Africa will only really be known to the generation that follows ours. What dramatic critics may "know," read or perceive in text/performance are the present various, diverse and contradictory complexities in the struggle against apartheid — one which, since February 1990, is still being waged. These complexities include hegemonic penetrations and their effects, as well as the variety of sometimes mutually incompatible oppositional modes resisting them which still traverse the South African terrain with no certain indication of the outcome. We may think here, to appreciate this, for instance, of the range of responses — particularly the trade union response — to *Township Fever*, or of Mbongeni Ngema's subsequent, probably frustrated reaction in a BBC television interview, that he was thinking of emigrating from South Africa. Ngema is in other ways a good instance of aspects of the problems I have in mind. As I noted earlier, he has been frequently accused (as Kente was) of commercialism and exploitation, by critics and practitioners with active partisan involvements in versions of the "popular" of their own. But again as I noted earlier his work has probably drawn more voluntary audiences from the townships than that of anyone else in the past decade or so — certainly much larger than any of the ventures with which these critics and practitioners have been associated, which they have actively initiated, or which they advocate. Theatre in South Africa particularly in the last one and a half decades or so inevitably involves different and often mutually contradictory discourses, emanates from theatre practitioners who themselves occupy multiple different positions, occurs in an increasingly fluid situation. Projects that endeavour to prescribe *what ought to be, must be or should have been done* in the name of the chimera of the "popular" have exhausted their original contestatory impetus. Instead, the foregrounding and exploration of theatre as the representation of *present* struggle, inevitably involving multiple positions, diversities and practitioners who themselves, have multiple different perspectives with which, dramatically and dialogically, to engage becomes, arguably, one of the vital undertakings at present urgently required in South African theatre studies.

REFERENCES

Cohen, Walter, 1985. *Drama of a Nation: Public Theatre in Renaissance England and Spain*, Ithaca: Cornell University Press.

Manaka, Matsemela. *Egoli*, Johannesburg: Ravan, no date.

Mphahlele, Es'kia, 1984. "Prometheus in chains: the fate of English in South Africa," in *The English Academy Review*, vol. 2.

Ndebele, Njabulo S., 1987. "The English Language and Social Change in South Africa," in *The English Academy Review*, vol. 4. Repr. in Njabulo S.

Ndebele, *Rediscovery of the Ordinary. Essays on South African Literature and Culture*, Johannesburg: COSAW, 1991.

Peterson, Bhekizizwe, 1990. "Apartheid and the Political Imagination in Black South African Theatre," *Journal of Southern African Studies*, Vol. 16, No. 2 (June 1990), Special Issue: Politics and Performance, ed. Liz Gunner, pp. 229–245. This volume has now been reprinted under the title *Politics and Performance. Theatre, Poetry and Song in Southern Africa* (Johannesburg: Witwatersrand University Press, 1994).

Sitas, Ari, 1986. "Culture and Production: The Contradictions of Working-Class Theatre in South Africa," *Africa Perspective*, New Series 1 (1&2): 84–111.

Sitas, Ari, 1990. "The Flight of the Gwala-Gwala Bird: Ethnicity, Populism, and Worker Culture in Natal's Labour Movement," unpublished paper presented to the History Workshop, University of the Witwatersrand, February.

Sole, Kelwyn, 1987. "Identities and Priorities in Recent Black Literature and Performance — A Preliminary Investigation," in *South African Theatre Journal* 1 (1), pp. 45–113.

Steadman Ian, 1986. "Popular Culture and Performance in South Africa," Durban: CCSU.

Steadman Ian, 1987. Editorial, in *Critical Arts: a Journal for Cultural Studies*, 4:3.

Steadman, Ian, 1990a. "Collective Creativity: Theatre for a Post-Apartheid Society," in Trump, Martin ed., *Rendering Things Visible*, Johannesburg: Ravan.

Steadman, Ian, 1990b. "Towards Popular Theatre in South Africa," *Journal of Southern African Studies*, Vol. 16, No. 2 (June 1990), Special issue: Performance and Popular Culture, ed. Liz Gunner, pp. 208–228.

von Kotze, Astrid, 1988. *Organise and Act*, Natal: Culture and Working Life Publications, University of Natal.

THE PERFORMANCE AESTHETICS OF TOWNSHIP THEATRE: FRAMES AND CODES

CHRISTOPHER BALME

The theatrical storm that erupted onto the international theatre scene with the arrival of *Woza Albert!* at the Edinburgh Fringe Festival in 1982 and which reached its zenith perhaps in 1988/89 with the unprecedented commercial success of the musical *Sarafina* has confronted the theatre world with an intriguing performance form. The black theatre from the South African townships evidently has the ability to function both in its autochthonous context as political theatre and seems as well to be able to transcend effortlessly cultural boundaries and communicate with equal effectiveness to Euroamerican audiences, or indeed, to audiences wherever the plays are performed. The key to this success seems to be the creation of a theatrical language which, in terms of its aesthetics and of the cultural codes it draws upon, can in fact speak many languages at the same time. The aim of this article is to examine the means by which this theatrical genre communicates on stage. The analysis will be based upon three works: *Woza Albert!* by Percy Mtwa, Mbongeni Ngema and Barney Simon, *Asinamali!* by Mbongeni Ngema, and *Bopha!* by Percy Mtwa.[1] Although this small selection cannot lay claim to being fully representative of the rich theatrical culture of the townships, the plays are certainly indicative of a certain phase in the development of township theatre, and their immense success, both in South Africa and abroad has made them in many ways synonymous with this theatre form.

Any examination of performance aesthetics must of necessity transcend a narrow adherence to textual analysis. While these plays

---

[1] These three plays have been published in *Woza Afrika! An Anthology of South African Plays*, ed. Duma Ndlovu, New York: George Braziller, 1986. All quotations from the plays refer to this edition.

are primarily textual in orientation, as opposed to musical or dance-oriented, their specific theatrical communication form cannot be construed from the dialogue alone. The interest here is not so much on what the works say but how they say it. The analysis will therefore draw on audiovisual materials: videotapes of all three plays have been consulted; production photographs; personal observation[2]; interviews with the author/directors and actors; and the playtexts themselves, which contain extensive stage directions. Used together with the audiovisual material, these playtexts can provide a reasonably accurate and comprehensive picture of performance conditions.

There is no shortage of historical overviews of the development of township theatre. Kavanagh, Coplan and Larlham[3] provide the most comprehensive surveys of Black theatre in South Africa, albeit with very differing emphases. All three and, in fact most other commentators, have recognised the aesthetic complexity of the genre; the debt to both the Western and African performance traditions; and the special features such as narrative modes, episodic structure, use of music and dance etc. With few exceptions[4] these comments do not, however, proceed beyond generalized observations. This is not surprising in the face of the relative novelty of the genre and the fact that the plays do not seem to offer the traditional literary approach to drama a great deal to work with. The terms "syncreticity" and "hybridity" have been mooted to describe this combination of African and Western forms. The ethnomusicologist David Coplan stresses for example the influence of Black American performance culture on Black South African urban culture and that its adoption and adaptation by Black South African artists represents neither "slavish imitation" nor

---

[2] There is as yet no generally acceptable scholarly way of including personal observations in theatrical analysis. Needless to say theatre scholars need to develop an equivalent of the ethnographer's field notes. Such an adoption of anthropological methodology for theatre and performance studies has been most energetically promoted by Richard Schechner. See his article, "Anthropological Analysis," *The Drama Review* 22:3 (Sept. 1978), 55–66.

[3] Robert Mshengu Kavanagh, *Theatre and Cultural Struggle in South Africa*. London: Zed Books, 1986. David B. Coplan, In *Township Tonight: South Africa's Black City Music and Theatre*, London: Longman, 1985; Peter Larlham, *Black theatre, dance and ritual in South Africa*, Ann Arbor: UMI Press, 1985.

[4] Cf. for example the article by Anne Fuchs: "Re-creation: one aspect of oral tradition and the theatre in South Africa," *Commonwealth* 9:2 (Spring 1987), 32–40. Fuchs argues that the actual structure of *Woza Albert!*, a product of workshop and improvisation, may owe a debt to the structure of Zulu folktales.

rejection of an indigenous heritage:

> It is rather the result of a creative syncretism in which inno-
> vative performers combine materials from cultures in contact
> into qualitively new forms in response to changing condi-
> tions, needs, self-images, and aspirations. In South Africa,
> stylistic elements from many sources have been recomposed
> into new frameworks of meaning, reflecting changing moral
> relations, systems of identity and value, and realities of power.[5]

Although Coplan is thinking here primarily of Black music, his
remarks can be applied equally well if we expand the parameters
somewhat to include impulses from the wider Euroamerican theatrical
context. Although the influences are somewhat different, the actual
process remains the same.

In the following analysis, the components of this syncretic
process in its performance products will be examined under the two
broad concepts of frames and codes. The term frame/framing has been
adopted and adapted from Erving Goffman's sociological study, *Frame
Analysis: An Essay on the Organisation of Experience*, to denote the way
in which theatrical communication is organised on a macrolevel. It will
be used to show how these plays organise narrative, execute shifts in
time and space, play with questions of genre, and organise relations
between performer and spectator. On the microlevel we will investigate the individual codes — linguistic, gestural, kinesic, aesthetic — at
work in the plays. Although Goffman's study is mainly concerned
with the way social experience is organised and perceived, he draws
on countless examples from the realm of theatre, cinema and radio
drama to illustrate his categories. The result is a comprehensive study
of the way theatrical communication functions and has functioned (the
historical changes are particularly important); he also provides some
examples of the very different framing conventions obtaining in Chinese and Japanese theatre, for example.

Goffman defines the framing process as follows:

> I assume that definitions of a situation are built up in accord-
> ance with principles of organisation which govern events —
> at least social ones — and our subjective involvement in them;

---

[5] Coplan, *op. cit.* p. 236f. Temple Hauptfleisch opts for the term "hybrid" to
denote essentially the same process. Cf. Temple Hauptfleisch, "Beyond Street
Theatre and Festival: The Forms of South African Theatre," *Maske und Kothurn*,
33:1–2 (1987), 175–188, here p. 177.

frame is the word I use to refer to such of these basic elements as I am able to identify.[6]

The act of framing or defining activities and situations is of course well-known; Goffman is, however, primarily interested in the processes by which we change and redefine an activity or situations: these processes of transcription and transformation he calls *keying*; changes in key are usually indicated by specific *cues* which establish when a transformation is about to begin and end. In analogy to Goffman we can say that on the most fundamental level, theatre works on three framing levels or categories. The following categories are my own and are not drawn directly from Goffman's analysis, although he does deal with some of the elements contained in them.

> –*Dramaturgical framing*, which informs, narrates, tells us where and when the action takes place, etc. Naturalistic drama has to utilize the device of exposition, with varying degrees of subtlety, to provide this information. Non-naturalistic forms have recourse to a large vocabulary of devices ranging from prologues, direct narration to banners and voice-overs. Temporal and spatial transitions within the action are also communicated in this way.
>
> –*Performance framing*. The sets of conventions which control the shift from the everyday world to the fictional world of the theatrical performance and the behaviour of both actors and spectators which obtains during the performance. On certain cues (lowering of house-lights, lifting of the curtain) the "theatre-goer" becomes an "on-looker" (Goffman's distinction[7]); the actor assumes his role and, traditionally in Western theatre, in so doing divorces himself in varying degrees from his personal identity.
>
> –*Generic framing*. The information provided to orientate the spectator as to what genre of theatrical performance s/he will be witnessing, which should in turn influence his activity as a spectator. For example, spectatorial behaviour will/should be different in a night-club show or music-hall performance than in the performance of an Ibsen play. Generic framing influences of course performance framing. It is a component of the "horizon of expectation," a term introduced by the

---

[6] Erving Goffman, *Frame Analysis: An Essay on the Organisation of Experience*, Cambridge, Mass.: Harvard Univ. Press, 1974, p. 10f.

[7] Goffman, *op. cit.*, p. 130.

theorists of reception aesthetics[8] to denote primarily reading strategies.

To begin with generic framing. We are principally concerned with how a Township performance identifies itself, the rules and conventions it sets up and by which it expects to be governed; i.e. on the level of production. The question of academic generic categorisation is one of secondary reception and not really central to the process of generic framing. As a footnote it might, however, be added that a feature of Township theatre has been that it has largely defied easy generic classification. The South African theatre scholar Temple Hauptfleisch articulates precisely this ambiguity when he marshalls the following epithets to describe *Woza Albert!*: "*Woza Albert!* employs the *commedia dell'arte* style as frame, but emphasizes the narrative element in a way reminiscent of *ntsomi* usage — *but* utilizing two narrators and thus setting up dramatic interchanges in something like vaudeville fashion."[9] The necessity to establish genre in a township setting is well illustrated by an anecdote Athol Fugard tells relating to the first performance of *Sizwe Bansi is Dead* in a township. Before the performance began, a member of the Serpent Players, Welcome Guru, held a speech in which framing conventions were explicitly explained: He warned the spectators that there would be no women, singing or dancing in the performance and that they would have to expect an evening of "normal theatre."[10] It is clear that the audience's "horizon

---

[8] Cf. Hans Robert Jauss, *Ästhetische Erfahrung und literarische Hermeneutik*, Munich: Fink, 1977, p. 18. The term is beginning to gain currency among theatre scholars: cf. Patrice Pavis, "Production et réception au théâtre: la concrétisation du texte dramatique et spectaculaire", in: Patrice Pavis, *Voix et images de la scène: vers une sémiologie de la réception*, Villeneuve d'Ascq: Presses universitaires de Lille, 1985; and Marvin Carlson, "Theatre audiences and the reading of performance," in: Thomas Postlewaite and Bruce McConnachie (eds.) *Interpreting the Theatrical Past: Essays in the Historiography of Performance*. Iowa: Univ. of Iowa Press, 1989, 82–98.

[9] Temple Hauptfleisch, *op. cit.*, p. 185.

[10] Athol Fugard, "Sizwe Bansi is Dead", in: *A Night at the Theatre*, ed. Ronald Harwood, London: Methuen, 1982, pp. 26–33. In the article, Fugard goes on to describe how Western conditions of performance framing were flaunted during the performance. Spectators made highly audible comments, came up on stage and congratulated the actors, and at the crucial moment in the play when Sizwe is debating whether to assume the identity of the dead man the audience entered into the debate and turned the performance into a heated discussion on the pass laws.

of expectation" was focused on a type of theatre formed probably by
exposure to the Black writer-director-composer Gibson Kente and his
Township Musicals or similar performances, in which singing, dancing and some kind of romantic interest are essential generic components. All three Township plays examined here take cognizance of the
fact that music and dance belong in the township context to the genre
theatre. Their adherence to a Grotowskian performance ethic and
aesthetic precludes them of course from utilizing the large scale resources of a Gibson Kente-style musical production. The opening of
Woza Albert! is perhaps the most successful example of generic framing
of the three plays in question:

> The actors enter and take their positions quickly, simply.
> Mbongeni sits on the tea-chests at the point they meet in the
> middle. Percy squats between his legs. As they create their
> totem, the houselights dim to blackout. On the first note of
> their music, overhead lights come on, sculpting them. They
> become an instrumental jazz band, using only their bodies
> and their mouths/double bass, saxophone, flute, drums,
> bongos, trumpet etc.[11]

Not only do they establish a Township theatre frame by performing *mbaqanga*-style music, but their exquisitely executed "poor
theatre" musical tour de force establishes for the audience the whole
performance style of the play. Within the opening scene of the play,
an acceptable, "traditional" generic frame is communicated, and at the
same time a new, "avantgarde" performance style is introduced and
perhaps made palatable. *Asinamali!* and *Bopha!* similarly set up generic
frames by commencing with music and movement and also introducing the structure and subject matter of the play. The opening song and
dance of *Asinamali!* is interrupted as each actor steps forward and
introduces himself, and in so doing establishes the narrative structure
of the performance. The opening scene of *Bopha!*, a police drill parade
which transforms into a dance, establishes the theme and setting of
Black police in a white police state with an impressive dance performance. All three plays demonstrate in their opening sequences the
importance of generic framing by means other than the purely dialogic,
expository tradition of Western theatre.

These examples make clear that the process of generic framing
in Township theatre glides over into *dramaturgical* framing. The open-

---

[11] *Woza Afrika!*, p. 3.

ing scenes convey not only generic information but also can set scenes as in *Asinamali!* and *Bopha!*. What the three have in common is the use of narrative framing ("*Rahmenerzählung*") to set the scene for the actual action. The so-called, and frequently remarked upon, "episodic" structure of the plays is in fact in all three cases more tightly knit than might seem apparent at first glance. The *Morena* story in *Woza Albert!*, around which the play revolves, is not introduced until scene 5 where it seems to be the product of wild phantasizing on the part of the two former prisoners who have met by chance in a train. It grows out of actual play-acting in the carriage and then assumes a dynamic of its own. In scene 17 the action returns to the train setting, perhaps to remind the audience that it is all just projections of wish-fulfilment on the part of the two ex-prisoners. Percy says to Mbongeni: "Ja, you've got a very good imagination. I really like your stories."[12] This setting of dramaturgical framing in a train carriage is not very dissimilar to the actual genesis of the play, which began as a conversation during a bus journey while Mtwa and Ngema were touring with a Gibson Kente production.[13] Scene 17 leads to yet another set of variations on the theme of Jesus Christ in South Africa culminating in the final graveyard scene in which Morena resurrects the heroes of the anti-apartheid movement. There is no shift back to the original frame setting in the train. The climatic song and dance of resurrection *"Yamemeza inkosi yethu"* shifts in fact to the level of performance frame; the fictional dramaturgical frame is left as the actors raise their arms in the ANC salute and, depending on the performance context, sing the ANC anthem together with the audience.[14] The utopian notion of resurrection at the end of

---

[12] *Ibid.*, p. 25.

[13] Percy Mtwa describes the initial idea for *Woza Albert!* as follows. "Now, on our way back, the cast was singing one of the songs that is in the play [Kente's *Mama and the Load*, C.B.] and we discussed the subject about religion largely. We fetched it up high from the cosmos and brought it down to that little black bus in which we were travelling and everybody, all of a sudden, was filled up spiritually, and people for the first time started talking about all the religious aspects affecting the South African situation. And it was then, the idea for *Woza Albert!* was born." Quoted in: "I've been an entertainer throughout my life . . ." Interview with Percy Mtwa conducted by Eckhard Breitinger. *Matatu* 2:3/4 (1988), p. 164.

[14] I say depending on the performance context. In the 1982 BBC documentary on *Woza Albert!* which includes some documentary footage of a performance in a township, the performance ends with actors and spectators singing the ANC anthem. A performance of Saira Essa's *You Can't Stop the Revolution*

the play is concretized in the political act of singing the (then) forbidden anthem with full audience participation.

In *Asinamali!* the initial process of generic framing, as already
noted, also overlaps with the dramaturgical frame. Each character
steps out of the energetic Zulu dance and song "*Heshe Nsizwa*" to
briefly introduce his story and thus why he is in prison, the setting for
the stories which will constitute the action of the play. Similarly, *Bopha!*
begins with a police graduation parade in which Naledi, the reluctant
Black policeman, introduces his story. This direct audience narration
(scene 2) frames the action to follow partly as a flashback (scenes 3 to
5); and partly as a continuation of the story after the graduation (scenes
6 to end):

> *Hanhle hanhle* [truthfully] I didn't want to be a policeman. I
> came from Qwaqwa. I came to Jo'burg because my brother
> Njandini was here, a whole policeman Sergeant. I wanted him
> to help me fix my pass, so that I can get a job, but he refused.
> *Kemuth amubi!* He is so madly in love with the police force
> that he wishes every member of the family to be like him.[15]

Within the brackets of the dramaturgical frame there are of
course a wide variety of devices to indicate a change of temporal or
spatial frame. The example given above of direct narration introducing
a flashback is just but one example. The plays make use of an excep-
tionally large vocabulary of scenic devices to indicate these transitions,
some of which are clearly indebted to modern media codes and can
be found in the techniques of the radio play and in those of cinematic
montage. An example of the latter occurs in *Woza Albert!*. The transition from scene 4 (a quarrel between two prisoners) to scene 5 (they
meet again by chance in a train carriage) is described as follows in the
stage directions:

> *Mbongeni pushes Percy forward on to the floor. Percy goes down
> with a scream that becomes a siren.*
> Blackout.
> SCENE FIVE
> *The siren transforms into train sounds.*[16]

I attended at the Young Vic in London ended in the same way, with the
audience standing in salute, if not actually singing along.

[15] *Woza Afrika!*, p. 231.

[16] *Ibid.*, p. 9f.

The joining of one sound to a similar sound by means of an edit is a well-known cinematic device to smooth a transition requiring a large jump in time and space. In *Asinamali!* Mbongeni Ngema operates with comparable media-related transitional devices. Frequently a song will anticipate a change of scene, either musically and/or textually. For example, the transition from scene 5 to scene 6 — Bheki's speech about the necessity of leaving his homeland and going to Johannesburg to find work — is effected first of all by the underlying song *"wemali egoli"* [my money is in Johannesburg]; the speech ends with the line: "let us go to their offices,"[17] by which time another actor has positioned himself in a chair: Scene 6 in the pass office can begin. In this example three different codes — musical, textual and visual — are employed to prepare and effect the spatial and temporal shift. Other devices common to the three plays are the use of theatrical objects, the clown noses in *Woza Albert!* and moustaches in *Bopha!* to depict whites, or the donning of an article of clothing. These changes are frequently done in full sight of the audience to indicate the change from one scene to another. A scenic device often used in *Bopha!* is frozen action: an actor or actors stand upstage with their backs to the audience waiting for their entrance.

Our third major category that of performance framing, the set of conventions governing transitions to and from the social world of the actors and spectators to the aesthetic world of the play in performance. Traditionally, in Western theatre there are strict rules and conventions governing the behaviour of performers and spectators; most modes of performance do not permit direct physical or verbal interchange between the parties. When this does occur, despite the implicit agreement to the contrary, one can speak of "frame-breaking," to use Goffman's term. There are of course a number of Western performance forms such as Music Hall, Melodrama, Night Club routines etc. where frame-breaking is a constituent component of the performance, where it is expected and in fact necessary.

Particularly since the Theatre of the Absurd and the experimental theatre of the 1960s, frame-breaking has become part of the performance vocabulary of Western theatre. Although by no means innovative anymore, the fact that devices such as a spectator being taken up on stage, a performer moving amongst the audience, an actor dropping out of character etc. can still have an, albeit mild, shock

---

[17] *Ibid.*, p. 196.

1. *Bopha!* Transition Scene 3 to Scene 4. Photo: Christopher Balme.

effect, testifies that the Western performance frame has still not fully accepted such conventions.[18]

Examples of frame-breaking abound in Township theatre. On the one hand the plays seem to be heirs to the iconoclastic frame-breaking experiments of the 1960s, on the other hand these "devices" may also derive from a non-Western socio-cultural performance tradition. The first example of frame-breaking is one which Goffman terms the role-character formula:

> The individual, in the guise of the character he is performing, comments on himself as performer or upon his fellow per-

---

[18] The Theatre of the Absurd makes such extensive use of frame-breaking and self-conscious, self-reflexive devices that Goffman would like to rename it "theatre of frames." The 20th century precursor is of course Pirandello, to whom Goffman also makes extensive reference. But also the Elizabethan and Jacobean theatre experimented with frame-breaking. Perhaps the most radical example is Francis Beaumont's *The Knight of the Burning Pestle* (1607) in which fictional spectators interrupt the action of a play, clamber up on stage and demand to see another play more to their tastes.

formers, or in other ways draws attention to what he ought not to be able to draw attention to — the role-character formula.[19]

Goffman is referring here again to a shock device. Since the Fugard/Kani/Ntshona play *The Island*, however, in which the actors use their own names, the relationship between role, character and actor in Black South African theatre has become a problematic one; that is to say, it has itself become a subject of reflexion and performance. In *Woza Albert!* and *Asinamali!* the names of the characters and the names of the actors are identical. This may be explained by the actual conditions of production of Township theatre. These works are grounded ultimately on the bedrock of the actors' own experience in the apartheid system and this experience is given theatrical form through an intensive improvisational workshop process. In a strict sense this dissolving of the distinction between actor and character is not framebreaking but the establishment of a new frame.

Actual frame-breaking, in Goffman's sense, is also used, most spectacularly in *Asinamali!*, for agitatory purposes. Bhoyi's description of the Asinamali protest in Lamontville becomes an accusatory interrogation of the spectators which directly addresses the multiracial composition of the audience. First the actors search out "government informers" in the audience, presumably black, and warn them. This is followed by the singling out of a white spectator for special treatment:

> BHOYI: That anger was not only the problem of Lamontville township [. . .] It is not only about the language Afrikaans. It is not only about rent increases [. . .] What is it? Hey! What is it? You. (*points to a white member of the audience*). You, stand up. *Hey mthatheni Bafana!* [Go for him boys!]
> ALL: (*jump up and go towards the person in the audience*) STAND UP!
> BHOYI: What is it! Talk! You think I'm playing games with you. You think I'm acting. Sit down. My friend. You've got to look for it. It's deep down in your heart.[20]

A spectator thus singled out might well wonder for a moment if it is only "acting." In the South African context the scene takes on a political significance of existential proportions. Not only does the

---

[19] Goffman, *op. cit*, p. 395.

[20] *Woza Afrika!*. p. 212.

spectator actually experience persecution purely on the grounds of skin colour, but s/he is forced to confront the fact that the political situation is ultimately every white citizen's affair and responsibility ("It's deep down in your heart").

While involuntary audience participation of this degree tends to be exceptional in Township theatre, many plays appear to permit, or indeed invite, audience response on a musical level. Again, in the context of Township theatre one cannot speak here of frame-breaking but rather of frame expansion to encompass a set of conventions from a performance culture where audience participation is the norm. The Xhosa *ntsomi*, for example, a traditional oral performance form, often has audience participation in the form of call and response chants built into the structure of the performance.[21] A cast member of *Asinamali!*, Thali Cele, has emphasized the essential difference and participatory nature of Township audiences: "When we played in the townships, it seemed as if the whole hall was on stage. By the end of the show, you couldn't differentiate. Every hall had become a stage. Everybody was participating — whistling, ululating, singing."[22] The special theatrical nature of this audience response is engendered by a fusion of political content and familiar musical codes. Especially the final scenes of all three plays utilize the combination of a rousing protest song, vigorous dance and implicit or explicit call for continued solidarity and struggle against apartheid.

This is a brief outline of the three major framing devices obtaining in Township theatre. Within this macro-framework we now want to look at some of the performance codes which have developed into characteristic features of this theatre form. Keir Elam has elaborated a very comprehensive catalogue of codes and subcodes sustaining theatrical communication. The major interrelated codes or subcodes are theatrical, cultural and dramatic ones which the spectator always applies to "decoding" the information being produced. Elam identifies twelve different "principles" — linguistic, systemic, aesthetic, ideological etc. — which may be involved in this decoding process.[23]

---

[21] For an analysis of the performance conventions of the *ntsomi*, see Harold Scheub, *The Xhosa Ntsomi*, Oxford: Oxford University Press, 1975.

[22] Quoted in Emil Sher, "Apartheid on Tour," *Canadian Theatre Review*, 50 (Spring 1987), 59–61; here p. 60.

[23] See Keir Elam, *The Semiotics of Theatre and Drama*, London: Methuen, 1980, p. 56ff.

Instead of following this highly elaborate "map" (as Elam calls it), it will be more useful to select a small number of subcodes which point up the particular syncretistic nature of Township theatre. Most models of theatrical communication have hitherto implied a homogenous monocultural situation of reception: producers and receivers of the theatrical product are members of the same culture. Township theatre, however, wherever it is played in South Africa, is addressing a polycultural audience: in the Townships the polyglot amalgam of various ethnic backgrounds; in mixed theatres such as the Market Theatre in Johannesburg, a predominately White or a balanced Black/White audience. And beyond South Africa there is the "world culture," as Percy Mtwa terms it,[24] which some Township theatremakers seem to have in the back of their minds.

Linguistic Codes

The multilingual nature of Township theatre is the area where the polycultural situation in South Africa is most apparent. One of the truly innovative features of this theatre is the fact that multilingualism is not just registered and reflected, for comic purposes for example, but can in a performance situation be implemented as a strategy to include or exclude sections of the audience, make statements about the linguistic nature of the power structures in South African society, and reflect generally on the place of language in a colonial situation. In a recent article, Temple Hauptfleisch has outlined the linguistic environment of South Africa and its transformation into a new set of linguistic conventions in Black theatre, into what he calls "a new poetry of the theatre stage, in a language born of the polyglot environment in and around our cities."[25] That this new poetry can draw on anything up to eleven "formally accepted South African languages" plus a variety of urban *lingua franca* such as *flaaitaal*, which are composites of various linguistic elements, is quite rightly seen as "an immensely rich mine for the playwright."[26]

[24] Percy Mtwa, "Interview," *op. cit.*, p. 166.

[25] Temple Hauptfleisch, "Citytalk, Theatretalk: Dialect, Dialogue and Multilingual Theatre in South Africa", *English in Africa* 16:1 (May 1989), 71–92, here p. 77.

[26] *Ibid.*, p. 78.

In practice, however, the language of communication is primarily English. David Coplan has discussed the quite complex reasons for the adoption of English as the theatrical language of Township theatres: "When questioned, playwrights respond that English is the only *lingua franca* understood in townships throughout the country, but their preference for it as a medium of communication has a deeper significance."[27] He goes on to analyse this "deeper significance" and finds three main reasons for the use of English. Firstly, the use of an "African" art form suggests strongly the separate development advocated by apartheid; secondly, it [English] helps overcome the sense of cultural isolation South African artists suffer from; and thirdly, the use of English enables Black artists to communicate their message, theoretically at least, to an international audience. Of interest here is when and why and in what dramaturgical and/or performance contexts other languages are used.

The multilingualism has a *mimetic* function in that it reflects the linguistic reality of the Townships. It can, however, also be used as a *dramaturgical strategy* for a variety of political and/or comic effects. In the latter cases African languages are used literally as "code", not in its semiotic sense, but in the everyday sense of an esoteric, secret system, to which only the initiated are privy. This device assumes of course a community of the initiated and is very much dependent on the performance context and linguistic environment; i.e. it is only useful if sufficient numbers in the audience can understand the languages spoken and the frequent linguistic code-switching.

There are countless situations in these plays where the multilingualism of the black actors/characters and that of the black audience demonstrates a situation of superiority over white characters who may speak only one, at the most two, European languages and certainly no African language. However, the use of language by white authorities as a vehicle of oppression is most vividly demonstrated in scene 2 of *Asinamali!*, where Bheki is tried and sentenced for a series of unrelated offences. A trilingual situation is depicted: the judge speaks Afrikaans, which is rendered into English by the court interpreter; the defendant understands neither language particularly well, and so fragments of these exchanges are translated into Zulu by a Court Orderly. He in turn *selectively* translates the defendant's responses back to the judge. Each rendering results in shifts and slants

---

[27] Coplan, *op. cit.*, p. 214.

of meaning until the defendant, Bheki, is struggling like a hapless fish in a net, enmeshed in legal procedures which are everything else but transparent. In performance this linguistic confusion is further under-lined by the fact that these exchanges actually gain momentum during the course of the trial until there is almost Babylonian turmoil.

This example of victimization where language is used as an instrument of oppression is more than compensated for by situations in which multilingualism creates an area of freedom in which revenge can be exacted and satirical attacks levelled at white society. Certain exchanges are clearly not intended for white consumption. For exam-ple, intertribal jokes are made in African languages. In *Bopha!*, Naledi sits "singing to pass the time" and sings in Zulu: "I'd rather be like Xhosas and Pondos/ and carry shit-buckets on my shoulders."[28] A similar remark is made by Zulu Boy in *Woza Albert!*: "*Yabhodla ingane yenZule ukuba okungu — MSuthu ngabe kudala kuzinyele.* [There burps the son of a Zulu; if it was a Sotho he would be shitting.]"[29] Also much sexually explicit language and humour is spoken in an African lan-guage and thus reserved for the African audience. There is a good deal of cursing in Afrikaans too, but of the nonliteral expletive variety, whereas elaborate sexual metaphors and descriptions are probably reserved for the African languages. In *Bopha!* for example, two black policemen speak Zulu in the presence of the whiteman one of them has arrested: "*Pis in die straat. An-eke ahamba abonisa umthondo wakhe obomyu yonke indawo.* [He was pissing in the street, he cannot expose his red penis all over the place.]"[30] The first part of the statement is in Afrikaans, and comprehensible to the culprit and the whole audience; the rest of the comment, however, is reserved for the Zulu speakers. Of course, the linguistic situation is not always completely so clearly demarcated. *Bopha!* includes a scene where Naledi's disparaging comment to his brother in Zulu about Captain Van Donder is in fact understood by the recipient:

> NAL: *Levatela leburu lena abuti man!* [This Boer is obstinate!]
> CAP: *Hey wie's 'n boer?* [Who is a boer?] *Njandini, polisieman of nie polisieman, BOPHA!*[31]

---

[28] *Woza Afrika!*, p. 235.

[29] *Ibid.*, p. 37.

[30] *Ibid.*, p. 244.

[31] *Ibid.*, p. 250.

This dynamic of inclusion and exclusion is also very evident in the extensive use of songs, not one of which is in a European language. The songs have other functions besides. They can serve such diverse purposes as affective arousal, political agitation, and the invoking of cultural and tribal tradition. But of course in all these categories the actual textual message, whether it be important or not, whether it conveys a note of political protest or a joke at the expense of the whites, for this part of the theatrical performance, black performers and black spectators are communicating directly, while the white audience, for the most part, can only guess at what is being expressed. *Bopha!*, for example, uses throughout the action a well-known protest song, "*Siyayi nyova*", in which the audience can and does join in.

Proxemic and Kinesic Codes

Anyone who has witnessed a performance of Township theatre can testify to the crucial importance of nonverbal performance devices. At times it seems as if the language generated by the actors with their bodies is equally if not more communicative than the actual words spoken. Percy Mtwa has stressed the central importance of the actor's body in their form of "poor theatre": "you are using your body as the only instrument you have, and that body which you have can be anything, can be a piece of sculpture, it can sing, it can be a song, it can be movement, can be sound, can be anything, that body."[32] Mtwa, one of the co-creators of *Woza Albert!*, articulates here how the actor's body functions as a dominant sign vehicle for the performance. In the context of the Western "hierarchy of theatrical devices"[33] we can speak of a shift in dominant function in Township theatre to privilege kinesic codes. The kinesic codes can range from sign language, to mime, to dance, to stylized, sculptured movement. On the basis of the following photographs taken during a performance of *Bopha!* we can illustrate three general, recurrent categories of kinesic codes found in Township Theatre.

The opening of the play with a dance or a mixture of music and movement. Dance is a constitutive component of the theatre form and

---

[32] Percy Mtwa, "Interview," *op. cit.*, p. 170.

[33] This notion was first formulated by the Czech, semiotician Jinřich Honzl; see his article, "The Hierarchy of Dramatic Devices" in: Ladislav Matejka and Irwin R. Titunik eds. *Semiotics of Art: Prague School Contributions*, Cambridge, Mass.: MIT Press, 1976, pp. 118–127.

2. *Bopha!* Opening dance sequence. Photo: Christopher Balme.

one of the most important elements which illustrate the syncretic nature of these plays, in which traditional African performance forms can be integrated. Here the physical training routines of the police academies are transformed into a Zulu dance, where the dance is not just an interlude but through the transition from the drill routines retains a clear connection with the action and theme of the play: the predicament of Black policemen in the apartheid regime.

In the following photograph a police band playing the South African national anthem is being mimed. The same device is used in the opening image of *Woza Albert!*. This is but just one instance of the extensive use of mime, but one which is actually drawn from the actors' experience of growing up in the Townships. Percy Mtwa describes how as teenagers he and a group of friends created a rock band without instruments:

> And then, somebody — just during that moment — started playing a song that was popular at that time — it was called Mr. Bull, it was very popular. And then he started miming it, playing the bass guitar with his lips and his voice and then another person started coming in with the drums, miming them as well and then, all of a sudden, there we were, miming

3. *Bopha!* Scene 1 *"Die Stem van Suid-Afrika"*. Photo: Christopher Balme.

> this song and what came out was something very beautiful.
> We went home. We started arranging it, putting it together
> and we performed throughout the school.[34]

In the following example physical action approximates cin-
ematic/photographic techniques. The photograph is taken from scene
13, the funeral scene, where the procession turns into a massacre as the
police gun down the mourners/protestors. The action and movement
is slowed down to resemble a slow-motion or freeze-frame sequence
in a film, a technique often used to depict scenes of violence and death.
Such use of stylized movement reinforces the intention of Township
theatre-makers to create strong, vivid images within the episodic structure. Percy Mtwa again: "These images that I present there on that
stage, it is like a photographer -pah!- and it is there."[35] Mtwa illustrates
with this example the productive reception of other media codes: the
lived experience of Black people is replayed to them via other media
and this experience is refashioned in a theatrical equivalent on stage.

---

[34] Percy Mtwa, "Interview," *op. cit.*, p. 160.

[35] *Ibid.*, p. 174.

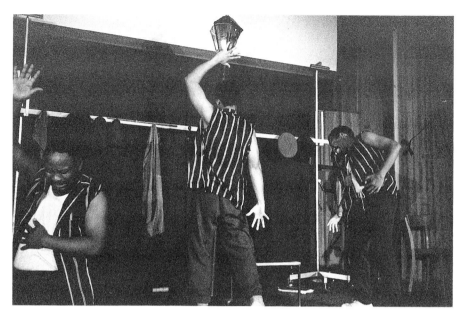

4. *Bopha!* Scene 13. Funeral March and Protest. Photo: Christopher Balme.

Conclusion and Outlook

Township theatre is astonishingly eclectic in its range of performance devices and codes. The formal devices examined here represent only one particular style of performance which is linked closely to Mbongeni Ngema and Percy Mtwa. One can find in the work of other groups a different theatrical vocabulary again: especially those groups espousing a more direct agitatory form of theatre have experimented with documentary drama, mixing film footage, with personal statements, with traditional African song and dance.[36] There is continuing experiment and work within the trade union movement, where theatre and drama are being utilized as means to help workers articulate their problems and even to rehearse strategies for specific situations.[37] The

---

[36] This is the approach taken in Saira Essa's *You Can't Stop the Revolution*, Upstairs Theatre Company, Durban.

[37] For a description of the genesis and reception of one such play, *Ilanga Lizophumela Abasebenzi*, devised by a lawyer, Halton Cheadle together with his defendants, and aided by actors from the Junction Avenue Theatre Company, see Keyan G. Tomaselli, "The Semiotics of Alternative Theatre in South Africa," *Critical Arts* 2:1 (1981), 14–33.

well-known Soweto writer/director/artist, Matsemela Manaka, has recently questioned the aesthetics of South African protest theatre which, he claims, overrides the cultural values of Africans and is more influenced by European than African culture.[38] In the light of the rapidly changing political situation in South Africa Black theatre artists will no doubt have to face the question of whether to preserve and elaborate on this tried and proven theatrical idiom or whether to pursue new paths and forms of expression in a post-apartheid society.

---

[38] Matsemela Manaka, "Thoughts on South African Theatre in Relation to Traditional Values and Protest." Paper presented at the conference, "Theatre and Politics in South Africa", 15–17. December, 1989, Bad Boll, Germany.

THEATRE FOR EXPORT:
THE COMMERCIALIZATION OF THE
BLACK PEOPLE'S STRUGGLE IN
SOUTH AFRICAN EXPORT MUSICALS

Jerry Mofokeng

In June 1987, a month before I left South Africa on a Fulbright scholarship to the United States, *Sarafina* opened at the Market Theatre. The
play was performed in the usual Gibson Kente style that was well
known to most of the township theatre patrons, with a thin storyline
puffed up by lots of sloganeering. It was a kaleidoscope of black
cultural expression, with slogans of the student protests and a storyline
of the student play featuring Mandela . . . it was a pot-pourri of
everything Kente had left in his satchel. I was surprised, then, when
I learned the production was already bound for New York.

I reached New York a month later and *Sarafina* had already
been widely publicized. Americans often asked me for my comment
on the production, but I avoided the subject, not knowing what they
wanted in theatre. Where I was hungry for dramatic theatre, the only
serious plays that I saw seemed to serve more as vehicles for stars than
expressive works about issues. The goal seemed to be to survive the
New York Times' review. Still, my guess was that *Sarafina* would not
make it in New York.

Sarafina opened at the Lincoln Centre Theatre. It was a HIT.
Within five months it opened on Broadway. One thing the play was,
was entertaining; one thing it wasn't, was illuminating of the South
African situation . . .

My studies at Columbia University reinforced my musings
about *Sarafina's* positive reception in the U.S. In a "Famous American
Plays" class, we discussed Kurt Weill and Maxwell Anderson's musical, *Lost in the Stars*, which was based on Alan Paton's novel, *Cry, the
Beloved Country*. Most of my classmates had read the novel at high

school or college. I had not. There we were, discussing a play that supposedly illuminated the struggles of my people, but the discussion only left me further frustrated. I was being engaged in an exercise where I had more work correcting the misconceptions in the play rather than expanding on what was in it. These encounters with *Sarafina* and *Lost in the Stars* prompted me to do my own investigation on the portrayal of apartheid's victims in plays and musicals which originated in South Africa. The international community, in sympathy with the victims of the cruel South African system, and perhaps in part out of curiosity and concern for the survival of these subjects, has been very accommodating toward the productions about South African blacks. Support for these productions was thought to provide a vehicle to educate the international community, to provide the black majority with an otherwise inaccessible outlet for cultural expression. This benign support was intended to contribute to the realization of the political aspirations held by the black people of South Africa.

In my view, however, theatrical expressions centering on blacks have first and foremost provided South Africa with a viable commodity for export, paradoxically bolstering and validating the state in the process. These consumer-oriented productions account for the presentation of blacks that conform to the demands of the market — blacks based on myth and prototype, often counter to the black experience. What is offered for consumption is frequently interpretation and presentation by others than blacks themselves. The imposition of a foreign form on black material also serves to facilitate international consumption and digestion.

For a long time blacks have not been recognized as artists in their own right. They have been neglected on the basis of their failure to adhere to established patterns of aesthetics in their art. This strangulation of black artists and academics has been accompanied by the breeding of a host of white academics and authorities against whom any black spokesperson is measured. *They* then become the articulators of our struggles and our aspirations — Alan Paton and his Jarvis character in *Lost in the Stars*; Donald Woods in the movie *Cry Freedom*.

Academics, dramatists, producers and critics are thus at the forefront of the propagation of a mythical black. In the same way that the theatre colonizes and sensationalizes the black man's struggle, the intellectual arena colonizes the theatre, issuing acclaim or condemnation based on their own academic criteria. Culturally and artistically dominant societies thus confer their own aesthetic prejudices onto subject cultures, using their own values to define those cultures and the way they represent themselves. The aesthetic is thus imported, perhaps implanted, in order for the commodity to be suitable for export.

Black people's history does not commence with the arrival of white people. Black people's identity is not defined by their victimization under apartheid, by the majority populace's relation to the minority. Black identity must be approached on its own merit, for if we are not understood despite apartheid, we will not be understood after apartheid.

Theatre is about more than just apartheid. It is about prejudice and racism; about the suspicion and fear of those unfamiliar and different from us. Theatre is about human identity, about human conflict. It is about human existence with oneself and in interaction with the outside world. It is knowledge of this wide canon of the theatre that will liberate us from the restriction of formulae.

Talent — especially raw talent — has had its stint in South Africa. The animal skins of *Ipi Tombi*, the drums of *Umabatha* and the exuberant youth and slogans of *Sarafina* have had their day. Now, it's time to outgrow the nappies. The curious pet of our theatre, the victim, needs to outpace the death throes of apartheid.

5. *Somewhere on the Border* by Anthony Akerman. Photo: Anthony Akerman.

THEATRE IN EXILE

ANTHONY AKERMAN

In 1974 I visited a small exhibition in Munich entitled *Theater im Exil*. The exhibits were not unusual; models of sets, costume drawings, original prompt copies. What was unusual was that all this work had been produced outside Germany between 1933 and 1945. During the 1920s and early 1930s Germany led the world in innovative and so-cially-committed theatre. Hitler put a stop to that. The exhibits were a moving testimony to the artists' perseverance, yet this question re-mains: what would they have achieved had they not left their country?

When the apartheid rulers assumed power there was no vi-brant, oppositional theatre that challenged their policies, so there was no call for a spectacular clampdown. The enactment of draconian censorship laws, not to mention a host of other laws which could be invoked to censor work, sufficed to keep the fainthearted in check should they ever venture from the rather straight and very narrow. By the end of the 1960s, with one or two notable exceptions, the theatrical landscape was arid. Apartheid laws presented black theatre practition-ers with a stark choice: remain amateur or go into exile. For those of us of lighter pigmentation the choice was more ambiguous. One could work within the (all-white) subsidised institutions and compromise oneself, work for slow change within the subsidised institutions, sur-vive precariously outside the institutions (still subject to the strictures of censorship and the Group Areas Act) or go into exile. This is how the cards were stacked in 1973 when I elected to leave the country.

My fate is by no means particular. I am one of a vast number of people who left South Africa over the past three decades. Whether we left to escape persecution or of our own free wills, exile was our shared fate. Theatre practitioners left the country for reasons ranging from professional ambition to evading the Angolan call-up. Most made their way to Britain, drawn by its theatre tradition and the fact that they spoke the language. That has been our loss and Britain's gain.

I left South Africa for a variety of reasons. I wanted to attend theatre school in Britain, I didn't want to work under the prevailing censorship laws in racially-segregated theatres and I didn't want to do army camps. I also took it all quite personally: I held a grudge against the country, fulminated at its mediocrity, felt impotent when confronted by its cruelty and cursed the fact I'd been born a (white) South African. The education and training I'd received was sufficiently Eurocentric to give me the illusion that Britain would be home from home. Perhaps I thought I could deny my past, become assimilated and acquire a new identity. This is not only a condition many South African theatre practitioners in Britain aspire to, but almost a *sine qua non* for survival.

Being a Colonial Boy was a handicap that could be overcome, but there was something more fundamental in me that resisted assimilation. Once I had left the country I began to discover my South African identity. Before starting theatre school I spent six months immersing myself in the London theatre. Ironically, of all the productions I saw the one that mattered most to me originated in Port Elizabeth: it was *Sizwe Bansi is Dead*. While I was a student I directed two South African plays: André Brink's *Pavané* and Athol Fugard's *People Are Living There*. Perhaps, as a stranger, I felt that when I did South African plays I had the edge over my British peers, but I was probably also motivated by homesickness.

Directing South African plays abroad is certainly not the prerogative of exiles. When Athol Fugard directed his plays for the National Theatre in London, or Market Theatre productions toured Europe, this had nothing to do with theatre in exile. Perhaps theatre in exile is little more than those productions mounted by practitioners living in exile, particularly when their work was banned in South Africa. Exile is the state of not being able to return. The reason for not being able to return may lie within yourself, but this is the essential distinction between the exile and the expatriate. While in Britain I worked with the Mayibuye Poets' Collective, the nascent cultural wing of the African National Congress, and this was a watershed for me. This placed me in the state of not being able to return. From this point onward I would be working in exile.

In 1975 the Dutch Anti-Apartheid Movement invited me to Amsterdam. No South African plays had ever been staged in Holland and I had proposed doing Fugard's *Statements after an Arrest under the Immorality Act*. By now I had an additional motive for doing South African work: as a political gesture. I believed, and still do believe, that plays can make something happen, can influence the way people think. A play like *Statements* . . . could help to raise the "indignation level," but it could do more than that. Unlike the political speech or the television documentary, it could provide audiences with a profound emotional experience. While being an unequivocal indictment of racism, it didn't present audiences with simplified moral coordinates. A moral universe of Good Guys and Bad Guys is one favoured by the B-Western and many of the activists who took no interest in the arts until "art as a weapon in the struggle" was incorporated into the anti-apartheid catechism. Working in a new cultural climate and a different language was a challenge I relished. I made a conscious effort to become integrated in Dutch culture and theatre. After three months I had landed my first directing job and managed to conduct rehearsals in rudimentary Dutch.

Eight months later I went into rehearsals with *Verklaringen na een arrestatie onder de Immoraliteitswet*. One of my first discoveries was that, although there were few apologists for the apartheid "philosophy" in Holland, in general people had a very sketchy understanding of the situation in South Africa. At the time, the received view was that Whites were the Bad Guys and Blacks were the Good Guys. And the Anti-Apartheid Movement didn't go out of its way to discourage this view; it was put to me that if you said the problem in South Africa was complex people wouldn't be as likely to donate money to the cause. The sophistry underlying this pragmatism is anathema to me. It's often argued that it's necessary for achieving political goals, but it's the kiss of death to art. Much of what passes itself off as "political" theatre is moribund proof of this.

My cast realised that inter-racial marriage was prohibited, but they knew nothing of the provisions, or the workings, of the Immorality Act. So it was going to be quite different from doing the play at "home." They didn't know the difference between a so-called Coloured (one of the characters) and a black person. And why indeed should they? Yet if they were to understand the play properly I had to initiate them into the mysteries of apartheid race classification. I spent a lot of time explaining things all South Africans know. Without this they wouldn't have an accurate understanding of the source of many of the characters' emotions. The production opened during the Art Against Apartheid conference held in Amsterdam in May 1978 and had a successful run.

About this time it was suggested to me that if I continued to direct Fugard plays I'd be labelled as a director who could only do

South African material. Pigeon-holing is probably universal, but it is particularly prevalent in Holland. However this wasn't the reason why five years elapsed before I staged *Boesman and Lena*. It had more to do with the nature of Dutch theatre which, during the 1970s, made a rigid distinction between repertoire theatre and political theatre. If you wanted to do a play about South Africa, you had to look to the political theatre. I worked intermittently in the political theatre until its demise in the early 1980s. There was great diversity in the political theatre; ranging from plays about sexuality in community centres to Marxism-made-easy presented to factory workers in their canteens. The quality of the work was uneven and invariably the message was more important than character, conflict, theatricality and ambiguity. I held back with *Boesman and Lena*. At the time I also felt the play didn't say enough; its indictment of apartheid was implicit rather than explicit and it didn't present a systematic analysis of the problem. I had learnt my catechism and I was making a good job of adapting. And yet I found it a haunting play. Finally, in 1980, I went into rehearsal; not with a political company, but under the auspices of the *Toneelraad* in Rotterdam. The title roles were played by two Dutch actors and Outa was played by the exiled South African actor, Joseph Mosikili.

By this time I'd come to know Dutch actors better. The performances they turned in were seldom spirited and impassioned. Rationality and caution ousted passion and poetry. As a South African I felt it was my task to give the performances a degree of authenticity. In this I was assisted by Joseph Mosikili and my South African costume designer, Linnemore Nefdt. Although the actors spoke Dutch, the behaviour of the characters needed something essentially South African. This belief doesn't derive from an interest in folklore. It's simply that a play like *Boesman and Lena* won't ignite if it's performed as if it were a Dutch play. But I also learnt that authenticity had to be used sparingly or you risk estranging your audience. For example, in 1978, when I translated the play with the Dutch writer Bert Schierbeek, I was adamant about leaving the Afrikaans intact. I thought it would bring the play closer to Dutch audiences, but by the time I went into rehearsal I knew the opposite was true. Most of it would be either incomprehensible or misleading. (An example from the play is the word "kaffer": it exists in Dutch, but simply means "lout" and has no offensive racial connotations.) So striving for authenticity had to be weighed up against how the audience was likely to read the signs. The semiotics of theatre can read differently for audiences in different countries.

In 1981 I directed Fugard's *A Lesson from Aloes* for a political theatre company called *Sater*. It was probably the most "Dutch" of the three Fugard productions and I went out of my way to sacrifice authenticity and historical accuracy to intelligibility. In Algoa Park, Port Elizabeth, in 1983 the Bezuidenhouts would have had a low wall around their garden. I had my designer do a high, fibrocrete wall with a wrought-iron gate. It was intended to suggest the beleaguered condition of Whites in South Africa. In itself this is not necessarily a misguided approach to design, but the production was fraught with self-conscious choices. I had assumed the Dutch habit of signposting and I didn't feel comfortable with it. I felt it was starting to erode my own authenticity. With the exception of the remarkable Cor van Rijn, who played Piet Bezuidenhout, the performances didn't ignite. I was less than happy with this production and I began to wonder if Dutch actors could ever do a South African play without emasculating it. In 1982 I wrote a play called *Somewhere on the Border* and I decided that if I were ever to stage it in Holland I would only do so with South African actors.

Directing South African plays in exile is one thing, writing them is quite another. I had directed British and Dutch plays, but I felt I would only write plays that dealt with the South African experience. Writing in exile is by no means unique to South Africans, but a significant part of our literature has been written out of the country. Writing in exile poses different problems for different writers. Your perception of your subject matter is filtered through memory, secondary sources, reportage. You're not there to jot down a casual remark passed in a supermarket. You can't visit a place to verify a street name. You don't know the price of a loaf of bread. You don't hear the languages spoken around you every day. So you have to cultivate memory. You have to remember and recreate. You spend hours in the company of other exiles, talking and remembering. You meet everyone who comes from home. You listen and make notes. You read every book and newspaper you can get hold of. You pore over maps. You collect photo books. You video every documentary and all the news coverage. You do your research like every other writer, but you can't go out and do it among your audience. The act of writing invariably requires withdrawal and for the exile the physical withdrawal is extreme. This can have beneficial spinoffs: one is given a detachment, perhaps an overview. I wouldn't have written *Somewhere on the Border* the way I wrote it if I hadn't been in exile.

The most obvious inhibiting factor would have been censorship. Self-censorship can only be verified when a writer voluntarily "edits" his text at a publisher's behest to ensure that it won't fall foul of the censor. (This rather indecent proposition was often put to, especially Afrikaans, writers during the 1970s.) What is it when the writer starts making these choices before he puts pen to paper? And isn't writing something you know won't be published or performed tantamount to shooting yourself in the foot? Of course, over the years many writers inside the country had pushed back the boundaries of the permissible by continually challenging a Directorate of Publications, which increasingly betrayed a desire to appear more liberal. However, when I sat down to write *Somewhere on the Border* in 1982, I knew that I would stray beyond the bounds of their "liberal" tolerance. I had elected to write about the military experience and I knew that what I would say and how I said it would incur the displeasure of those upholding the *status quo*. Although the playwright has no monopoly on the interpretations of what he writes, I would venture that *Somewhere on the Border* implies that the South African military establishment dehumanised young men by inculcating racism, sexism and fascist doctrines. The last scene in the play is based on the 1978 SADF raid on Cassinga, a refugee settlement in the south of Angola. During this raid 160 men, 295 women and 300 children were massacred and their bodies dumped in a mass grave. The official version not only made no mention of these statistics, but also claimed Cassinga wasn't a refugee camp. The play didn't set out to prove the raid had taken place, but to explore the effects of such a raid on the characters. Nonetheless, reference to the SADF killing children was bound to be considered "objectionable."

The protagonist of the play, the liberal Campbell, makes a series of choices in order to survive, which culminates in shooting a wounded SWAPO guerilla in cold blood. Once in the military, personal morality is sacrificed to the greater evil. If this had the effect of discouraging young men from doing national service, it wouldn't constitute a misreading of the work's intention. The language presented a particular challenge to me. I enjoy recreating the speech patterns, syntax and vernacular of a period or place, but I particularly felt that most plays set in the military had never fully exploited the linguistic potentiality. All institutions have their jargon and slang and that in the military is proverbially obscene. However, most plays set in the armed forces have indicated this rather than exploited it. (In the late 1950s and early 1960s when British playwrights wrote about their national service, they had to contend with the Lord Chamberlain.) I wanted to use the language of the barrack room in all its obscenity, but

I also wanted it to function as an indicator of attitudes and fears.

When I wrote *Somewhere on the Border* censorship didn't impinge on my consciousness. I knew that was the least of my worries when I considered production possibilities. My chief concern was to find financial backing. When the play was completed and had elicited favourable responses from South African readers, I felt the need to send it home. I was tempted. Wouldn't it be possible to stage it in South Africa? In June 1983 I sent a copy to Athol Fugard. It never reached its destination and a few months later the *Government Gazette* promulgated the fact that it was "undesirable" in terms of Section 47(2) (a) & (e) of the Publications Act, 1974. When I made inquiries I was informed that the language "was not only vulgar but will be offensive to the reasonable and balanced reader." It was deemed prejudicial to the safety of the state because "in the closing parts of the book (sic) the South African Armed Forces are placed in an extremely bad light." The script was examined as a publication and not a public entertainment and I was informed that "a play could be staged if the parts which were found offensive are deleted." This concession seemed absurd. Even words like "fart" and "balls" were listed as offensive. If this play were bowdlerized it wouldn't even cast a shadow. And how should you begin to delete the closing parts? The conclusion of a play usually contains its meaning. In other words, the play could be staged provided it "meant" something else.

My response was complex. I was in exile. I had left the country to get away from all this. I had written the play free from the restrictiveness of censorship. When I heard the news I was rehearsing the play with a South African cast in Amsterdam. The Directorate of Publications was an absurd and remote institution with no jurisdiction over what I was doing. I was told there was some distinction in having the play banned. It enhanced my credentials. What further proof was required to demonstrate that I was one of the Good Guys? And yet I was not indifferent. I was rather stunned. Apart from any "political" motive, producing South African work in exile now had another meaning for me. It had everything to do with the meaning of my life; being an exile and, irrefutably, a South African. My relationship with South Africa had become a significant part of my identity. I had come to see myself as a South African playwright. This preemptive banning effectively meant that my play didn't exist in South Africa. Had it been banned after a few performances it would nonetheless have *existed*. I felt marginalised, a sort of echo in the void. What I felt most deprived of was the possibility of engaging in a dialogue with South African audiences. I now realised that I'd had them in mind all along when I wrote the play.

The Dutch Ministry of Culture and the Amsterdam City Council provided funding to stage *Somewhere on the Border*. I registered a foundation called Thekwini Theater as the production company. Performances were sold to theatres throughout the country. All productions have to tour in Holland, as it's policy to disseminate "culture" to the regions. This may be a laudable policy, but it has many drawbacks. If you receive state funding touring is mandatory. It is given an additional financial incentive by subsidising regional theatres to pay a good flat rate for a production. A run in Amsterdam, where you can seldom acquire a theatre for longer than two weeks, is never lucrative. Amsterdam is a cosmopolitan city with the audience most suitable for this play, but we also had to tour to smaller provincial towns. The further you are from Amsterdam, the less English audiences understand.

It was my decision to do the play with South African actors. This had as much to do with my desire to work with South Africans, as it had to do with my conviction that they would do it better than Dutch actors. The cast I assembled came from Amsterdam, Paris and London. My costume designer and stage manager were also South Africans. After eight years in the Dutch theatre it was strange to rehearse in English again, but it was a relief not to have to explain South Africa to the cast. The rehearsal space was virtually transformed into a barrack room; steel trunks, helmets, boots and rifles. There was physical training, instruction in stage fighting and military drill. The militarisation of rehearsals was a bittersweet irony, as most of the company had left South Africa to escape the army. This was truly exile theatre: a company composed almost exclusively of South Africans who couldn't or wouldn't return, working on a play that was banned at home.

The production was well received, although it was accessible to a smaller audience than the Dutch-language productions. Ironically, now that I was working with South African actors, I was constantly asking them to tone down their accents in the interests of intelligibility. Obviously the finer points of South African slang were lost on Dutch audiences, but there was something more fundamental that eluded them. The first preview was a litmus test of this. Half of the audience was Dutch and the other half was made up of South Africans. Salvos of laughter came from the South Africans, but the reason why the Dutch didn't laugh as much wasn't just that they didn't get the jokes. They were appalled by the violence, the sexism and the racism portrayed in the play. They felt laughter was inappropriate. This is a culturally-conditioned response. The South Africans were probably more appalled because they were intimate with the ugliness depicted, but to them laughter wasn't an inappropriate response. To those brought up in totalitarian societies laughter often means something else; humour can be subversive or a way of exorcising the horror. This is something South African satirists know only too well. Dutch audiences were receptive to the play, but you could always pick out the South Africans in the house. The most memorable performance was given for an audience of South Africans attending a conference on South African military aggression in the front-line states. This brought home one of the inherent contradictions of theatre in exile. A theatre without an audience has no *raison d'être* and theatre in exile comes precariously close to that condition. It's a wonderful thing to reach audiences in different countries, but it's a sorry thing to be cut off from your own people.

The success of *Somewhere on the Border* and the fact that a number of exiled South African actors lived in Amsterdam seemed reason enough to continue working together. I was in no hurry to get back to directing Dutch-language theatre. Thekwini Theater could be a home away from home; a production company for South African theatre practitioners living in exile. I was working on a new play set in the South African exile community in Amsterdam, called *A Man out of the Country*. As it also featured a Dutch character and reflected the experience of exiles in Holland, I thought it would speak more directly to Dutch audiences. If Thekwini Theater could raise funding to produce one show a year, there would be continuity and something to build on. I applied for funding for my exile play.

By the time I staged *Somewhere on the Border* political theatre in Holland had run its course. Dutch theatre practitioners looked to German dramatists and directors for inspiration. Since the mid-1980s Dutch theatre has moved towards form-conscious, directors' theatre. Productions tend to be overdesigned, overlong and overacted. Under the circumstances our chance of getting funding for a play which made no pretention to being overtly experimental seemed rather slim. When *Somewhere on the Border* was up for funding it was put to me that it would be more interesting if the black actor was played by a white actor and the soldiers were all played by black actors. This was a personal view, and an asinine one to boot, but the man who expressed it was also a member of the advisory board to the Amsterdam City Council and his vote against us resulted in a considerable financial shortfall. We had decided not to go ahead with the production of *A Man out of the Country* if we weren't fully subsidised. On the one hand it gives rise to financial nightmares and on the other we felt a principle was at stake. As it happened, the recommendation to the Ministry of Culture was negative and that to the Amsterdam City Council was positive. We were offered less than half of what we needed. We returned the money and a number of years were to elapse before the play was staged. Quite subjectively, we experienced this as a form of censorship. So we resolved to do a South African play anyway; on the dole and a shoestring. I had been particularly excited by the way Joseph Mosikili and Ian Bruce (as Marais) had worked together in the final scene of *Somewhere on the Border*. I also wanted to direct a Fugard play with South African actors, so I suggested *The Blood Knot*. In a way it seemed an obvious choice for reasons of economics and casting, but it proved to be a seminal production for us. Not only did we have a long rehearsal period which enabled us to sink deeply into the play and not only did the performances signal a breakthrough for both actors, but it also afforded us the opportunity to present a statement about brotherhood in South Africa. The story of betrayal, guilt and the possibility of redemption delineated in the play is really what all South Africans need to work through if we want to give a meaningful content to the new South Africa. For us it was a labour of love in the truest sense of the phrase. What else kept us going when we performed for basic costs, in tiny provincial theatres, in sub-zero temperatures, on a concrete stage with Joseph Mosikili mostly barefoot? We did that for love; love of the work and our love for South Africa. And for those members of the audience who were still in their seats when we came in to strike the set; people who were devastated and needed to speak to the actors. Shortly after we opened, a Dutch production of Fugard's *Master Harold . . . and the Boys* opened in Amsterdam. This production reduced the characters to stereotypes and seemed to be fundamentally at variance with the play's argument. Sam's final speech to Hally, in which he offers him a chance to redeem himself after his betrayal, was played with such derision and anger that audiences were left with a different message: there is no chance of reconciliation between Blacks and Whites in South Africa. This was an outsider's view and one I would still contest. There was no place in our work for such glib cynicism. At the risk of sounding sentimental I spoke of the love invested in *The Blood Knot*, but that's what made this production special; the love the actors felt for their characters, each other and South Africa. And exile gave that love its intensity.

Although we kept *The Blood Knot* in our repertoire for a number of seasons, hopes of giving Thekwini Theater continuity as a production company faded fast. Without funding it was not viable. Now that I had worked with South Africans I had no relish for directing Dutch actors again, so I earned a living as a literary manager at RO Theater, the repertoire company based in Rotterdam. During that period the only South African play I directed was Fugard's *A Lesson from Aloes* in Mexico. I'm not sure if this could be called theatre in exile, but it was the first South African play ever to be staged there and the cast rose superbly to the occasion. It was gratifying to have a second shot at the play and get right what had gone wrong in the Dutch production.

In 1989 I was asked by Joost Sternheim, the late artistic director of Frascati Theatre in Amsterdam, to direct *A Man out of the Country* in a season of showcase productions of new Dutch plays. The fact that the play was set in Amsterdam and I was a naturalised Dutch citizen made it Dutch enough for him. Frascati could only provide facilities and a minimal budget. I now agreed to stage the play for a fraction of the amount I had once returned to the Amsterdam City Council. It seemed a bitter irony, but an unperformed play doesn't exist and, five years on, I still felt as much urgency to stage it as I had when I had finished writing it. It wouldn't have been possible without the love and commitment of the actors, who worked for a tip.

A Man out of the Country was written in exile and is about the exile experience. Exile is a state of conflict. The exile is constantly in conflict with his surroundings. In the play the conflict is externalised in a failing love relationship between a South African man and a Dutch woman. The other source of conflict in the play is between two South African men. They are friends and one of them has decided to return to South Africa. The play is set in 1979. The title derives from the aphorism, "You can take a man out of the country, but you can never take the country out of a man." Exile is an existential dilemma; who are you, what have you become, where do you belong? This is the facet of exile the play sets out to explore and it was something familiar to most of us in the company.

In 1986 a group of actors based in Bloemfontein took a production of *Somewhere on the Border* to the Grahamstown Festival. They made none of the cuts required by the Directorate of Publications. The reviews they received obviously gave them some measure of protection, although there were incidents; military police confiscated the uniforms they wore as costumes on the opening night in Cape Town and in Johannesburg two actors were severely beaten by members of the CCB (Civil Cooperation Bureau) hit squad. I felt emotionally torn. It was incredibly gratifying to read the reviews and yet it was crucifying not to be there. I applied for a visa and was refused entry the day before I was due to leave.

President de Klerk's speech of 2 February 1990 sent shock waves through the exile diaspora. We were deprived of a certainty; the certainty of not being able to return. It's a curious paradox, as we had been sustained in our exile by the conviction that we would one day be able to return. During these years we had been coming to terms with our identity as exiles. Now we had to discover a new identity. I was granted a visa and renewed my physical acquaintance with my home after an absence of seventeen years. But something else was waiting for me on my return. The Performing Arts Council in Durban (NAPAC) invited me to direct *Somewhere on the Border* for the Loft Theatre Company. Working with South African actors, on South African soil, for South African audiences was a healing experience. My exile was ended.

So what would I, and others who shared my fate, have achieved had we not spent so many years in exile? Any answer to this question will be purely speculative. It's rather like wondering what your life would have been like if you'd got a "proper" job and married the girl next door. Many of us who were in exile certainly did get things done. We were exposed to so much more than those who remained behind in a country which became increasingly isolated from the rest of the world. Obviously, many of our actors, who were disadvantaged on the labour market because of their accent or their first language, would have experienced less unemployment at home. Those of us who wanted to produce South African work soon discovered that other countries had their own problems and that one South African play every so often was more than enough. Perhaps our output would have been greater if we'd not been in exile. But I'm speculating. Bertolt Brecht wrote his best plays in exile. Would he have written those plays if he had stayed in Germany?

MY LIFE IN THE THEATRE OF WAR:
THE DEVELOPMENT OF AN ALTERNATIVE
CONSCIOUSNESS

MATTHEW KROUSE

When I was young, growing up in a small industrial town on the outskirts of Johannesburg, it became fashionable for white parents to send their children to elocution lessons. Our English is flat and nasal, and many parents spared no expense in altering this in their children through intensive grooming. Elocution lessons happened in most white church and school halls once a week, from about 3 pm onwards, after school. Children were usually dropped off by their mothers, after lunch, or were walked to elocution by their servants. Sometimes one stayed behind after school and did homework in a classroom until the elocution teacher arrived. Then hour-long classes would take place in the hall, either privately or in small groups. I remember an epileptic kid had a fit in elocution once, and the elocution teacher held his tongue down with a wooden ruler. When he revived the class continued and the teacher seemed unruffled.

A favorite mime improvisation game among these very strict colonial elocution teachers, was called "After the Bomb." In this theatre exercise the unfortunate child would have to hide under a table, anticipating the bomb, until the elocution teacher made a terrible bang, by clapping hands together or banging a book on her desk. Then the child would have to silently enact the shock and horror of emerging from a bomb shelter to find everything familiar in post-apocalyptic destruction.

So popular was this little charade with the teachers in our town that, when it came for the annual adjudication of students in our region, "After the Bomb" was a prescribed exercise. The regional adjudication was an evening event, complete with interval, and tea and cakes. Prepared poems were recited, play scenes were enacted, and then came the miming of "After the Bomb." On the stage of our

6. Matthew Krouse and Robert Colman in *Famous Dead Man*. Photo: Matthew Krouse.

bleak school hall, one by one, about fifty children acted it out. The audience consisted of parents, grandparents and siblings, all gathered to inspect the development of their children's English and dramatic skills. On the far end of the hall, at an elevated desk in the aisle, sat two ghostly adjudicators, a hooded lamp lighting up their evaluation forms. The adjudicators would ring a bell. Then backstage a prim official would usher a child onto the stage.

The enactment of "After the Bomb" was usually quite one-dimensional. The child would creep onto the stage, horror-stricken, where he or she would find mother dead, father dead, dog dead, house blown to bits, clothes gone, and so forth.

Then after the whole examination was over the adjudicators would briskly walk to the stage, enthusiastically, while the community applauded themselves into a frenzy. The formal adjudication would follow as each of the two adjudicators delivered lengthy appraisals of each student's work. That is when the dames of the colonial stage enjoyed their greatest moments. They did great renditions of "After the Bomb," correctly, for hours, as the teenage boys whistled catcalls, mothers became emotional, and fathers sat sternly.

"After the Bomb" was, of course, quite a meaningful display of theatre for the whites who were living with the constant threat of resistance from their black underlings. It had significance as a ritual acknowledgement that there was a threat, and it was a theatricalised response to the official war psychosis that had, ever since the Second World War, institutionalised public fire-drills, suburban defence teams, and so forth.

For me, at any rate, it was probably my experience of elocution lessons that helped me decide that I could pursue a career in the theatre. And so I went to Johannesburg to study drama. Years later, as a conscript, it was my grounding in theatre that helped me to become a singer-dancer in the entertainment corps of the South African Defence Force. It was here that I had my experiences of army drag, being a Master of Ceremonies, singing for army pageants, and so forth.

At the same time, I worked in an army media centre where a great deal of war photography was processed. I was a scriptwriter and I spent over a year producing training videos and slide programmes on nursing procedures for military nurses. Here I was in the fortunate position of being shown hundreds of pictures of wounded soldiers, in operating theatres and in the field. Once, I became alarmed when a series of photographs arrived on my desk of an unusual operation that described, to me, the horror of the war in its extremes. They were photographs of a young soldier, unconscious on an operating table. He had suffered an accident while jumping off an armoured vehicle. He had attempted to throw his rifle to a friend before alighting, but the friend had miscalculated and the rifle fell to the ground. The butt bounced on the ground and a shot went off. As the boy jumped off the vehicle he connected with the barrel of his own gun, and his anus was blown out. The photographs were of the unconscious naked youth, lying on his back with his face covered, legs spread in the air, as a nurse held his scrotum aside for the benefit of the army photographer.

For obvious reasons I stole these slides, and years later, in an anti-conscription play under the auspices of the ECC (End Conscription Campaign), I projected the slide of this unfortunate victim, much to the ire of the South African Police.

The opportunities for performance, in the mid-1980s when I graduated from forced conscription, were much enhanced by the existence of a venue in the midst of the city called The Black Sun. It was here that I and my partner Robert Colman staged our play about the life of Hendrik Verwoerd called *Famous Dead Man*. It was a successful satire that told the story of Verwoerd, the architect of apartheid, in cabaret form. It was a scathing attack on the assassinated leader, written and performed by two angry youths who were hardly prepared for the scandal it inspired.

On the opening night of this play, South Africa's strange contradictions manifested themselves. The cabaret theatre, where the play was staged, adjoined a Greek restaurant where a rightwing political group was holding a rowdy dinner. The manager locked the door of the theatre as the first performance began.

So successful was *Famous Dead Man* that my partner and I, along with our pianist, were invited by an enterprising entrepreneur to perform our satire in Durban, in an auditorium of the Natal University.

When we arrived in Durban our efficient promoter had already hung a good few hundred posters on the street poles and trees of the city. Many of them, apparently, were hung alongside posters advertising a public meeting of the rightwing AWB (*Afrikaner Weerstand Beweging*).

The poster for *Famous Dead Man* contained the eye-catching slogan, "Sex, Jokes, Filth and Verwoerd." Offended, a rightwinger from Durban phoned the surviving daughter of the late Prime Minister, Anna Boshoff, who reported to the press, on 28 September 1986, that she would "speak to the right people." We found ourselves in major articles in the papers, being threatened with our lives. "My father did a lot towards the end of his life to bridge the gap between English and Afrikaans people, so I don't know why the English must attack him," said the daughter of Verwoerd.

On our return from Durban, an interesting experience awaited us. As we drove into Johannesburg city I remember seeing newspaper headlines of the daily press. One poster displayed rudely, "MINISTER GETS CABARET SHOW BANNED." I knew then that we were in hot water, for our run of the play was to resume in Johannesburg. The following day, on 30 September, the manager of The Black Sun was served a banning order from the state censors which read, "No further performance is permitted," in terms of three governmental decrees. The play was banned for obscenity, blasphemy, and for inciting South Africans against Afrikanerdom.

Without delay, Robert Colman and I seized the moment to write and perform another satirical sketch in a revue to take place in the bar of a suburban hotel — the Oxford Hotel — this time under the auspices of the ECC. This show was called *Noise and Smoke*, after the Brechtian cabaret of the same name, and it was here that we included the slide of the unfortunate conscriptee who had lost his anus.

The night before this anti-conscription revue was to take place, the dirty-tricks department of the South African police had arrived at the hotel in an anonymous-looking white panel van. An armed man in a balaclava held up the hotel receptionist while others spray-painted graffiti slogans all over the exterior hotel walls. Upon arriving at the venue for our rehearsals the following day, we were beset by the horrific image of the Oxford Hotel clad in crude slogans, most of them reporting "Viva ANC" or "Fuck conscription." Of course, it appeared to any innocent passer-by that the defacement of this genteel suburban hotel was caused by militant young leftwingers.

Our performance of *Noise and Smoke* nevertheless went ahead, and a contingency plan was made, that in the event of an emergency the escape route would be through the hotel's kitchen door, which would be left open. Needless to say, the police invaded the theatre that night, and we actors dashed for the escape route only to find that all entrances to the Oxford Hotel had been barred. The actors Robert Colman, Irene Stephanou and I, were cornered by the police and interrogated for a brief spell in the hotel's kitchen. Then I was singled out as the "kingpin" of the event, and removed from the theatre for further questioning. It so happened that, in my pocket, I was carrying the photographic slide which had been part of the show. It was the slide I had stolen from the army. As I was ushered out of the theatre, by four policemen, I wedged the slide out of its plastic holder, inconspicuously put it into my mouth, chewed it and then swallowed.

In the foyer of the hotel pandemonium reigned. A press photographer was slapped by a policeman and her film was confiscated. I was told by officials of the ECC to cooperate with the police who wanted to remove me from the pavement to their van, so I could be taken to their police station for questioning. I didn't like the idea, and, seeing an opening I ran away, down the street where, coincidently, I found a friend of mine about to leave in her motorcar. When asked under what law the performance was being closed, the police said, "breaking the laws of the State of Emergency."

In the interim, my close group of friends had travelled from the theatre to my apartment where they forced open my front door and collected personal effects that might have incriminated me, should my home have gotten searched, like banned books, written scripts, and so forth.

Later that night I was taken to the bohemian housing settlement of Crown Mines where my close friend lived. There Robert Colman and I hid for a couple of days while the storm around *Famous Dead Man* and *Noise and Smoke* raged. "Actors in Hiding" reported the press. In the end, we were offered a free appeal by two humanitarian lawyers. In order to facilitate the appeal we had to perform our satire for the censors who were to sit in a full house to judge the merits of the play.

On a weekday, one afternoon, Robert Colman and I performed *Famous Dead Man*, again at the Black Sun, as part of our public appeal. Then, later that same week we travelled to Pretoria's Appeal Court to listen to the appeal and to hear the verdict of the censors. The country's major satirist, Pieter-Dirk Uys, as well as the prominent song-writer Des Lindberg, were called upon by our lawyers, to deliver a critical appraisal in favour of our play.

Three full cars drove to Pretoria. In the courtroom, the humorous, cutting phrases from the play were bandied about. Its harshness was in the spotlight as suited old men listened to the lines, "Oh I've always wanted to fuck a future Prime Minister. Oh, the man in my life who could change a nation. Oh, Presidents and Parliaments make me so horny. Oh, if I could fuck a Prime Minister I would probably live forever. Jesus, Eva Braun should've had my fuckin' luck!"

This was, of course, quite embarrassing for us, the playwrights. Our play was being examined, criticized, word for word. The poor censorship board, present in a full force of about ten people, mostly clergymen and military personnel, tried desperately not to break out in uncontrollable anger as prop dildos and underware, in the colours of the South African flag, were held up for all to see. And then, at the height of the proceedings, in walked the daughter of Verwoerd, Anna Boshoff, quite regally, accompanied by a legal representative and her daughter. They sat, glaring at us; and then eventually they walked out early, in the same flurry that had heralded their arrival. And nothing could save the play. It was banned, without being offered the cuts other offensive plays had been offered in the past. But the final verdict was that Hendrik Verwoerd, as a deceased politician, could not be defamed, and so Colman and I were spared a further legal trial for defaming an almost religiously revered South African politician.

The tribulations of *Famous Dead Man* raise the question of whether authority is above criticism, and what the "reasonable" constraints of criticism should be.

A year later, in 1987, the events here described were included into the script of an alternative feature film directed by Andrew Worsdale called *Shot Down*. In this film I had the good fortune of acting as myself, and further, of re-enacting the bannings and the interrogation I had experienced. Needless to say, *Shot Down* was banned shortly after its completion; and remains banned today. But it was also banned for the inclusion, in the film, of another short alternative film called *De Voortrekkers*. *De Voortrekkers* itself has a stormy little history, one that I'll recount in the anecdote that follows:

While serving in the South African Defence Force, I teamed up with the film producer Jeremy Nathan and the cinematographer Giulio Biccari to write the eight-minute, black and white film commemorating the anniversary of 150 years since the Great Trek, that movement into the interior of South Africa, by the Dutch pioneers who colonised the Cape. One afternoon, while working in the barracks, I received a telephone call from Jeremy Nathan who reported to me, in a worried voice, that something terrible had happened. We had been writing our film *De Voortrekkers* at a student home in the high density university suburb of Braamfontein. At the same time, the owner of the house had lent a room to a marimba band of twenty black youths from Cape Town who were to play a season in a jazz club in the city. It was on the 15 June 1985, a day before the commemoration of the June 16 student uprisings, when a policeman on patrol witnessed a number of these black youths emerge from this Braamfontein house. The policeman suspected these youths to be political militants and he called on the military intelligence to come and search the house within which our script lay, in a brown envelope, waiting to be filmed.

I have been told, subsequently, that about ten policemen descended on the Braamfontein house that day, armed with automatic machine-guns. They lined up all the children of the marimba band outside in the garden, then they made the children kneel with their hands behind their heads while they did a thorough search of the premises. In the course of their search they found the script of our film *De Voortrekkers*. Then they radio'd for the assistance of more informed members of the intelligence squad. Two arrived, apparently students of Witwatersrand University, which was one block away.

The script of *De Voortrekkers* was confiscated, along with a series of photographs of me, naked, lying splayed upon a monument to the fallen soldier, in Barbeton. In our absence the intelligence police vowed that they would get to the bottom of our script that contained a central scene of Dutch pioneers copulating. That was the last we saw of the intelligence police, but we had to put our plans to make this short film on hold.

In 1987, as I have recounted, we did gather together enough financial resources to make our film *De Voortrekkers*, with its central contentious scene of pioneers copulating. In order to facilitate the setting we hired the use of a farm outside Johannesburg, as well as an ox-wagon, the form of transport the pioneers used, before which we intended to film our scene. The ox-wagon was to be delivered to the farm before the shooting began, and the crew was to travel to the set early to prepare for the shoot. I functioned as the art director of the film, and when I arrived on the farm I found that the hired ox-wagon had been delivered, and had also been vandalised by some politically conscientised local farm-hands. On the body of the wagon numerous slogans were spray-painted, like, "Fuck the boers," and so forth. I remember reflecting, then, on the other moment in my life when graffiti like this had mirrored the serious divisions between South Africans.

We completed our filming of *De Voortrekkers*, which to this day is one of the more successful underground films to have been made during the emergency period in our history. So successful was *De Voortrekkers* that various commercial venues and festivals inside South Africa made application to the censorship board to show it. The state censors had seen *De Voortrekkers* as part of the feature film *Shot Down*, and, well prepared for the application, they immediately banned the film. On the 28 November 1989, Jeremy Nathan was served with a banning order for *De Voortrekkers* which stated that the film "intrudes on the privacy of the sex act," and that a short instance of homosexuality depicted in the film is "indecent and obscene." The censors reported that, "in a short film, with 85% undesirable, there is no way to pass *De Voortrekkers*." (sic)

One year after the making of *De Voortrekkers*, in 1988, I was part of the group of frustrated artists who formed the City Theatre and Dance Group of Johannesburg. The lack of opportunity for alternative independent productions necessitated a new approach to self-sustainment in the theatre, and so five of us, with the composer and musical director Shaun Naidoo, formed the company with the intention of staging large dance dramas, which we did. It was under the auspices of this group that I co-authored the controversial play *Sunrise City* with directors Chris Pretorius and Mark Fleishman.

Sunrise City was about that monolithic cancer on the horizon of culture, Sun City, a gambling den and tourist mecca set in the impoverished bantustan of Bophuthatswana. In the play the workers of an imaginary bordello called Sunrise City rebel, deserting their overlords, decadent brothel keepers, leaving them destitute and short of a work force. The libretto was set to music, with a chorus line of five beautiful scantily-clad actresses. Knowing the theatre-going habits of moneyed South Africans, we were certain that this play would draw a large audience, and so we booked our troupe (17 people) onto the stage of the largest music hall in the city, the Market Theatre's Warehouse. The dancing was choreographed by the award-winning choreographer, Robyn Orlin. The overriding intention of the play was to confront the issue of why South Africans needed to travel a hundred kilometres, to Sun City, when they could witness all the gambling and nudity they desired, at home.

Needless to say, *Sunrise City* was banned. On the 4th of May, 1988, the management of the Market Theatre was served with the banning order which stated that,

> The viewer is dragged into a vision of corruption and vice. Female breast nudity, simulated copulation movements, sadism, lesbianism, crude and profane dialogue abound. The performance is mediocre, without any artistic or dramatic merit and in the opinion of the committee has only been created as a peg for banal obscenities. Evil triumphs over good and there is no corrective message.

Again, blasphemy, obscenity and the inciting of racial groups against one another formed the basis of the banning. Again, a defence team was contracted and a public appeal was lodged. And again, I got the opportunity to see one of my works dissected before the staunch and uncompromising censorship board, at their Appeal Court in Pretoria. This time, though, the censors suspended the play, pending their judgment, thereby allowing it to run its course for approximately a fortnight. An immediate 2–18 age restriction was to be enforced at the box office. The effect of this was to encourage the general public, who appeared to follow the press publicity closely. The performance, in its venue which seated four hundred, was sold out and we were able to pay for the legal appeal which was a costly process indeed. Finally, *Sunrise City* was shut down early, and I was left without work, wondering whether the laws of the country would ever change to allow a modicum of self-expression.

In 1988 I encountered political cultural activism for the first time when I was invited to the launching of the Progressive Arts Project, which took place at Witwatersrand University. It was at the height of the cultural boycott, and activists were attempting to establish structures inside the country that could reflect broader aspirations for democracy. At that time there were many small groups debating the various roles of cultural production, most importantly, the pressing need to incorporate working-class culture into the mainstream entertainment industry. At that time there was a dearth of opportunity for the numerous community groups that had sprung up in the townships. Many groups, as well as individuals like oral poets and dancers, found that there were no venues in cities that would provide facilities for the culture they were producing. Certainly, the regional performing arts councils weren't providing platforms then. The debates were stormy and engrossing, particularly on the role of individualistic artists who didn't identify with the mass movement taking place, as well as the manner in which local culturalists should conduct the cultural boycott. Those were the stormy days when the Cultural Desk would hold public debates around applications for artists to either enter or exit the country. I must confess, here, that with my experiences in the censorship realm, I felt a distinct sense of pleasure in knowing that the alternative cultural movement was exerting a fair degree of muscle in deciding for itself the route of the emergent South African arts.

From these discussions, various smaller groups emerged, ones that would meet in the evenings to discuss ideas for a common par-

ticipation in cultural production. The interesting aspect of this arrange-
ment was that the time had come for white professional dramatists,
dancers and musicians to meet with their black counterparts who,
invariably, were working men and women with an interest in culture,
an interest that they sometimes could not afford to pursue. But the
resilience of these working class participants can be witnessed in the
manner in which they formed choirs, workshopped plays and presented oral poetry at the various commemorations of the political
struggle. Almost every weekend we would travel to a venue in a
township church or school where recitals and performances would
take place. Once I even found myself performing my own poetry on
the stage of the Johannesburg City Hall before two thousand miners
of the National Union of Mineworkers, at the public commemoration
of the Kinross mining disaster.

     With this experience, I noticed how styles and forms of cultural
expression and resistance were evolving. For me, the days of outra-
geous political satire were over. They had been replaced by a well-
supported form of agit-prop, an oral testimony that did not discriminate
between the professional practitioner and the grass-roots worker.
Although the message was instant and somewhat unrefined, it presented itself as a measure of identifiable solidarity, a few simple words,
effectively juxtaposed to create a form that has become unique to South
African culture.

     It was then that I decided to form my own agit-prop perform-
ance group, of approximately five people, which was called The Re-
Action Group. With this group we did performances for various benefit
organisations, against capital punishment, censorship and conscription, and so forth. In form, we borrowed elements from previous
political satires which we coupled with the new form of oral poetry
that was emerging from the townships. Again, we suffered a fair
degree of intimidation from the authorities who would phone our
employing venues and organisations to threaten us with arrest should
the show go on. But in every instance the show went on, even though
we knew that somewhere in the audience sat a plainclothes policeman
making mental notes.

     In 1988 I was approached by a committee member of a cultural
group who invited me to join in preparations for the 70th birthday of
Nelson Mandela, who was the world's most famous political prisoner.
I agreed to do some coordinating and was told that a secret meeting
would take place at a well-known Johannesburg hotel. I wasn't told
which hotel to go to, but only to follow a man holding a folded

newspaper under his arm, someone I would see on a streetcorner somewhere in the city.

When the day of the meeting came about I did indeed find a lone ranger standing with a newspaper at the busy city intersection, during working hours. I was quite frightened as I followed him, up a hill and into the foyer of a large five star hotel. Once inside the hotel we stood at the elevators, silently, not acknowledging each other. Eventually a lift arrived and we proceeded to the seventeenth floor. The lift doors opened and I followed the leader to an inconspicuous hotel-room door which seemed to open as if by providence. Once inside the hotel room I was aghast. There before me were approximately twenty people, all jovial, making plans for the large concert to take place at Wembley stadium in London, and for a smaller concert that would take place simultaneously at home.

Meetings like this one were to occur on a weekly basis for at least two months. Once a week I would follow a man with a newspaper to another venue where the same group would meet, bringing feedback about preparations for the celebration of the Mandela birthday. It was quite absurd. Once the meeting had gathered, a lookout was posted in the hotel passage. Then sandwiches and tea would be ordered from the hotel reception. Ten minutes later there would be a knock on the door and the guard would usher in a waiter bearing a trolley of refreshments.

In this group, certain coordinators were given different tasks. My task was to see to the press releases that would be circulated to the media concerning the event. To achieve this I was asked whether it would be safe for a handful of individuals present to meet at my house to draft the press releases. I agreed and set a date for the meeting.

On the morning of the meeting I awoke and looked out of my window. There on the pavement, outside my house, was a man inconspicuously watching my abode. Later, he was joined by another, and then another. Eventually I had four guards watching my house. I was not sure whether they were in favour of the meeting or against the meeting, and I remember sitting at home that day just waiting for something bad to happen. Eventually, at the arranged time, there was a knock on my door and about five activists arrived. I ushered them into my lounge where we were to sit and draft the press release.

I was informed, then, that the South African celebration of the Mandela birthday had been banned. This had some bearing on the nature of the press releases we were to draft, and so, we took the opportunity to write some scathing lines about the infringements on freedom of speech. Those were the days when diatribes against "The Regime" were always accompanied by accolades bestowed upon, "The People."

With the concert banned, it was decided that a press conference would be held to draw attention to the banning and to allow some expression of celebration in favour of the Mandela birthday. It was decided that the press conference would be held at the Market Theatre in the large Warehouse auditorium where, only months before, our play *Sunrise City* had been banned.

On the day of the press conference I arrived at the Warehouse early to hang, on the cyclorama, a gigantic banner of Mandela's face. It was a banner that was supposed to have hung on the stage of the banned outdoor concert. It looked absolutely monumental, dwarfing the Warehouse stage. One by one, invited representatives of various governments arrived at the press conference, bearing telegrams from their governments abroad. I was delegated to a desk where the foreign representatives were to hand me their well-wishes. I remember, when the first representative arrived he asked the chief coordinator where he should hand in his message. "Give it to that General there," said the chief coordinator, pointing to me in jest. From that moment all the foreign representatives arrived, and, mistaking me for a major revolutionary, they all respectfully called me, "General."

Then, in a flurry of activity, Winnie Mandela arrived, attended by her Mandela Football Team, about twenty township youths, wearing bright yellow tracksuits. The press conference went ahead with a good few dozen international television crews videoing the event. I was instructed to take to the podium where I stood for a full ten minutes reading the international messages of support.

After this, two mammoth postal sacks of birthday cards from around the world were hoisted onto the stage. The Mandela Football Team then flew into a frenzy, throwing hundreds of these pretty cards into the air while the world watched in anticipation.

Following the release of South Africa's leaders, and the unbanning of our political organisations, I have had the opportunity to run in the streets in mass rallies, along with thousands of others, in the most theatrical celebration this country has seen. I have also had ample time to reflect on the absurdities of the South African censorship system that, today, is somewhat void of the harsh direction it defined for itself in the past.

Today, I receive the censorship bulletins from the state. They come to my office in frightening regularity, full to the brim with titles of books and cultural artifacts that have been banned, unbanned, given age-limits, held at customs, and so forth. From my rather privileged perspective I find that I am more ignorant of the effects of censorship, now, than when I first got banned. This is because the spectacle of politics runs its course, regardless of the desires or powers of ordinary people.

But one thing is certain: Today, hundreds of lesbian and gay books get banned. It is almost as if, having missed their previous target, the censors have defined yet another. It is strange, but official homophobia appears to be replacing official racism and fear of communism. The banning of political ideas is being replaced by the banning of already otherised sexual identities. At the same time, homophobia in South African society is so widespread, that from no quarter will state censors ever be challenged on this note. This is alarming because it indicates, to me, that in many ways the struggle for human rights is far from over in South Africa. If the freedom to love is indeed part of that struggle, then perhaps ours has just begun.

WHAT IS A TRIBAL DRESS? THE *"IMBONGI"* (PRAISE SINGER) AND THE "PEOPLE'S POET." REACTIVATION OF A TRADITION IN THE LIBERATION STRUGGLE

PETER HORN

Describing a visit to the Transkei in 1977 Nadine Gordimer asks the question: "What is a tribal dress?" and answers: "Something in a constant state of change since Africans began to wear anything." The Dandy's and Dadaist's esoteric law of aesthetics — "style is a combination of incongruities" — which she discovers in contemporary African dress, applies equally well to all other expressions of African culture in a post-colonial situation.[1]

The intrusion of colonialist culture and the destruction of the pre-colonial social structures radically change the pre-colonial culture of the African populations of Southern Africa: the remnants of the pre-colonial culture lose their all-embracing validity and become "traditional" or "folk" culture in opposition to an "élite" or "ruling class" culture, which installs itself as the dominant norm and marginalizes all "variants" as slang.[2] As far as literature is concerned, this division coincides essentially although not completely with the division oral/written culture. While "folk" culture is by no means as stable or even stagnant as some descriptions of it would have us assume, under the

---

[1] Nadine Gordimer, "A Vision of Two Blood-Red Suns." In: Nadine Gordimer, *The Essential Gesture. Writing, Politics and Places.* Edited and introduced by Stephen Clingman. Cape Town, Johannesburg: David Philip, 1988, p. 194; The term "post-colonial" is used here in the sense in which Bill Ashcroft, Gareth Griffith, Helen Tiffin, *The Empire Writes Back. Theory and Practice in Post-Colonial Literatures.* London, New York: Routledge, 1989, p. 2 have defined it: "to cover all the culture affected by the imperial process from the moment of colonization to the present day." While I am aware of the problem of lumping Canadian, Nigerian and South African cultures under the same term, I still find the term useful to designate certain common features of all these cultures.

[2] Cf. Ashcroft, Griffith and Tiffin, [note 1], p. 7.

conditions of colonialism, where this culture fights for its survival first against the "élite" culture, then even more desperately against the "mass" culture of capitalism, it acquires traits of purism and conservatism, traits which militate against those artists who try to develop the existing culture dynamically. Various forces — both African nationalists and well-meaning or less well-meaning colonialists — attempt to "preserve" the *status quo ante* of a subjugated culture.[3] Daniel Kunene writes about the changes in tradition, which came about by the wars of dispossession as follows:

> Creating a militant poetry in the African languages is a challenge that faced the oral poet in the nineteenth century as the Boers encroached more and more on the Africans' land during the so-called Great Trek and beyond. The contemporary young activist poet of the seventies and eighties can take courage from, and also feel humbled by, the fact that his activity is nothing new. He has a tradition to fall back on. He has poetry of high calibre that used powerful imagery and direct exhortation, that was created in the heat of the wars of dispossession. His courageous forefathers resisted the invaders, and his artistic predecessors immortalized them in his poetry of praise. He is therefore able to measure his own efforts against his glorious past.[4]

D. Dingiswayo takes up this theme when he says: "Cultural struggle has always formed an integral part of efforts of the oppressed in the fight for democracy and national liberation."[5] And the resolution

---

[3] Cf. David Coplan, "Popular culture and performance in Africa." In: *Critical Arts. A Journal for Media Studies.* Vol. 3 (1983), No. 1, p. 1.

[4] Daniel p. Kunene, "Language, Literature and the struggle for Liberation in South Africa." In: *Staffrider.* Vol. 6, No. 3 (1986), p. 37; on the poetry between the first generation of resistance poets — Mqhayi, Jolobe, Vilakazi etc. — and the most recent group of popular poets described here, see Jacques Alvarez-Péreyre, *The poetry of commitment in South Africa.* Translated by Clive Wake. London: Heinemann, 1984; Detlev Th. Reichel, *Schriftsteller gegen die Apartheid.* Berlin 1977; Nadine Gordimer, *The Black Interpreters. Notes on African Writing.* Johannesburg: Ravan, 1973; Ursula Barnett, *A Vision of Order. A Study of Black South African Literature in English 1914–1980.* London: Sinclair Browne, 1983; Dennis Brutus, "Liberation and Literature"; and Don Mattera, "Some points about the literature of liberation in present-day South Africa". In: *South African Literature. Liberation and the Art of Writing.* Evangelische Akademie Bad Boll, pp. 13–16, pp. 17–22.

[5] D. Dingiswayo, "Culture and the national struggle" In: *Spark. A Progressive: Sinclair Browne, Arts Project Publication.* Kengray n.d. p. 2.

of the CASA (Culture for Another South Africa) conference in Amsterdam (1987) echoes this strain:

> Recognizing that culture is an integral part of the national democratic struggle, the national democratic movement therefore asserts that the role of cultural workers is inseparable from the overall struggle against apartheid as well as the moulding of the future non-racial, non-sexist, unitary and democratic South Africa.[6]

I would like to describe here the experience of such a popular culture as I observed it in the Western Cape[7] and elsewhere in South Africa during the eighties, focussing on the function of "poetry" within that culture. Various cultural forms (music, dance, poetry, drama) appeared both within the context of political and trade union meetings and in the form of "cultural" events with a clear political connotation. Elements of this culture were taken from "traditional" culture and its transformation in an African ghetto (traditional Xhosa songs and dances) but also from "foreign traditional" cultures, such as the marimba players. Other elements come from a generally Afro-American black culture (jazz) with a strong South African flavour (the jazz of Basil "Manenberg" Coetzee) while others again parody certain elements of "mass" culture (the rock and roll of the Oaklands Band). There is no easily discernible, distinguishing sign which subsumes such widely differing expressions as the Mavis Smallberg Dance Group and the songs of Ivan Lucas, the poetry of Sandile Dikeni and of Keith Gottschalk, except perhaps the overtly political nature of practically all the material performed, and its performability.[8] At about the same

---

[6] Quoted in Dingiswayo, [note 5], p. 2.

[7] A recent anthology of this culture is Ampie Coetzee and Hein Willemse, *Iqabane Labantu. Poetry in the emergency. Poesie in die noodtoestand.* Johannesburg: Taurus 1989.

[8] While performance is seen as an essential element in music, dance and drama, poetry is not necessarily seen in this light. Cf. Ian Steadman, "Culture and Context: Notes on Performance in South Africa." In: *Critical Arts. A Journal for Media Studies.* Vol. 2 (1981) No. 1, p. 1ff. See also Ian Steadman, "Performance Research: A select bibliography. In: *Critical Arts. A Journal for Media Studies.* Vol. 2 (1981) No. 1, pp. 60–65. Attempts by critics brought up on the individualistic poetry on the printed page of poetry books to evaluate performance-oriented political and public poetry of the popular kind which I try to describe here will tend to fall into all kinds of traps and prejudices.

time (the 1980's) in the Western Cape I, too, began to read poetry at large political meetings and May Day rallies. Performance poetry like this has now become an integral part of struggle culture in South Africa.[9]

In this context, the *imbongi*, oral poetry, thought by many to be a dead tradition or the preserve of chiefly praises, resurfaced as a voice of ordinary black workers and their struggles from about 1984. Of course the techniques and rhythms of the *imbongi* tradition had never really been dead. On the 29th April 1990 — at the ANC Rally in Lentegeur, Cape Town, at the time of the first talks about talks between the ANC and the Nationalist government — Christopher Toise, a traditional *imbongi* and a political leader of the squatters in Cape Town, called out the traditional praises of Mandela:

> When two bulls clash, with one a speckle-back beast,
> go round its hindquarters, to check its back is arched.
> Slimlegged buck from the house of Madiba that sports its
> white patch
> they desire to annoy him, pat his crown, little thinking he's
> raging.[10]

The trade union poet Mi S'dumo Hlatshwayo, for example, had learned this technique in the baptism in words of fire through the *eCibini*, the St. John's Apostolic Church, an independent African church of the poor.[11] One of these modern praise singers, Mzwakhe

---

Cf. Nick Visser, "English Studies in Transition" and "The Critical Situation and the Situation of Criticism," and Michael Vaughan, "The Critique of the Dominant Ideas in Departments of English in the English-Speaking Universities of South Africa." In: *Critical Arts. A Journal for Media Studies.* Vol. 3 (1984) No. 2.

[9] Among the many other poets who regularly read at political meetings, trade union gatherings, funerals and popular cultural festivals one could single out Jeremy Cronin, James Matthews, Mavis Smallberg, Nise Malange, Mongane Serote, Pascal Gwala, Sipho Sepamla, Mandlenkosi Langa, Gladys Thomas and Joan Baker.

[10] Christopher Toise, *Hail, offspring of the predator.* Recorded by CASET 1990. Translated by Abner Nyamende, revised by Keith Gottschalk.

[11] See the introduction by Ari Sitas to Alfred Temba Qabula, Mi S'dumo Hlatshwayo, Nise Malange, *Black Mamba Rising. South African Worker Poets in Struggle.* Durban: Worker Resistance and Culture Publications, 1986, pp. 1–7.

Mbuli, has in the meantime achieved pop star status, and his audio cassettes sell as well as his collection of poems. As a public and political poet, Mzwakhe Mbuli relies heavily on all the techniques of a rhetoric which derives, on the one hand, from the African evangelical and revivalist churches and, on the other hand, from the traditional *imbongi*, but to carry a message which — at least superficially — is neither revivalist nor traditional. Anybody who has seen and heard Mzwakhe Mbuli perform in a political meeting, at a funeral or in concert, cannot but be struck by both his charismatic presence and his performance.[12]

The rhetoric of the *imbongi* makes its appearance in Mzwakhe Mbuli's poetry, for example, in the traditional similes and metaphors of a rural community in close contact with an untamed nature, when the invincibility of the people is demonstrated with the following widely quoted image:

> The people are like crocodiles in the river;
> and no one can fight crocodiles inside the river;
> South Africa why therefore buy time?
> When crocodiles are against you;
> Why give chase to lizards?[13]

On the other hand, the isolation of the poet in jail is described in terms of banishment into the untamed wilderness with its dangerous beasts of prey and poisonous snakes:

> Cut-off from the world of human beings;
> And brought closer to the world of lions and mambas.

The modern *imbongi* is re-cited in *Hansard*,[14] in the protocols of political trials, and in the very prison regulations, which control his life after

---

[12] Mzwakhe Mbuli, *Before Dawn*. Johannesburg: COSAW, 1989. Cf. my review of this volume in *Staffrider* vol. 8, nos. 3 & 4, 1989, pp. 185–193.

[13] Mbuli, "Crocodiles", [note 12], p. 39f.

[14] Cf. Keith Gottschalk's poem "Prejudicial to the peace & good order." In: *Emergency Poems/Imibongo Yenxakeko/Noodgedigte*, which refers to an incident in the white House of Parliament, where his poem "For Ashley Kriel whom they killed by Hazendale" (p. 43) was quoted to demonstrate the agitatory role of poetry in the struggle. While in prison he was interrogated about his poem "Ode to the statue of Jan van Riebeeck" (p. 76).

being condemned. Thus Keith Gottschalk's[15] poem "War Memorial"[16] celebrates the victory of Jeremy Cronin and Breyten Breytenbach:

> they probably don't know it yet,
> but this place
> has a calli-graphic,
> a sort of war memorial,
> to Jeremy Cronin
> (Marxist, seven years),
> Breyten Breytenbach
> (Budhist, seven & a half years).
>
> go past the reception desk
> graced by two delicious monsters,
> (manned by two undelicious monsters);
> enter the contact visitors' room,
> look at the wall on your right -
> I mean the new Regulasie 4(f):
> "no letter
> containing a poem
> shall be forwarded
> from a prisoner
> to the outside
> or from outside
> to a prisoner"

Itself part of a cycle of prison poems (*Noodgedigte*) it creates by its reference to other prison poets a continuity across the discontinuities of popular culture in South Africa: it contains an alternative literary history *in nuce*. Solidarity in this context means the assurance: "A person is a person because of other people," as the title of one of Cronin's poems states ("*MOTHO KE MOTHO KA BATHO BABANG*").[17]

---

[15] Gottschalk has developed his own personal style of performance with a full range of gestures and even quick costume changes, which is much appreciated by his audiences, and which successfully transforms the written page into the experience of his listeners. He is not an oral poet, in the sense that his poetry is first written down and then performed and in the sense that he does not improvise, except in a limited way. He does, however, adapt his poetry to the occasion, and writes new lines and stanzas practically for each major new performance. Some poems have lines where the poet alludes to current events and here he replaces the names of latest victims of police brutality etc. during performance.

[16] Gottschalk, [note 14], part of his prison cycle "Noodgedigte".

[17] Jeremy Cronin, *Inside*. Johannesburg: Ravan Press 1983, p. 18.

Another of these young poets, who is both immensely popular and a very gifted writer and who draws both on the traditional craft of the oral poet as well as the modern consciousness of the current participant in the freedom struggle, is Sandile Dikeni. Just returned from a spell in prison for his political activities, he addressed his oppressors in his poem *NDIM LO!* (Here I am back!):

> Murderous advocates of Genocide
> Oppressors of my black blood
> Dogs that maul without Pride
> Hit me now, hit me hard
> I say Ndim lo[18]

He is a poet "who makes no secret of his involvement in the situation he is talking about, of his partisanship, of the subjective nature of his creations."[19] Similarly Mzwakhe Mbuli disdains the "armchair cultural workers who can only communicate with the masses through the newspapers, TV, or through books bought in a bookshop," and demands: "they must be there everyday with the people."[20] Similarly Alfred Temba Qabula — dressed in a colourful African costume — sees himself in his famous *"Izimbongo zika Fosatu"*[21] as a traditional healer and sage:

> Listen I am a Sangoma,
> You [FOSATU] have come to me so that I tell all about you
> I have thrown my bones and called on my abalozi.
> My bones and my abalozi tell me this:
> Yebo, you have good and handsome sons
> Also they are intelligent and quite healthy.[22]

The poetics of the *imbongi* has not yet been written, despite some useful prolegomena, and I do not pretend that I am capable of this task. Praise poetry is a genre shared by all the peoples of Africa south of the Sahara,

---

[18] Sandile Dikeni, "Ndim Lo!" In: Coetzee and Willemse, [note 6], p. 56.

[19] Daniel P. Kunene, *Heroic Poetry of the Basotho*. Oxford: Clarendon Press, 1971, p. xiv.

[20] Mzwake Mbuli, "Cultural Organisation — What is it and why?" In: *Spark. A Progressive Arts Project Publication*. Kengray n.d. p. 5.

[21] Which he started to perform in 1984 at trade union meetings. Cf. [note 11].

[22] Qabula, "Praise Poem to FOSATU", [note 11], p. 12f.

and probably by all human beings in the past.[23] "For thousands of years panegyrics of the kind [. . .] have been the medium of expression for the sentiments of homage, appreciation and thanks."[24] Forms of the *imbongi*, the praise singer, can even be traced back at least in written form to UrNammu, the founder of the third dynasty of Ur.[25] When a Sumer king is praised[26] as a "true off-spring engendered by a bull, speckled of head and body," as a "mighty warrior born of a lion,"[27] the metaphors are similar to those we heard in the praises of Mandela,[28] as are other common devices of oral literature, i.e. linking, cross-linking, parallelism,[29] cross-parallelism,[30] anaphora, kenning etc.[31]

---

[23] Cf. Ruth Finnegan, *Oral Literature in Africa*, Oxford Library of African Literature, 1970, Ch. 5, Panegyric, pp. 111–146.

[24] A.C. Hodza and G. Fortune, *Shona Praise Poetry*. Oxford: Clarendon Press, 1979, p. 1.

[25] Depictions of "court minstrels" go back even further into the past, into an age before the invention of writing. Cf. Samuel Noah Kramer, *From the Poetry of Sumer. Creation, Glorification, Adoration*. Berkeley, Los Angeles: University of California Press, 1979, p. 59.

[26] According to the praise songs, "the king of Sumer and Akkad was the perfect ideal man: physically powerful, distinguished looking, intellectually without a peer, spiritually a paragon of piety and probity." Kramer, [note 25], p. 65.

[27] Kramer, [note 25], p. 60f.

[28] A few random examples from *Black Mamba Rising*, [note 11]: "You [FOSATU] are the hen with wide wings / That protects its chickens" (p. 9); "FOSATU you are lion / That roared at Pretoria North" (p. 10) (Qabula); "The Black mamba that shelters in the songs / Yet others shelter in the trees!" (p. 30) "here are the workers coming like a flock of / Locusts" (p. 30) "You powerful black buffalo, / Powerful with slippery body / The buffalo that pushed men / Into the forest / In bewilderment the police / Stood with mouths open." (p. 32) (Hlatshwayo).

[29] A typical example would be from Mqhayi's *Vide Ityala lamawele* (1953, p. 98):

> *Ndingumntu nj' int' ehlal' ihambele?*
>
> *Ndingumntu nj' int' ehlal' ihlal' ifuduke?*
>
> *Ndingumntu nj' int' ehlal' ihlal' ihlal' igoduke?*

Quoted from Qangule, [note 24], p. 14.

[30] Cf. Hodza and Fortune, [note 24], p. 91.

[31] Julia Kristeva has described the *blazons*, laudatory utterances in the courtly literature of Southern France, which belong to a phonetic culture, character-ized by repetitive utterances and enumerations, originating in the fair, the

Many of the stylistic features of these ancient songs can still be found in present day Sotho, Xhosa, Shona or Zulu praise songs.[32] Physical power, courage and bravery are attributes highly valued.[33] Even if "the traditional praise-singer, the *imbongi*, is at work in the name of a new chief — the union"[34] and even if the subject of his song is nowadays often "a metaphorical warrior in a metaphorical battle,"[35] the *imbongi* remains, he still "writes with his spear."[36]

When he is asked to "write" poetry in the Western sense rather than to "perform," Sandile Dikeni breaks into a sweat:

> In the night
> droplets
> of light
> sweat
> confirms my fight
> I refuse to write
>
> I'll rather speak
> climb my voice to the peak
> of mountains
> that block my vision
> of worlds still to venture
> or just whisper

---

market place, the public square. Cf. Julia Kristeva, *Desire in Language. A Semiotic Approach to Literature and Art.* Edited by Leon S. Roudiez. Translated by Thomas Gora, Alice Jardine and Leon S. Roudiez. New York: Columbia University Press, 1980, p. 53.

[32] E. W. Grant, "The Izibongo of Zulu Chiefs," *Bantu Studies*, Johannesburg, vol iii, No. 3, July 1927, pp. 201–44; G. P. Lestrade, "Bantu Praise Poems," *The Critic*, Cape Town, vol. iv, No. 1, October 1935, pp. 1–10; G. P. Lestrade, "Traditional Literature" In I. Schapera (ed.), *The Bantu-Speaking Tribes of South Africa*, London 1937, pp. 291–308; I. Schapera, *Praise Poems of Tswana Chiefs*. Oxford Library of African Literature, 1965; T. Cope, *Izibongo. Zulu Praise Poems*. Oxford Library of African Literature, 1968.

[33] Kramer, [note 25], p. 66.

[34] Hein Willemse, "Poems speak of militant working class." In: *South*, Cape Town, 19th March 1987, p. 18.

[35] Daniel P. Kunene, *Heroic Poetry of the Basotho*. Oxford: Clarendon Press, 1971, p. xiv.

[36] Traditionally the *imbongi* carried a spear: "*Wabhala ngawo kwavel' imihobe neziny' iincwadi*" ("He wrote with his spear and poems and other books appeared"). (Yako 1977, p. 33), here quoted from Qangule, [note 24], p. 25.

to reach the hungry ears
of hundreds and thousands
that still want to hear.[37]

Sandile Dikeni, like Mzwakhe, is a performing poet, whose
work needs to be heard as well as read. Only when the poet steps onto
the tattered stages of the people and performs his poem is the cycle of
creation complete, as Gottschalk makes clear:

now: world premiere.
venue: paintpeeled hall in ghetto.
air conditioning: six smashed windowpanes.
interior decor: wiremesh on windows.
                        flydirt on lightbulbs.
                        newjacket on police informer
audience preference: less piano, more forte.

let your voice take command: plead, resonate, thunder.
they laugh, applaud, crowd round.
afterwards we put our work away
& walk back into the world.[38]

Even if he no longer "paces gracefully in his leopard skin
kaross," he still "stamps upon the ground churning up dust."[39]
There is no clear dividing line between the *imbongi* and the
evangelical rhetoric of the African churches, since the African evangelical rhetoric itself draws heavily on traditional figures of speech,
and since the rhetoric of the preacher has an underlying similarity to

---

[37] "In love with a critic." Most of Sandile's poetry, though widely known
through his readings to mass audiences, has not yet appeared in print. He
kindly provided me with manuscripts for this article.

[38] Gottschalk, "Crafting a poem," [note 14]; cf. Peter Horn, "Written poetry for
performance (Jeremy Cronin, Keith Gottschalk)". In: Reingard Nethersole
(ed.), *Emerging Literatures*. Bern, Frankfurt am Main, Paris, New York: Lang,
1990, pp. 162–172.

[39] That is how Tayadzerhwa depicts Mqhayi performing *imbongi* in heaven
after his death:

Seyibonga kwaPath' izitshixo!

Man' ixhentsa kuqhum' uthuli!

Iwunduza ngamabal' engwe!

Quoted from Qangule, [note 24], p. 16f.

the rhetoric of the tribal sage.[40] The use of the anaphora and parallelism in Mzwakhe Mbuli's *Creative than Before* and many other poems
is both biblical and indigenous:

> I am more creative than ever, ever before;
> I am more calm than ever, ever before;
> I am more composed than ever, ever before;
> I am more cautious than ever, ever before;
> I am more careful than ever, ever before;
> Yes. I am more creative than ever, ever before.[41]

The *kenning*, a device known to most oral poetry including
Anglo-Saxon, and other complex games of verbal repetition structure
the flow of sermon and *imbongi* alike.

But this "poetry" has a new self-assurance which does not
politely ask the English masters whether it may use a word or phrase
in this way or that. Mafika Gwala states: "with regard to the state and
the role of English, who owns it? Is violence between black and white
culturally adaptable? How does one use English as a site of struggle?"[42] The re-making of English in the image of Africa is apparent in
the bold grammatical structures which are bound to give sleepless
nights to purists. The boldness of this new poetry is best appreciated
in Sandile Dikeni's "*TRIBUTE TO ANGOLA,*" in which he addresses
the white soldiers destabilising the neighbouring country and support-
ing Savimbi:

> Sons of Van der Merwe
> haven't you heard
> haven't you heard the voice from the bushes of Angola
> haven't you heard the voice of Alexander Kalishnikov
> bellowing like the thunder in the mountains of Mathole

---

[40] Rhetoric has become something of a swear-word in contemporary academic
criticism, with implications of dishonesty, simplification, moralizing, and
politicking. Perhaps it is time to remind critics that from the Greeks to the
Romans, from the Medieval poets to the Renaissance and far into the Age of
Enlightenment rhetoric was the repertoire of skills and techniques which the
poet (as well as the public speaker) would use to structure and embellish his
communication.

[41] Mbuli, [note 12], p. 43.

[42] Mafika Gwala, "Towards a National Culture." Interview by Thengamehlo
Ngewenya. In: *Staffrider* Vol. 8, 1989, p. 72.

whispering hollow
like the wind
blowing in the dark forest of Hoho
giving birth to goose pimples on Malan himself
saying softly
go home, go home to apartheid
tell them of the resisting spirit of Angola
tell them that Savimbi is nothing
but a dog
dog that whimpers in fear
a fear for the sons of the Cuban revolution
of the advancing sons of Dos Santos
[. . .]
Luanda shall remain free
as long as Africa lives
the lives of the children of Africa
shall be defended
until there is no more America

Admittedly performance poetry like this is a powerful tool for educating people, creating a sense of unity and enriching political struggles, and both the Mass Democratic Movement and the government have understood the potential of such art.[43]

The *imbongi* rhetoric does, however, create a problematic, of which many proponents of people's culture seem to be either unaware or which they see as merely intellectual and academic nit-picking. On the one hand Mzwakhe Mbuli's lyrics by example do contest a number of poetic and emotional spaces which in the past have been the exclusive territory of reactionary forces. Until the advent of black theology and liberation theology, revivalist and evangelical rhetoric essentially turned the mind of the listener away from his daily struggles and tried to locate him in relation to another world of just retribution which would make up for the hurts of this world. But even liberation theology and its rhetoric do not abolish the ultimate authority[44] to which people have to bow, even if that authority is portrayed as inimical to

---

[43] Cf. Durban FOSATU Cultural group, "Culture and the workers' struggle." *South African Labour Bulletin*, 10.8.1985.

[44] In fact, it merely has to link to the Xhosa traditional line of authority: God — ancestors — king-people (father) — mother — children.

the existing political, social and ethical order.[45] D. Dingiswayo reminds us that the "connection between identity and culture makes culture 'the very foundation of the liberation movement' (Amilcar Cabral). One of the strongest forces that binds people of different and even opposed classes together into a single nation is a common culture."[46] And he points out "that [culture] is the basis of a people's sense of identity. [. . .] This sense of identity can cut across class divisions."[47] But that use of culture in a national rather than an internationalist sense has its inherent dangers. The recourse to traditional symbols and forms of discourse can be an equally powerful force both in the promotion of popular struggle and in the promotion of reactionary nationalisms and chauvinisms, and the recent history of Africa is full of "liberation struggles" which benefited neo-colonial élites and international capital under the exclusion of the workers. "The impetus towards national self-realization in critical assessments of literature all too often fails to stop short of nationalist myth."[48] While not to contest this appeal to traditional and national values would be foolish, to do so uncritically can only serve the purposes of a new ruling class.

We must not forget that all genres have a content which is located in the form, and which cannot easily be filled with a new content. The rhetoric of salvation, while it assumes the individual efforts of the Christian, promises inevitable happiness and the final fulfillment in a utopia hereafter. It both creates expectations, which will be difficult to fulfill in a liberated South Africa, and attitudes amongst the listeners of being the target of revelations by prophetic voices, rather than the thinking subject, capable of deciding his/her own future. That negates the very democratic grass-roots structure of the South African struggle against apartheid. Equally, while the *imbongi* has traditionally been used not only to praise the king, but to express

---

[45] Examples from *Black Mamba Rising*: "Go and represent us because you are our Moses –/Through your leadership we shall reach Canaan." (p. 14) "Hero deal with them and throw them into the Red Sea." (p. 14) (Qabula); "On our side are your/Brothers even at the new/Jerusalem/Let it be workers! They Say,/Heaven above also/Approves." (p. 29); "Together we would/Give respect to God and not/To dollars" (p. 39) (Hlatshwayo).

[46] Dingiswayo, [note 5], p. 2.

[47] *Ibid.*

[48] Ashcroft, Griffith and Tiffin, [note 1], p. 17.

criticism,[49] the tendency of affirmative rather than critical thought in this type of poetry should be problematic in organizations which see themselves as democratic, i.e. that strive for the fullest development of all its members to participate in the debate and the decision-making of the organization.[50] Even if the poet now attributes the symbols of authority to the people, their organizations and their leaders, the very act of attributing authority is problematic in the democratic field. While the praise of a leader like Mandela must be seen in the context of the need of a strong unifying national symbol, Keith Gottschalk's *Praise Poem to the African National Congress* creates visions of a popular Messiah in the very form of the litany:

> Born Prince, you became the people:
> Student, you taught your teachers;
> Lover, you chose your wife;
> Youth Wing, you organised the Elders;
> Volunteer-in-Chief, you defied apartheid;
> Charterist, you proclaim these Freedoms;
> Trialist, they call your patriotism treason;
> Prison reformer, you boycotted potatoes;
> Envoy, you traveled through Africa;
> Miner, you work underground;
> Lawyer, you defend the nation;
> Accused, you indict the law;
> Captive, you held a government captive![51]

---

[49] The praise-singer is "a social critic and a repository of traditional values." Qangule (1979), p. 86.

[50] Cf. Kelwyn Sole, "New Words Rising." *South African Labour Bulletin*, 12.2.1987 points out that praise poetry is usually thought to be related to traditional and ethnic power (e.g. Matanzima and Inkatha). He does, however, also point to the use of praise poetry since the *Mfecane* to criticize collaborators, as well as to the traditional *imbongi*, Hlongwe, who was active praising Champion and the ICU (Industrial and Commercial Workers' Union) in the 1930's. An example of a conservative (patriarchal and hierarchical) concept of the rule of law can be found in Mqhayi's *UDon Jadu* (1967, p. 82): "So then it is explained to the man / the law that is passed at the royal place / and he in turn instructs the family / all the members of the family to obey it, / the children to obey their mothers; / their mothers to obey the chiefs, / the chiefs to obey God." *Ityala lamawele* (1953, p. 63) adds: "Their mothers should obey the men, / The men should obey the chiefs" Quoted from Qangule (1979), p. 64f.

[51] Gottschalk, [note 14], p. 127.

In the context of negotiations which to a large extent occur at a distance from grass-roots political organisations (however much the leadership can claim the allegiance of the majority) this is not entirely unproblematic. The question of leadership, the possibility of a "personality cult," is dealt with by Ari Sitas in his poem *Motto*:

> Beware
> what you ascribe to leaders
> you take from the people.
>
> Take from the leaders
> give to the people
> for leaders are colourful flags.
>
> They wave and waver as the wind blows
> as people work the bellows
> and make the whirlwinds thunder.[52]

"Unions emerged," not because there were leaders, "agitators," but "on the back/of a galloping grievance" of the people themselves. It was the Mass Democratic Movement which after all forced the nationalist government to the conference table.

In his poem, "Organizing the people," Kelwyn Sole makes us aware of the difference between the rhetoric of grass-roots democracy and the politics by acclamation which so easily supplants it in reality:

> We have no need to vote;
> the answer's clear.
> Who was that coughing
> in the thirteenth row?
> Take her out.
>
> Our merchant and student delegates
> at their last night meeting
> triumphantly constituted
> the party of the working class.
> – Will someone tell the working class?
> Perhaps we *do* need to vote,
> after all.[53]

---

[52] Ari Sitas, *Tropical Scars*, Congress of South African Writers, 1989. Cf. my review of this volume in *Staffrider*, vol. 8, nos. 3 & 4, 1989, pp. 193–199.

[53] Kelwyn Sole, *The Blood of our Silence*, Johannesburg: Ravan, 1987, p. 77.

The posturing of those who appear on the stages all too easily supplants the will of the masses, who are left to merely acclaim the leaders they have to trust:

> The rest of you:
> Trust us.
> Roll call is easy.

Mere cynicism is not a politically productive stance. In any case there are other traditions in the struggle in South Africa which need to be nurtured and strengthened in the vitally important years ahead.

Each tradition is a constant struggle against forgetting and apathy. Teachers, lecturers and theatre managers know only too well, how difficult it is to inspire enthusiasm about past and present culture. Only where a people consider themselves to be embattled, does it become easier to project the culture of that people as an essential terrain of ideological struggle for hegemony: in such a case culture becomes relevant far beyond the very limited circle of "culture lovers." In the case of the present culture of the South African struggle the nature of the cultural struggle was highlighted for everybody by means of bannings, the ban on meetings, and judicial restrictions. Thus a Luxurama performance of September 1985 was dramatised for all participants by a magisterial order forbidding the artists to praise or criticise any form of government — an order which was promptly ignored — and the presence of the police force in Wynberg near the cinema before, during and after the performance. In a similar way a performance at Cine 400 in Rylands on the 16th of December 1985 was marked by a magisterial order forbidding any gatherings and the proposed candle light demonstration. During the performance the audience learned of a clash between the police and demonstrators in Belgravia Road and of the arrest of John Issel and his wife. Under conditions like that "culture" takes on a meaning and a relevance which it otherwise rarely has, except perhaps in the case of the cathartic experience of isolated individuals.

Music, songs, dance and poetry resonate and channel powerful collective emotions of fear, anger, hate, love and identification. I think it would be correct to say, that the learning that takes place in a situation like this is directed to creating an active collectivity which learns to handle its fears and aggressions, its anger and its identifications and projections. It is a reaffirmation of the threatened collectivity in the face of potential violence rather than the creation of new insights into the fabric of a society. Under a condition of an extremely repressive regime the organising of such performances of popular art and the reading of poetry within the context of such "Concerts against detention,"' "Concerts for the Unemployed," "Concerts for the sacked teachers of WECTU"[54] becomes a focal point for the creation and strengthening of solidarity, while remembering and transmitting the memory of those who suffer under this regime links up those who are assembled and those who have been cut off.

What is necessary now, however, is to create a climate in which neither a neo-colonial democracy of mere appearances nor its cultural adjunct, "mass" or "commercial" culture, can flourish, a culture, which despite its popular elements and wide acceptance amongst the labouring masses is built on ideological subjugation. A true democracy demands a working class culture, one which grows out of the modern forms of resistance (political party, trade union, cultural struggle) and which might draw on "folk," "élite," "missionary" and "mass" elements, but which is essentially different from all these. The beginnings of such a culture are evident in Trade Union locals and other democratic grass-roots organisations like Civics.

Like real democracy, popular art is participatory. Working class culture recognizes and rewards the particular skill of an artist or performer, it does not make him into a "star," and by lessening the barrier between "artist" and "non-artist" encourages all members of the audience to become performers, in the same way as it encourages all workers to participate in true political decision making.

---

[54] The acronym WECTU means Western Cape Teachers' Union.

THE WORKERS' THEATRE IN NATAL
[A talk to the COSATU regional structures in Natal, November 1992]

ARI SITAS

I

We start from a simple fact: that all we have are our bodies and what our brains redraft as stories. There are no resources, no sophisticated venues, no hype.

What brings us together is a desire to use whatever talent we have to create an event or a play, so that we communicate something we believe in, to our broader community.

II

Most of us are from the factories, the shops and mines — many too are unemployed — our bodies therefore bear the marks of our conditions of life. History has carved its powers on us — what we eat, how we sleep, what we drink, how we dance and how we work shape our physical abilities. These bodies are all we have. Better: these bodies are what they left for us.

Thin or heavy, stunted or overbulging, wrecked by industrial accidents or coughing from "brown lung", most of us don't look like the kind of stars one watches on TV or in the movie-houses.

Our voices too are not as neat: they sound like some enormous lathe has scraped our vocal chords, or some industrial lubricant was poured down our gullett.

Those clumps below our wrists are our hands — thickset and able to do two or three things we get paid for.

We need to use our bodies the way they are, the way they have been shaped, the way history has given them to us. Let us not be cowed by what the media put forward as correct, handsome, beautiful or real.

This is what they are and they can speak and move and haunt the world.

Despite all that most of us have been schooled from early childhood in movement: the use of our bodies in dancing in ceremonies, in parties, for recreation and also for honours and trophies; the use of our voices in choirs, in oral poems and singing groups, the use of our abilities in sport and in mimicking and teasing oppressors. We have powers and talents that are rich despite our predicaments. All these are the raw material for our performance.

Our popular theatre starts from the way we move and can move and the way our musicality and rhythm has shaped us.

III

We also start from the fact that we also have all that our brain can help us remake as stories.

We usually make plays that are rooted in our experiences as people in a racist and exploitative system. We use stories that are born out of our daily toils or out of what we heard has happened to others. We believe that our lives are more than calculations in an employer's account book, or statistics in someone's census.

In this way, the Dunlop play started from the stories about the struggles for union recognition and it grew into a broader project through the memories of older workers about life and work in the 1950s and 1960s. In this way too, in our estimate thirty five plays were created in this region within COSATU's structures in the last six years.

When we discuss experience, we do not only mean the step by step account of one's life and its meanings! We also mean our dreams and daydreams! People think that we are everyday of our lives working in front of machines doing repetitive work that kills our minds, our lives. Most of us don't! Most of us let our hands do the one-two-three screw the screw, then breathe, one-two-three screw the screw then breathe . . . whilst our minds wander off into our private theatres where we are (unlike in our lives) the powerful ones, the loved ones, the heroes, the oversexed ones, the free.

Of course, these daydreams at work are also dangerous and can cost a finger or two because of the lack in concentration. What I mean is that daydreams too are part of our experience we can use in plays alongside our nightmares and worries.

In a similar vein there is a rich trove of traditions that reach back to the heyday of the Zulu kingdom and before, traditions too that involve the many interpretations of the Bible, as an oral text in the rural areas as a reader in the urban, and in all these there are stories and parables, symbols and poems, tragedies and comedies.

In our workshops we have used all of the above time and time again. For example, the domestic workers' play that was performed by COSATU culture course students for Women's Day in 1990 started from workshops around the traditional stories of "*uhlakhanyana*" – the trickster of Zulu folk tales. Then the workshops moved towards trying to keep the spirit of the trickster, the resolute survivor in the modern context with women workers taking the foreground. In the end a story around the abilities of a rural woman to manipulate crises in her struggle to survive.

In short, in making plays about the way our lives are marked, we use every resource and tradition available for our cultural formations. And as Astrid Von Kotze pointed out in the book *Organise and Act — The Worker's Theatre Movement in Natal*, we keep on making them for a purpose: not to make money, not to impress the powers-that-be, not to receive a licence of competence from anyone, but to assist in the effort to drag ourselves out of the murk of exploitation and ugliness into a better future.

IV

The way we have been making plays and the way we will continue making plays is one that demands our full participation. We argue that everyone of us has some talent, some spark to make our imagination light a fire.

Our workshops to make a play are very much like our traditional song patterns, like *isicathamyia* or better like jazz: the project leader introduces a theme and everyone in smaller groups improvises around the theme, responds to the theme from one's experience and sometimes, changes the theme altogether.

Of course many have written plays and get groups together to perform them; others have very strong ideas about plays and need others to help them realise them, but in most cases these plays develop in workshops.

Most themes for a play come from red hot issues in the daily struggle of working people and the unemployed: the Dunlop play was born out of the struggles for union recognition, the Sarmcol plays out of the need to popularise the dismissal of a thousand workers in Howick for the broader community, the Spar play out of a strike situation, *Qonda* out of the need to express how violence was affecting workers in Umlazi and so on.

V

We also understand that there are great obstacles to our work — very few people have the time and energy to involve themselves in making plays and other cultural activities for great lengths of time. Shiftwork, transport problems, fear, household responsibilities and so on make our work very difficult.

Also the following statistics tell a lot — we selected the same number of cultural activists in the labour movement in Natal for every two years from 1986 onwards. In this way we gathered facts on 120 of them (about 20% of all the names in our records).

The aggregate results are as follows

1. Deaths   6.6%
2. Homelessness due to persecution/incl. burning down of home   18.3%
3. Assaults, Skirmishes and violent combat/incl. hospitalisation
   (but not death)   50.0%
4. Unable to practice, rehearse or organise events in their
   community due to victimisation or violence   39.2%
5. Still active in cultural work   38.7%
6. Job Loss/Retrenchment   23.5%
7. Able to Improve Life-chances and jobs BECAUSE of creative
   involvement   17.5%
8. Still in their old jobs   40.8%

If we break down the statistics according to group-years, the results are even more horrifying:

	1986	1988	1990	1992
1. Deaths	15%	15	0	0
2. Homelessness	35%	25	25	15
3. Assaults etc	45%	65	80	85
4. Unable to etc	30%	40	70	80

(figures rounded off for exposition)

Although the direct killing of activists has declined and the need to flee one's home registers a decrease, the occurence of violence and conflict increases dramatically. This reflects the changing patterns of conflict in Natal's townships. Whereas in the early days activists would be targeted and be killed or flee for their lives, now such targeting has met with organised resistance to the effect that 85% of all participants have personally been involved in clashes.

Whereas in the old days a group of vigilantes could march into the Mpophomeni township, kidnap key activists, like the Sarmcol play's Simon Ngubane and execute them, last year one of Mandini's main creative dynamos, Marrasta Shabalala was hospitalised after a fierce gunbattle when attackers tried to invade at night and "clear-up" an "ANC/COSATU" house.

It is no surprise then that the "themes" chosen by groupings of creative workers in Natal correspond with many of the "uglinesses" outlined above: extortion, violence, exploitation, unemployment, destruction of family life, in short what this world had made of our lives and how we kick back.

VI

Despite the difficulties in making plays and the little time people have in their working weeks to surrender themselves over to such making, the workshops and improvisations in each project take a long time to complete. Participatory methods of constructing a performance/story demand a lot of discussion and many hours of shifting and changing. Usually it is the urgency of a deadline that completes the work, and such deadlines arrive from trade union and community offices with no thought about the niceties of "letting the work grow, organically".

Still, within whatever limits we try and use workshops to create a culture of play-making that demands everyone's contribution. Each participant has to become a performer, thinker, planner and story-teller. Like in the Sarmcol Workers Cooperative (SAWCO) Cultural group we need ensembles/groups of people who are not just performers, but who are critical and reflective grassroots teachers.

We do not need the vulnerable fodder our institutions produce, those deficient lackeys and clones, those unformed psyches and playthings that are made available to the grand egos of (shrink, ouch) theatre directors. We need tight-knit groups who could teach and think and dance.

Perhaps the Sarmcol Workers Cooperative's (SAWCO's) plays

are a case in point. *Bambatha's Children* and its predecessor *The Long March* need no advertising: they have been hailed and praised throughout the country. Through their stubborn efforts and mishaps, their wavering organisational ability and often their successful interventions, they have managed to perform their play in all the nooks and crannies of black community life. For tens of thousands of people *Bambatha's Children* is an example of committed and powerful theatre. Rooted as it is in the rituals of resistance of Natal, it is seen by ordinary people as part of the unending saga of struggle since the poll-tax insurrection of 1906. So is their latest contribution: *Mbube* — a play about the hostel violence and a challenge to perceptions of "Zulu-ness".

Their achievement and popularity at grassroots level is beginning to resemble a political version of a Gibson Kente and a Mbongeni Ngema. Their work has also touched every creative person who has worked with them. They have also struck a chord of admiration in a broader critical community: very few would disagree with Nadine Gordimer singling out their plays as exemplars of a drama that most closely succeeds in being a "people's literature". The power of SAWCO's improvisatory movements, song-cycles and narratives is arresting and songs like, *Ngikhumbula abazali* or *Bazali bami sengikathele* are great recreations of rural roots and influences.

What is and was admirable was that a humble group of children from labour tenant families from the Midlands, people evicted from the farms, swatted down in factories, chased out of work, sometimes on the brink of starvation could turn their lives, and their ancestral traditions into a local and a universal experience. They were communicating to a new generation of creators from Port Shepstone in the South to Mandini in the North. They did that masterfully. That they did that all the way to Glasgow and Warsaw is admirable too.

What should haunt people further are the furies that animate a group like the Sarmcol one — what *does* sustain a band of travelling players to move from the starvation days of 1985 to now, after 5 years of "success" to be earning R37 a week. Both in 1985 and 1988 the workshop participants had to be fed before every session otherwise their state of malnourished inertia could not be broken. Nevertheless, the ever-presence of unemployment and hunger did not stop some peculiar utopia or dream animating them to keep on keeping on. What for? Of course, the applause and recognition must have played a strong role; their attachment to a community and a struggle must answer for the rest. Whatever the answer we put forward, all this marks a little victory for art. 5 years are a long time and their destination cannot be some laughable outreach community service proposed by a parastatal's performance council. Even if the group collapses out of sheer exhaustion and poverty, their influence will linger for many years to come.

VII

Fashions come and go: a few years ago the workers' theatre movement was given a lot of prominence in the dominant media; the timing was perfect for exposure in the midst of defiance, revolution and violence! Cultural élites incorporated it as part of the canon at a time when they felt vulnerable and in need to identify "downwards". Now, the tide has changed: it is not fashionable anymore, these plays are "passé" and belong to another era — they were boring and tedious after all.

Look at the following table, it traces the media exposure of worker plays: in 1986, the highpoint of "publicity" there were a hundred and twenty features on workers' theatre, seventy of which, were in the "establishment" press. If we take 1986 as the highpoint, this is what happens

MEDIA EXPOSURE OF WORKER PLAYS

1986	120
1988	48
1990	29
1992	5

Similarly, 50% of all those involved in 1986 managed to move out of their factory jobs and find more demanding forms of employment *due* to their creative work. By 1990 this drops to 10% and thereafter to 0%.

Finally, these changing fashions do not correspond with a diminished cultural activity pattern in Natal: whereas of the 1986 group only 40% remain active, the 1990 group features a 70% participation rate.

These people, men and women workers, larger than any statistic are contributing in their small way to the survival of a vibrant grassroots culture with strong roots in Africa's performance traditions; at their best they will innovate. At their worst they will try and communicate something important to themselves and their organisations.

VIII

I started by stating that all we have are our bodies and what our brains help us recreate as stories. Through them, something special has happened in Natal despite the violence.

"AN INTEREST IN THE MAKING OF THINGS."[1]
AN INTERVIEW WITH WILLIAM KENTRIDGE.

Q. People know you both as an artist, as a film director and a maker of plays. I know that you were trained as an artist and after that you went to Paris to study mime and drama with Jacques Lecoq. What made you do that, why did you choose suddenly to change directions?

W.K. It wasn't really a change of direction; my working in all these different areas has as much to do with indecision as with anything else. When I was studying politics as a student at Wits, I was at the same time going to painting classes at the Johannesburg Art Foundation and working with Malcolm Purkey with Junction Avenue Theatre Company, initially in productions like *Ubu Rex*, and then in *The Fantastical History of a Useless Man*. I decided I would have a period of study. This fruit salad of different activities seemed untenable. It was the choice between going to an art school, a film school or to a theatre school. And in the end I chose the theatre school, partly to test whether I was going to be an actor (which the school very quickly succeeded in clarifying). For some years I resolved to stick to only one or other of these activities. But in the end I always lapsed. I think that at a different level it has to do with an interest in the making of things. For a while there was quite a gap between the sort of theatre work I was doing and the drawings I was doing, but now there is less and less a gap. The current production of *Woyzeck on the Highveld* is a mixture of drawings and film-making and theatre. At times I thought about it simply as a director, another time I thought it's just a drawing that has gone into other directions as well. Over the years there have been specific ways of working which have to do with painting or film-making or with theatre and there is a greater transference of strategies of working from one form into another.

---

[1] This interview with William Kentridge was given to Geoff Davis and Anne Fuchs at his home in Johannesburg on 15th September 1992.

Being able to play with space

After I had come back from Paris at theatre school and had decided I wasn't going to be an actor and I wasn't going to work as a painter and I had to restrict myself to one craft, I thought I would be a film-maker. So I spent several years as an art-director of other people's films, learning the craft. And only after, I think, three years in the film industry did I go back to the studio and start drawing again. But one of the things that I learnt for example, or that became very clear when I was working as an art director on a series of really terrible low-budget films that were made here, was the way in which the space in which people moved, in this case we were talking about film-space, was so completely arbitrary and changeable. The fact that one's normal, renaissance sense of perspectives, how rooms are created, was completely interchangeable once you just used moveable flats for walls that you could shift and change. My general upbringing of a central light-source, also from renaissance perspective, traditional art-making, becomes changed when you are lighting a completely artificial space with whichever light sources you want. And that sense of being able to play with light and space which was really part of the craft of inept film making at the time, translated itself very directly into a way of being able to deal with space, particularly interior space, when I went back to making drawings. So the drawings that emerged from the film work very much had to do with the freedom that came from being able to play with space. Before that I had always been terrified of the space that my figures had to inhabit. They either lived in a very rigidly renaissance perspective grid or simply in a field in which space had been omitted, by simply having a straight horizon line and the figures juxtaposed on that. That was one direct way in which film-making influenced the drawings.

An idea of engagement with the world as starting-point

Q. What you've been saying is that you have been creating meanings from a synthesis of art forms. Could you tell us something about the meaning that you are creating?

W.K. I think that the meaning is always ambiguous, it's both necessary, but secondary. For some artists, working on a canvas, the mark is primary, well, there's enough pleasure in the physical sensation of a mark being put down on a canvas for that to be an end in itself, and in that trajectory goes a huge strain of art-making in the century. For me that pleasure,.that central pleasure, whether it's a film or a piece of theatre or a drawing, is absolutely essential, but it's not the primary motive behind it. For me to work, it's necessary for there to be an idea of meaning or an idea of engagement with the world as a starting-point. Now I mean this in a very specific way. For example, if I have a blank sheet of paper, it is impossible (in the sense that I would feel lost or would be uncertain of what I was doing) for me to simply put a lush charcoal mark or smudge across the sheet of paper. It needs a point of engagement; I would say, for example, "right I'm going to work with a figure and I'll be drawing a shoulder," so that means I have a shoulder in my head that is being drawn for me to have a sense of purpose in making that mark on the drawing. It is not vitally important for me then that it's an accurate shoulder or that it's a specific shoulder but the fact that there's a connection between making that mark and something in the world gives it a sense of reason, and removes the completely haphazard nature of making the mark. Once that mark is done, there's an enjoyment of that on the paper. There has to be a point of engagement with the world. So that which relates to things outside of the history of art is what it is that makes me interested. It had to do with domestic situations, it had to do with power relations in South Africa, it had to do with class relations at different points. But in a sense those are points of entry into starting the work.

A formal and technical problem

Once that's begun, the interest is always in what at one level is a technical or formal question. How does one continue from that point of entry? How does one get the particular piece of work to make sense? In a film like *Johannesburg — Second Greatest City after Paris*, I had started with two characters: Soho Eckstein, who was a businessman who in many ways refers to my paternal and maternal grandfathers if I think of it now, so there's a personal point of contact, and Felix Teitlebaum, who is represented as the naked, alter ego figure. Both of which were dream images that came up, but the important point was that there were points of entry into the film. Once they were there I was confronted with a formal, technical problem, how do I link these two characters together and what is the story going to be? And then elements came in from a number of sources, one was a simple narrative connection. I would give them a woman in common, the wife of one and the lover of the other as a way of connecting those two figures.

That was one point of connecting. The second would be a technical one. What, within that medium, within that particular form of animation, works? And one of the things that works in that particular medium is the creation of large crowds that can grow from the charcoal marks. So these two elements which in a sense are at the heart of the meaning of the film, start off without their presence there being given by a programme of meaning at the start of the project but by things which have arisen in the process of making it — a formal solution to a problem of how to link two characters and something that is suggested by the actual technique itself. So that's a sort of an impure origin of elements of meaning. However, having stated that that's the origin, once they are there, they have obviously got to coalesce and make sense. The hope has to be that my unconscious, the sorts of pushes and pulls that are pushing me through the world to where I am now — upbringing, reading, all of one's constructed history — in the end work too, if I am loosened, free and responsive to the hints within the work itself, in the end create something which does have a meaning, which isn't simply incoherent or a series of chance associations.

I didn't start off saying, well, I want to do a film about two men and their rather distant relationship to each other which is mediated by the view of a starving crowd in front of them. It started as much less precise and impure. And in the end of course it has to make a meaning or people don't respond, but it's a risk that that sort of work takes: that the work has a fairly private or idiosyncratic origin of reference. But presumably the background I'm coming from, or the range of references that I'm drawing on, are not so unusual that other people can't link into them and that they become fairly easily readable.

To give another example. In the production of *Woyzeck on the Highveld* there is a sequence in which Woyzeck has to lay a table. The corresponding scene in the original is that of Woyzeck shaving the Captain, which for the puppets is too clumsy and messy. And when I did the sequence, it started with an animation of objects moving round a table, getting more and more out of control; a metaphor for Woyzeck's inability to cope with the world. At that stage it wasn't completely clear whose table it was going to be. It was really a sense of playing with animation that could work on a screen and that would have a relation with something happening on the acting surface below the screen. At that stage I think there was the idea that the Captain eating at his table was going to take up a large part of the play which was going to be constructed around the Captain's dining room table. But it was very much a game that was being played, by myself, of what objects could be brought on, how could they move. It didn't have a root directly in the play, it didn't have a root when I was doing it in my head directly in any particular personal history.

One's unconscious is a step ahead

Now that the sequence is finished and Woyzeck performs it, I realize very strongly that it has a direct reference back to an old manservant who used to serve, at my parents' table, when I was a child, to his panic and inability to deal with the niceties of bourgeois etiquette around a table. But that in a sense is something that I have recognized once it's finished in *Woyzeck* and it's one of the reasons why that scene works powerfully.

In the same way, it was only a while after I had completed some of the Soho Eckstein films that somebody reminded me that in fact I had drawn that same character many years ago in one of the first series of prints I did. This was a series of linocuts of my grandfather in his three-piece pin-stripe suit sitting on Muizenberg beach from an old family photograph. Those linkages backwards, or those meanings being found when the work is done are very important — I'm always interested in the area in which meaning comes, it's not something that's just storyboarded and scripted in advance, it's between programme and it's also not obviously complete chance. It's not putting a pin down in the middle of a dictionary and using that as the reference material. It's somehow that one's unconsciousness is a step ahead, or makes connections which are there. For me an actual metaphor for that way of understanding the construction of meaning in work would be conversation; where, on the one hand, you could rehearse a sentence before you utter it and you simply perform something you've thought out in your head — which would be like planning a drawing or a piece of work entirely in advance and performing it. But generally one has a vague sense of what one is going to say but one relies on one's brain and tongue to put coherent grammatical sentences together which you can't anticipate entirely at the beginning but which make sense at the end.

But more than that, very often in the activity of that conversation, in that physical activity of talking, new thoughts develop. Things that you didn't know at the beginning make sense at the end. And that way of working seems to me very important in the way of constructing the meaning, both in the drawings and in the animated films and to a certain extent in the theatre. In theatre work it's harder if you start with somebody else's script. In film work it's impossible if you are working with a large film crew. You have, in terms of time and cost, to have planned everything in advance. But with the animated films where it's simply me and a piece of charcoal and a sheet of paper and a camera in a studio alone, it's very easy to start a sequence without knowing necessarily how it links together and how it will end. I think that's my general relationship to meaning.

Workshop theatre: a successful strategy of overcoming one of the factors of apartheid

Q. You have a very personal vision of the world which comes over in all your work. Could you explain perhaps what you were doing with Junction Avenue? When you were doing workshop theatre with other people, how did you fit in? Do you prefer working on your own now, directing *Woyzeck* perhaps and being the master of everything?

W.K. Well, I think the vital part of workshop theatre in South Africa in the '70s and '80s, was that it was a practical and workable and successful strategy for overcoming one of the factors of apartheid, which was to make different people completely ignorant of the details of the lives of large sections of other groups in the country. So that I, growing up in the northern suburbs, knew a little of the life in the backyard, less and less about what happened in Soweto, almost nothing about what happened in rural Africa, in the rural parts of South Africa. The workshops and those play situations in which those different parts of the world were able to come together were a basic information-sharing strategy. It was an essential and very successful way of overcoming a problem and where it worked at its best (for me in productions like *Randlords and Rotgut*) you had different pieces of the world coming together, each one close to its own particular touchstones. It would have been inauthentic if I had tried to put myself in other positions to write the dialogue. I think that great writers, that's obviously what they do, they are able imaginatively to put themselves in the position they've never been in and the better the writer, the more authentic, the happier we are to go with the journey that they are proposing. For me that was an essential and a very valuable part of workshop theatre and when it still works, it is an excellent way of work happening.

What it did lead to, what it does lead to, is some softening of the edges particularly if one is dealing with sensitive material. And when you have strong people with strong feelings around in different productions, often there is objection to lives which they can't identify with personally. But as the material gets closer and closer to me, I get more and more interested in it, like in Junction Avenue's production *Tooth and Nail*. I find it more and more difficult to accept the compromises that come from accommodating all participants' views. In the *Woyzeck* production there has certainly been input as I would imagine there is in most productions from the actors, and in terms of the design and making of the puppets. Of course there was not just an input — it was a real collaboration. But overall it was very important that I felt it was my vision, my story, to be able to push into shape, the way it would as if I were simply working on a drawing.

Transposing Woyzeck

Q. What for you has been the particular fascination of the work of Büchner as a revolutionary author in 19th century Germany and his play *Woyzeck* and how have you tried to transpose that to South Africa? Where did you see the possibilities?

W.K. I think again we had started work on *Woyzeck* and the play was nearly finished before I actually remembered that when I was at High School I had done a series of poster and set designs for a hypothetical production of *Woyzeck*, as a High School art project. I think I had heard a recording of the opera which had fascinated me and I'm sure the photograph of Walter Berry in his beret as Woyzeck on the record cover was a key. When we decided that we were going to work together on a production, Basil Jones, Adrian Kohler from Handspring Puppets, and myself, *Woyzeck* wasn't by any means a starting point. We were going to work on something together and initially it was assumed we would write a new piece. But I'm not a writer, and I just got more and more traumatised and terrorised by the idea of having to write a play. In the first notebooks — it was eighteen months ago — and before the word Woyzeck had come up, the characters that were present already were: someone with the megaphone (because that has been an image present from a series of drawings which has its origin in a photograph of Lenin speaking into a megaphone I had seen in John Willet's *The New Sobriety*. Also one often sees that horn in Max Beckmann paintings). So that character comes from somewhere between that photograph from the 1920's and a Beckmann painting. That was one character that existed. The character of Woyzeck is similar to the character that I used in a version of Hogarth's engravings called *Indus-try and Idleness*. First of all he becomes Lord Mayor of Derby Road, the street in Bertrams adjacent to the house I live in. And I had also used this particular man as an actor in a short film called *T. & I.*, Tristan and Isolde, making a version of the opera in which he wears a herring-bone coat walking across the landscape. So this character who had also been in various drawings was definitely going to be in the play. Initially he was going to be carrying a huge load on his back, a bit like a Goya drawing of someone, an Atlas character carrying a pack on his back. So *he* was present, then there was going to be the usual businessman, Soho Eckstein, as he has been in the animated films, who was going to be in the script. These were all characters that I was interested in turning into three-dimensions as puppets and taking them out of the drawings.

Another starting-point of the project was a sense of the land-scape, of the terrain which is really south of Johannesburg, an area and landscape which is defined by industrial detritus, by failed civil engi-neering projects. And at various stages we looked at some Mayakovsky plays, at the *Mystery-Bouffe*, looking to see whether we could rewrite the *Mystery-Bouffe* for puppets. *Woyzeck* came up as an idea and when it came up, we thought O.K. that sounds great as a starting-point, but it was really only going to be a starting-point. At one point we had extra characters, we had the Captain's wife, we had the police Captain, we had the Soho Eckstein character seducing Woyzeck's wife at some stage and it became a completely different story. We had a puppet that was going to eat everything on the table, a puppet that would expand to the width of the stage. Also we had someone with a huge mega-phone that was such a size we could operate glove puppets inside the bowl of that megaphone as a sort of stage within a stage. So there are still things to be done.

But once it came down to the nuts and bolts of saying: How is the story going to be done? What is it going to be about? It became clear that there was more than enough on our plate, tailoring it all down. And at that point, with very minor changes the play transposed not just effortlessly onto a South African context and absorbed the set of characters that were there in advance of that particular production. The new ones, obviously, are the doctor who hadn't been in my scheme, Maria, and the accordion player Andries. Although the accordion player, who hadn't been in the list of characters in my head, had been there present as a character in film scripts that I had written and in a series of drawings. The newspaper woman, the sort of deathlike figure was again something which came from drawings and once we had that puppet she had to be given something to do, so she was given some of Margaret's lines, so it was fairly easy, it wasn't as if the play had to be wrestled into finding the characters that one could transpose it into, those were prior to it.

Working with puppets

Q. What to you is the importance of using puppets?

W.K. Well, in this production of *Woyzeck*, we'd started with the idea that we were going to use animation and puppets and that small scale of theatre rather than saying we want to do *Woyzeck*, what's the strongest way to do *Woyzeck*? But the idea of the puppets was that, if one was working with a rough technique of these drawn landscapes and drawn environments (we could have chosen for example just simply to film the terrain south of Johannesburg and use that for our backdrops), we needed the characters to match this roughness, so that there wasn't a huge distinction between what you saw on the screen behind and the puppets in front. And that was obviously, both in terms of scale and in terms of breaking away from naturalism, far easier to do with puppets than with fancy cosmetics or actors. There's also a sense in which when the manipulators are visible and next to the puppets which they are in a large number of significant scenes in the puppetry play, they are not simply obstructions getting in the way of seeing the play) they act as aides to the action and chaperones to the story being told which, in terms of what happens to the character of Woyzeck, creates a different meaning too than we would have achieved from simply using an actor.

Q. It's rather like an alienation effect though, in that it breaks the illusion of the puppets when you see the actual mechanics of the manipulation.

W.K. I don't think I agree with that. No, even when you don't see the manipulators, one is very much aware that these are not live people and that these are puppets you are watching. When you actually see the manipulators with them, in a way you are usually able to accommodate their awkwardnesses and the things they can't do; I'm constantly fascinated by the circle one goes: one's looking from the performer's face saying the lines next to the puppet through to the puppet and back to yourself. And although one's very aware, and sees quite clearly the artifice and how it's all done, how the manipulation is done and where the voices are coming from, nonetheless essentially one's attention is on that puppet as the agent of the play.

Q. Seeing a South African version of *Woyzeck* as a European it's very interesting to see the sources of personal inspiration you have been talking about and the local South African inspiration, and two of the items which have interested me is, one, the music and the second is the figure of Harry who comes to the door every day. I wonder if you could say something about these two local figures.

Harry, the South African Woyzeck

W.K. First of all, Harry, the man on whom the character is based is Derek Buys. He lives in the neighbourhood where I live in Bertrams which is a fairly rough, inner-city area of Johannesburg. At one stage in his life he was a Maths teacher, but now he is essentially, I suppose, a down and out hobo, very much known in the area, very much based in the area, and I have used him as a model for a number of drawings and pictures. Woyzeck came from the drawings and not directly from the man, but he's certainly present through the drawings round through the production. That was one sort of local talisman making sure that, yes, this is the way such a character could be in the world. I mean Woyzeck in Büchner's play is very much more part of a clearly stratified society. Woyzeck is employed as a private in the army. In South Africa if one is actually talking about the bottom of the social pile, if somebody has a regular job and a regular income, he is relatively speaking part of a privileged group. And the huge bulk of the population, increasingly so, are people at the edge or below that, who've got jobs for a short amount of time and who don't have a regular place to live or live in squatter settlements. They are the informal part of the economy rather than people who can rely on health benefits or anything that even Woyzeck could have had as a private in the army in Germany in the 1830s. So that I think that change of social position in our production is an accurate one. To have had Woyzeck as a soldier in the South African army would have introduced a far greater number of distortions and abnormalities into the relationships of the story than it does this way.

The music of the play

In the *Woyzeck*, we started off with a sketchbook or a cassette of hundreds of different types of music from Algerian music to Siberian choral singing to Zulu jazz from South Africa to massed choirs and eventually what it boiled down to was that almost none of the stuff on the sketchbook tape worked except for some unaccompanied cello music which seemed to have the roughness and the edge to be accommodatable to the roughness and the edge of the puppets. And the other music came from a fragment of a film which I had seen about eight years ago called *The Two Rivers*, a documentary on Venda and Johannesburg, which had in it a very memorable fragment of an accordion singer somewhere in Johannesburg playing his accordion and singing. I think a connection in my head then was that in that documentary the accordion singer had a beret pulled down very low on his head and a completely desperate look in his eyes and that had a very direct link back to the image the Woyzeck of the cover of the record from my childhood. But I think it had also something to do with the particular quality (but I don't know whether desperation is the right word) but a very moving, strange quality of the singing.

So although the music is a hundred times removed from Alban Berg's music, it seemed immediately to have the right passion in it. What followed was simply a process of trying to find that music: taking a cassette of the actual sound-track of that fragment of the film, finding someone to take a small cassette-player with that cassette into Soweto, Katlehong, Alexandra, to play his cassette, to see whether anybody could either play music like that or knew of someone who could. After a week or so, we had two accordion players, who claimed to be able to play that exact piece of music which they could not quite (but they did play a very nice Jim Reeves song that became one of the pieces in the play). One of them claimed, however, to have taught the particular person on the cassette and recognised him on the tape. This, the Jim Reeves musician, then set off into Alexandra township and emerged triumphantly two days later saying he'd found the accordion player. And on the next Saturday morning I was taken to a particular corner in Park Station where indeed he was playing. This was eight years on and he was somewhat unrecognisable because he no longer played an accordion; he has a little Honda petrol generator which powers an electric drum kit and electric keyboard and he now plays this very electronic, different music to what he was playing then, but still surrounded by huge crowds, doing astonishingly well as a street-musician. He then came into the studio and armed just with his accordion sang the songs which are the basis of the play and which again for me are a very good touchstone. I think they are all versions of Methodist hymns but with a retuning of certain key chords in the accordion, so it does not sound like an accordion played in other parts of the world, and with a quality of voice that we would not have got otherwise. At one level I suppose the key elements of the play are the way Woyzeck's persona and the music are very much rooted in the streets of Johannesburg.

The question of audience is paradoxical

Q. Now could you say something about how theatre might develop as an art form in a new South Africa and linked with this, what about theatre audiences, what kind of audience are you writing for? Or would you like to write for?

W.K. I suppose the question of audience is paradoxical. I would like to keep going on these journeys which are idiosyncratic, started without a sense of particular audience, but I suppose in my head if I assume that these are the things that interest me or the connections that I would find interesting, it would presumably be people with a similar range of references and an ability to make the connections between different points, the hope is that the theatres would be full and packed with everyone. Of course one of the idiosyncrasies or one of the ironies which is to be remarked, is that very often people get anxious about other people saying, "well it's fine, I managed to understand what you were doing, but I'm sure that an audience that doesn't know Büchner or that hasn't seen a lot of video projections won't be able to understand." And in fact one finds that an ability to read works of art that are unconventional extends over a very broad range. The fact that the theatre we're doing isn't proscenium arch, curtains opening onto a box set makes it strange only to people who are used to proscenium arch, curtains opening onto a box set of a living room. To people who have neither seen that sort of theatre or any other, it will be in no way stranger, so I think the question of how one finds an audience has to do with a great deal of things which are over and above the particular nature of the play. It has to do with intangibles or how word gets out about different pieces of work in different communities, in different areas.

If we don't get an audience for *Woyzeck* here in Johannesburg the main thing it will do, is make it very difficult to do more work like this. Productions which do brilliantly well on Broadway or in the West End of London, like *Death and the Maiden*, stagger along here. Productions do wonderfully in one theatre and then get transferred to another theatre like the Paul Slabolepszy, which was filled in Rosebank and is still striving to find its audience at the Market . So those things are real intangibles. To try to, as it were, design one's audience in advance of the play, the way people do if they are making a film, when you start with your distribution and end with your scripting, either you've got to be very sophisticated and skilled at doing that or you've got to do what you want to do and hope you can find an audience. I think there seems to be a general, world-wide phenomenon of theatre audiences getting smaller, and I think that South Africa doesn't appear to be an exception, but on the other hand, theatres don't need the sort of audiences that films do for plays to happen.

Productions like Sarafina *are an exception*

Q. Would you consider working with people like the directors of *Sarafina* for instance, Black Consciousness theatre directors such as Matsemela Manaka or Maishe Maponya? Do you think that you could work with people like that? Just as when you were talking just now about Junction Avenue you were talking about different experiences coming together. Might you then get — it's very difficult to talk about a popular audience as we don't know what a "popular" audience means — but I suppose a black audience?

W.K. Yes, I think I would have difficulty working with a second director on a theatre project. I'm not quite sure what it would mean; now I certainly don't have a problem working with Maishe Maponya or Matsemela Manaka as black theatre directors. I'm certainly not a proponent of white consciousness, but I presume it would depend on the project and the particulars of what we would be doing together. But I'm not sure that that is enough to find a popular audience. I mean I'm not sure that Matsemela Manaka finds a mass audience, or that Maishe Maponya finds a mass audience. They are not doing Gibson Kentes. They have some impact and a large exposure in foreign festivals overseas, here they struggle, I think, in the same way that any white directors do. Productions like *Sarafina* that can run for months and months and months to full houses in large theatres are an exception and I don't know what someone like Gibson Kente is doing now, but it seems that the productions which he had which ran for years and years and years to full houses travelling around the country as far as I know are not happening in the same way.

Q. On the whole then you would think that theatre in South Africa would go the same way as theatre world-wide? That is, it is an elitist art form.

W.K. I'm not sure that there is necessarily an immediate correlation between a marginal art form and an elitist art form. I don't think it has to be restricted only to the very wealthy, say, who could come and see it. I think that what you have got is a small group of people, who are interested in theatre who become a fairly sealed audience. I don't think you are going to get your whole City-state to come and watch your performance. You get that with certain pop concerts and here even not with many pop concerts.

Workers' theatre as marginal theatre

I've done some stints with workers' theatre. We once did a play called *Dikitsheneng* (In the Kitchens) which was a farce of non-recognition about a domestic servant in a house whose place is taken by her boyfriend when she goes on leave, but no-one notices the difference. And we performed this at church-halls and at school theatres around Johannesburg and did one performance for a large annual gathering of the domestic workers employment programme DWEP, 3000 domestic workers all together in a huge hall. This was our bringing theatre to the masses. My job was to stand at the back of the theatre with a red track suit and wave it whenever I couldn't hear the actors so that they knew the people at the back couldn't hear. It turned out that one of the actors simply didn't look my way at all and the other, Arthur Molepo, had this look of growing and greater desperation as he bellowed louder and louder, and the production disappeared into the hall. It could not be seen, could not be heard, it was a minor, strange aberration going on at the far end. And working with Ari Sitas in Natal, I acted with Ramolao Makhene in a play called *Gallows for Mr Scariot Mpimpi*. I played the part of Mr Fatman in my brother-in-law's pin-striped suit and again it worked just fine when we were performing to 50 shop stewards in a small contained space. Then we tried to perform on the back of a lorry at Curries Fountain at the Annual FOSATU General Meeting. Halfway through the production someone with a trumpet in the crowd started playing and everyone followed him like the Pied Piper round and round the stadium. The actors were left stranded, performing their lines to the wind. The theatre which was done there, worked but in a marginal, particular way not in the way that cinema does, not in the way that television does, not in the way that a full-scale pop concert does.

I'm interested in large-scale extravaganzas where one's video screen is gigantic and one's speakers are enormous and can be seen and heard. I think that that has got as much to do with megalomania as wanting to find a popular audience. I think that to say that something is marginal is not to say that it doesn't either have meaning or isn't important in its effects. And that I can only say from a personal point of view; I have to think of what are the different things or how is it that I construct myself. A lot of it has to do with particular books that one reads, remarkable experiences in theatre or films, particular pieces of music as well as broader social factors. Perhaps this is an exception, and there are a very limited number of people who are that fashioned by cultural artifacts that they come across. I don't think so.

TOOTH AND NAIL. RETHINKING FORM FOR THE SOUTH AFRICAN THEATRE

Malcolm Purkey

As South Africa celebrates the real possibility of the death of apartheid, the South African theatre movement faces a crisis. It is in danger of losing its central dynamo. All of the most powerful South African theatre of the last forty years, from the early work of Athol Fugard through the work of the Space Theatre and the work of Workshop '71, to the spate of international hits that have recently emerged out of the Market theatre, have one thing in common: all were generated out of a profound and critical reaction to apartheid and its manifestations.

Post 2nd February, 1990, and the onset of hard-nosed negotiations, South Africa presents engaged theatre makers with the most complex of challenges. How do we move beyond the reactive apartheid critique? How do we transcend the stock response and the slogan, and begin formulating a comprehensive cultural response to the times? South African society is in a state of the most rapid and complex transition. As apartheid cracks up, and the possibility of a new order, based (we hope) on the will of the majority, emerges, oppositional theatre makers face profound questions.

* As apartheid gives way to a new form of government, can theatre makers protect and increase their hard-won relative autonomy, allowing theatre to maintain its responsive and critical role which has been so central to its particular quality, or will theatre be expected to be subservient to the new order of things?

* Can oppositional theatre maintain its vibrancy and strength, even as its traditional subject, apartheid, finally shows signs of crumbling?

* Is such a thing as objective partisanship possible? That is, can theatre be involved in the struggle for transformation, reconciliation and national unity, and strike a necessary critical distance at the same time?

* Is the so-called, and to my mind narrowly named "Protest Play" finally exhausting its meaning and potency?

* Can we move from a "protest" to a "post-protest" literature? Can our literature and theatre become *pro*active rather than *re*active?

* Can we rethink form and find new content for the new South African theatre? Can we build on the remarkable developments of the last four decades?

* How do we prepare to make a theatre that contributes to a post-apartheid society?

The Junction Avenue Theatre Company play, *Tooth and Nail*, created over six months in 1988 and premiering at the Market Theatre in February 1989, represented an attempt to address some of these questions head on. In the following pages, I will attempt to give an account of the making of *Tooth and Nail* and compare it to Junction Avenue Theatre Company's previous play *Sophiatown*.

In its fifteen year history, Junction Avenue Theatre Company has created a number of original plays. From *The Fantastical History of a Useless Man* which opened in 1976 at the Nunnery Theatre, Wits, to *Sophiatown* which premiered at the Market Theatre, Johannesburg in 1986, from *Randlords and Rotgut* to the "people's plays" *Security* and *Dikitsheneng*, from *Marabi*, based on Modikwe Dikobe's *Marabi Dance*, to *Will of a Rebel*, an expressionist exploration of the life and work of Breyten Breytenbach, the company has been driven by a passion to improvise stories which critically reflect the mad world of apartheid in all of its manifestations.

All these plays have been created collectively in theatre workshops, usually over a period of six months, the group meeting three or four times a week at night, after the members have completed time in their more conventional jobs. Research, oral testimony, yoga and theatre games, exercises and African dance, music workshops and the study of sociology are some of the strands that have made up the eclectic whole designed to unleash the creative energies needed to forge a workshopped play.

I have always regarded the theatre workshop as a very special idea with a particular meaning for South Africans. In international theatre debates this century, we have had many powerful arguments for the value of collective play making and the magic of the sacred workshop space, but in South Africa a vital additional element is added. The workshop space in South Africa is a space where South Africans can momentarily leave the monster of apartheid behind them and meet as equals, without prejudice, to work creatively together.

7. Ramolao Makhene in the stage play *Sophiatown* with Siphiwe Khumalo in the background. Photo: Ruphin Coudyzer

This may sound idealistic, misguided and impossible to some, but in the case of Junction Avenue Theatre Company the workshop has provided a most creative environment. Over the years the plays we have created have been very well received both nationally and internationally.

Most of the work the company has created has been conceived as militantly oppositional and locates itself firmly in the anti-apartheid tradition. We have taken on the task of revealing "hidden history" and telling stories from the point of view of the oppressed. In taking on the question of history and telling those stories the state wants hidden, the company has largely relied on a model for theatre making that is based on a strong concept of character development and narrative structure and is indebted in part to a kind of social realism and in part to the theories of Brecht.

In *Sophiatown*, for example, although there are relatively realistic characters involved in a domestic drama, chants, political slogans, shouts and *a capella* songs break up the narrative, intervening almost arbitrarily in the action. An attempt is made to distance the audience momentarily from the emotional action and generate a critical perspective and new awareness. In the company's shorter plays such as *Security* and *Dikitsheneng*, the characters are broader and more representative, almost as if they were stock characters from a melodrama, but the structure of the play has largely involved the unfolding of a story in a fairly conventional way.

When Junction Avenue Theatre Company embarked on the making of *Sophiatown* in July 1985, there was a sense of deep-rooted optimism in the company about South Africa's future. This was not a calculated or well thought-out position, but rather an emotional response to the period just proceeding. The general insurrection of the period 1983 to 1985 had shaken the very foundations of the state. At last it seemed that it was possible to overthrow apartheid. A spirit of revolutionary optimism was in the air.

Everywhere people were liberating small corners of South Africa.

In spite of the brutality which inevitably accompanied such a revolutionary uprising, a sense of euphoria was generated from this most palpable evidence of the emergence of people's power.

In our haze of emotions we thought that liberation was around the corner. To many of us the future seemed immediately possible and simple.

Sophiatown was created in that spirit.

In spite of its subject matter, the destruction of a Johannesburg suburb because it was freehold and non-racial and perceived by the apartheid state as a threat, there resided in the very heart of the play, a positive, joyful and forward-looking energy. This energy clearly generated an empathetic reaction in our audiences wherever we played, and we played in many centres both nationally and internationally. This energy and heart won us large audiences and made the play very popular, but was not without its contradictions. A major critique of the play was that it was nostalgic and ameliorated the sordid conditions of the real *Sophiatown* in its portrayal. Other critics, deeply supportive of the work, found it a powerful and complex piece of political theatre. It was argued that the warmth and heart of the play generated the kind of large and responsive audiences that give plays such as *Sophiatown* their full meaning.

From 1986 to 1988, Junction Avenue Theatre Company toured *Sophiatown* to major international festivals such as the Berlin Festival, the Zurich International Theatre Festival, the Toronto Harbour Front Festival, the Glasgow Mayfest, the Chicago International Festival, anti-apartheid festivals and conferences in France, and university and community festivals in America and Europe, as well as playing a month at the Hampstead Theatre in London.

On these tours the company was exposed to directors and creators such as Kantor and Pina Bausch, companies such as 'Oh La La Human Steps' and Carbon 14 from Montreal, and leading experimental companies from the USSR, Eastern Europe and Latin America. All these companies revealed to us that the emergent theatre language of the late twentieth century is a highly complex, sophisticated, imagistic and abrasive one.

For some of us, the implications of this exposure to world theatre were profound. One cannot be so isolated so long from major international theatre movements and tendencies and then be exposed to them in such a forceful way over a relatively short period without being deeply influenced in ways that we cannot yet fully comprehend.

It is inevitable that exposure to this theatre language should have exerted a powerful influence on the members of Junction Avenue Theatre Company. Some of us in the company were very intrigued with the imagistic and formal aspects of the work we saw, and wanted and still want to experiment with these forms to transform Junction Avenue Theatre Company's theatre language. We felt we needed an extended and enriched theatre language to deal with the times we were living through. Simple dramatic through-lines and straight forward narratives, even when broken up with Brechtian interventions, did not seem enough.

The revolutionary uprisings that had taken place through the eighties had brought with them a whole series of new media images. Most notable were the mass funerals of the Eastern Cape, but everywhere the townships were on fire. 100,000 people rising to their feet in one voice is a completely palpable image of people's power. Upturned cars on fire and burning bodies leave an indelible impression on the mind. The emergence of the Zola Budd and the Casspir, new police and riot police uniforms, gas masks and riot helmets, wooden replicas of AK 47's, and the dreaded necklace with its connotations of witch-craft and burning at the stake, all provided photographers in particular, but artists in general, with a subject of the most powerful and devastating sort.

By the middle of 1988, there were subtle but far-reaching changes in experience and consciousness in the collective mind of Junction Avenue Theatre Company. These changes, plus difficulties with personal relationships, made more intense by the demanding tours we were undertaking, and the consolidation of political tendencies within the group that had not seemed to matter before, as well as new difficulties in the conditions of production, plus our recent exposure to some of the best theatre the world had to offer, were profoundly shaking up the company. Many of the things we had taken for granted were being challenged.

In spite of the international success of *Sophiatown*, members of the company were expressing the need to experiment with new forms and newly conceived content. It had become clear that the material and social conditions which had driven the workshops of all previous Junction Avenue plays had begun to change. We were very conscious of the difficult questions that South African theatre faced and is still facing.

The *Tooth and Nail* workshop was set up to explore all these issues and challenges. Wherever possible Junction Avenue Theatre Company have tried to put the difficult questions facing us under a creative spotlight in a workshop situation, turning, as it were, our liabilities into our assets.

Tooth and Nail's form represented a radical departure from the narrative structure we had so often used. The play was conceived of as a series of fleeting images, made up out of almost 100 fragments of all aspects of South African life. Song, dance, chant, imagery, obsessional repetition, fictional language, opera pastiche and puppetry contributed some of the formal language of the fragments, and in keeping with Eisenstein's ideas about collision in the cinema or the theories of the Surrealists, each fragment was intended to derive much of its meaning from juxtaposition with other fragments. Each fragment was conceived of as very short, some only lasting thirty seconds and most lasting no more than a minute or two. The overall effect we wanted to create was one of a barrage of contradictory statements and pictures, abstract sound, cold ideas and impenetrable flashes of meaning that somehow threw light on the deeply confused historical moment we found ourselves in. By the late eighties we were sensing great change, and we wanted a changed theatre language to try and deal with the experience.

While it was clear that the South African theatre had forged for itself a powerful performance style of ease and energy, which has a profound resonance for international audiences, we have tended to create this theatre in relative isolation, cut off by the cultural boycott until now from some of the most interesting contemporary theatre and performance experiments taking place in the rest of the world.

This isolation has not seemed to matter until recently, but if I am right, and the tradition we have been forging has temporarily lost its way, then we are in need of rejuvenating input.

Our issue-driven theatre is highly attractive to many Europeans and North Americans, who seem to have long lost contact with the processes by which they are governed, empowered and disempowered. These audiences tell us they detect a complex mixture of ease and commitment in contemporary South African performances, which, apparently, European actors work long years for. The sources for our theatre are rich and varied, and generate extraordinary performance, but they cannot retain their stimulating strength for ever.

Some of us in turn are attracted to the highly sophisticated theatre languages that are emerging on the cutting edge of the festival circuit.

It seems to me that the way forward for the South African theatre lies with a theatre which remains issue-driven, but understands that the empty words of an anti-apartheid theatre no longer have resonance and power for audiences who have been exposed to this forty-year history, and are deeply immersed in the complex issues of transformation which the current political situation has thrust onto the agenda. We are no longer only fighting against the state in a broad anti-apartheid struggle. We are now faced with the complex task of what we want to fight for. These questions of our

future have to be battled out in the cultural arena, as well as the
political.

Every possible political grouping from the ultra left to the
extreme right is demanding allegiance, and we are hard put to read the
signs. How do we read the signs? This concern became a recurring
theme in the workshop we were setting up.

Learn to read in the dark, become good readers of the signs.

The original idea for the *Tooth and Nail* workshop, imposed
from above and quickly abandoned, was to make a revolutionary
opera in five parts, each part in turn governed by the principles of air,
water, fire, earth and atomic waste. Each section was to consist of
twenty fragments which were to allow deeply contradictory glimpses
and flashes of South African life. The whole was to run continuously
for 100 minutes.

The intellectual brief set out for the group was as follows. We
would take as our starting point the deeply resonant quote by the
Italian theorist Gramsci:

> The old is dying and the new cannot be born; in this inter-
> regnum there arises a great diversity of morbid symptoms."

Gramsci's words seemed so extraordinarily applicable to our
own situation.

In the words of the play, we live "in the bitter times between
the old and the new" and new morbid symptoms still appear daily.
Now more than ever.

Consider the content of the newspapers we were confronted
with daily as we prepared *Tooth and Nail*. Family murders in the
Afrikaans community, the murder of comrades by comrades, the
hunting of witches in the Northern Transvaal, clear evidence of hys-
terical reactions and psychopathic withdrawal in the community, refuge in decadence and alcohol, the emergence of neo-Nazi groups such
as the AWB (*Afrikaanse Weerstandsbeweging*) desperate speculation that
a white homeland could be built, a collapsing economy, the abuse of
funds and the abuse of newly gained power, the assassination of the
most gentle of souls, and so on and so on and so on. All this made up
part of our daily life, which seemed to be becoming increasingly frag-
mented. How could we give expression to all this new experience?

Moving from a narrative structure to a play built out of fragments without obvious structure, a playful manipulation of slippages
of meaning and a complex juxtaposition of images, each designed and

placed to negate the other, was a highly unusual move for the company, and what we created in *Tooth and Nail* was not without contradiction.

On the one hand, we wanted aspects of our work to be difficult and opaque, for we wanted to make a theatre which was not easy to co-opt. On the other hand we wanted to make a play as popular and populist as our previous work. Theatre for the majority implies popular and accessible forms, but the then current theatre seemed bankrupt to us. We wanted our work to be new and difficult and popular all at the same time. We tried to turn certain concepts derived from Brecht to our advantage. In his refutation of Lukács Brecht had argued as follows:

> We must not derive realism as such from particular existing works, but we shall use every means, old and new, tried and untried, derived from art and derived from other sources, to render reality to men in a form they can master . . . . New problems appear and demand new methods. Reality changes; in order to represent it, modes of representation must also change.[1]

We embarked on a project to radically change our modes of representation, without successfully rendering reality in a form available for mastery. Many found the play too difficult and inaccessible, though many others were deeply excited by the new form and the challenging ideas. By the time we had reworked the play by invitation for the 1991 Grahamstown Festival it seemed much less opaque. History had caught up.

In the end the theatre piece consisted of some 70 fragments, dominated by image and puppetry, each fragment ranging from one minute to ten minutes in duration, and linked by a loose narrative, which ran as follows: ten characters are on the run from the floods of blood unleashed by the apartheid armies. They do not all meet up with one another, but pass each other in the night as they continue on their journeys. One of the main characters, Sifiso, is a political activist who, as a central unifying force, tries to engage all the characters in building a survival craft for the future.

---

[1] Bertolt Brecht, "Against Georg Lukács," in *Aesthetics and Politics*, (London: Verso, 1980) pp. 81–82.

8. Saul the photographer (a life-sized puppet manipulated by Basil Jones) in *Tooth and Nail*. Photo: Ruphin Coudyzer

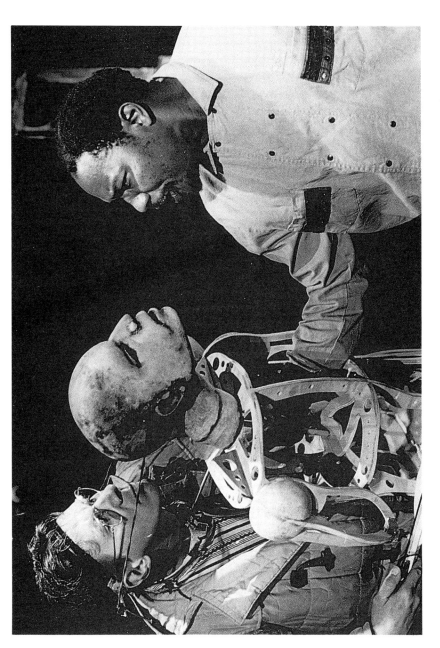

9. Saul I and Saul II with the Activist (Ramolao Makhene) in *Tooth and Nail*. Photo: Ruphin Coudyzer.

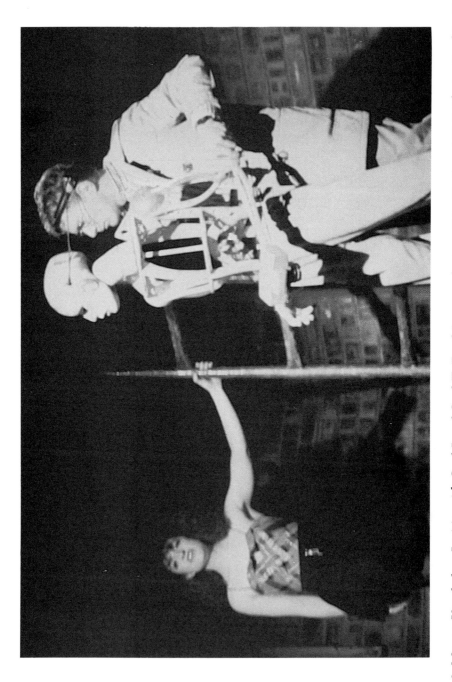

10. Megan Kruskal as Letitia with Saul I and Saul II (Basil Jones and puppet) in *Tooth and Nail*. Photo: Ruphin Coudyzer

The metaphor of the floods and the need to build a survival craft was consciously rooted in myth and the play consciously attempted to link the ancient stories of floods and arks to a present day reality in South Africa.

While it is possible to read the metaphor in several different ways, we wanted the floods to refer to the apartheid system of repression and the violence it unleashed. The survival craft symbolised the various different attempts by the resistance movement to fight the system over the last eighty years. Many of the fragments were labelled history lessons.

As Sifiso says, in one of his main speeches,

> Everywhere there are floods of blood. Some will survive, others will die. But blood will not run for ever. We need to believe in the future in spite of all. What is the history of our people? A series of survival craft. We need to build an unsinkable survival craft.

The closing words of the play are his:

> Build with care. Build slowly. Everybody know each other's work. For the murders will not yet stop.

Sifiso's journey through the apartheid landscape is plagued with danger and violence. Hooded figures, brandishing torches, pangas and knives, relentlessly pursue him, finally closing in on him. The security police hunt him down and he is interrogated and tortured.

In the play, Sifiso is juxtaposed with a character/image called Saul, the artist-photographer, who is caught up in the central issue facing artists in South Africa. Can one remain neutral? What does it mean to be engaged?

Saul was embodied as a double image. The part was played by a full-sized puppet attached to an actor (brilliantly designed by the Handspring Theatre Company who collaborated on the project). Saul played out the role in two conflicting voices. The actor and the puppet are bound together by the ropes used to operate the puppet. In his opening monologue, Saul states in his first voice:

> I need my freedom to express the wonders of the world. Fear of the dark, a delight in flight, the jewel-like quality of Amazonian frogs . . . .

Saul's second voice contradicts, he wants the artist engaged in struggle.

Later Saul says

> These times are very extreme. We have to be very rigorous. Everyone wants us to work for them, make images only for them. Some want my pictures for their war, some want my pictures for their pleasure, some want my pictures to bury themselves in. Others, who want their brutality hidden, don't want me to take pictures at all.
>
> I want to make pictures only for myself. If they are truly for myself, then they are truly about the times. Everything is fragmented now, broken into little pieces. I want my pictures to be about those little pieces . . . .

Other characters on the run from the floods include:

Madelaine and Angelo, a white bourgeois housewife and her faithful black manservant. This couple only communicate with each other in a pastiche of famous opera arias and are tied in a bittersweet and seemingly unbreakable bond of a master-slave relationship. Madelaine and Angelo, Madelaine locked into a wheel barrow pushed by her manservant, provided moments of comic madness.

A *ménage à trois* consisting of Letitia, a pleasure-loving, neurotic white woman, her husband Manfred, an advertising executive, and Letitia's lover Mandla, a black yuppie who works for South African Breweries. Their power struggles revolve around the issues of sex, race and class. A triangle of lovers caught up in the sweet and destructive powers of antagonism and love.

Mandla and Manfred are rivals in love and work and come to represent the new middle class that the state, capital and the mainstream media so desperately want to create.

Much of the research for these characters was based on media images, especially as used by the breweries. What is the dominant message? Young trendy white and black executives with newly acquired mobility are going to make the new age. Power will be shared in a token way by a middle class that is no longer defined by race but by wealth.

Mandla is caught up in the anxiety of his upward social mobility, and its implicit betrayal, and he seeks out Sifiso for advice. In a comic fragment he expresses the wish to get involved.

> Sifiso, Sifiso, ek het n probleem, is ek a yuppie? A topshayala? Ek wil zabalaza . . . I want to be in the struggle . . .

In the end Mandla's social aspirations seem to defeat him.

On the other hand Manfred, in the last moments of the play, is revealed as a balaclava-clad right-wing vigilante. In a most brutal way he asserts his right to a place in the future.

> I have only one thing to say. My name is Manfred. I am very meticulous, very careful. I keep my balaclava neatly folded in my underpants drawer. And who says I don't have a future?

The threat is evident and the moment is reminiscent of the sentiments and images of the emerging neo-Nazi movement in South Africa.

In some ways, Letitia, the third wing of the triangle, typifies white paranoia. Living a life that fluctuates violently between fear and hedonistic pleasure-seeking, Letitia also represents a freedom that comes from living on the edge, constantly in the present. She is a creature of flight. In the opening sequence, she is running away from Mandla, screaming, like a frightened animal.

> LETITIA: It's a revolution . . .
> (Mandla tries to placate her and counter her perceptions.)
> MANDLA: It's a veld fire . . .
> LETITIA: It's a revolution . . .
> MANDLA: It's a veld fire . . . .
> LETITIA: It's a flood . . .
> MANDLA: It's another Johannesburg rainstorm . . .

Locked in this conflict of antagonism and love, Letitia reverberates with dual tensions of desire and withdrawal. In her *Song of Hopeless and Dangerous Dreams*, she sings of her need to black out the bitter moments of the present and escape into a world of pure pleasure, only to find that everything, including pleasure, turns to fragments and dust. Echoing the words of Sifiso, she too urges us to be "good readers of the signs." Letitia, however, can never escape her essential hedonistic impulses, even if they are perverse. Caught in a perverse contradiction, she both feeds off and is destroyed by the violence that surrounds her.

> I love the violence that surrounds me . . . the blood of the streets runs in my veins . . . I'm in the fast lane, the fast lane . . . and I want to go faster.

In the final moments of the play, both her lovers declare what they want from a relationship with her. Mandla admits that all he wants from her is power over a white woman. Manfred will chain her up and love her for ever, if only she will let him.

Predictably, Letitia offers no future, "but let's have a sweet, sweet present."

There are two mothers in the play: a white mother and a black mother. Both have children who have left them to engage in the struggle: Saul as a photographer/observer constantly and obsessively in dialogue with himself, and Thandiwe, who is recruited into the revolutionary army. Thandi dies in detention, and in keeping with the theatrical representation of the spirit world that we were exploring, returns from the dead to recount to her mother how she was murdered on the tenth floor of John Vorster Square.[2]

The conflict between Busisiswe Khuswayo, earth mother and spiritual healer, and her daughter Thandiwe provides a representation of the generational conflict that forms such a crucial part of South African experience. Thandiwe, like so many of the 1976 generation of students, cannot understand her mother's passive response to the brutality of the state. She repeatedly and defiantly rejects her mother's notion of spiritualism. Her mother wants to heal with water. Thandi's own logic of struggle leads her systematically to one course of action, healing with fire.

Sifiso comes to fetch her to join the revolutionary army and in one of the most poignant moments of the play, Busisiswe screams,

> BUSISISWE: Who are these people who call my daughter? She is the only one I have. Bafa Bonke. They all died. . . . You are calling my daughter to her death . . .
> THANDI: Mama, I will die if I stay here . . . Let me go.
> BUSISISWE: I named you Thandi . . . Love . . . and now you go to war.
> SIFISO: That is the only way to love, mama.

Thandi is murdered for her commitment and comes back as a spirit to graphically describe her detention, torture and death. Ironically, she has been drowned in a bucket of water. Her last words to her mother are,

> THANDI: And I say to you, the time has come to heal with fire.

---

[2] Johannesburg Police Headquarters.

This time, her mother replies,

> BUSISISWE: Hamba Kahle, Thandi. The time has come to heal with fire.

Thandi's message, 'Heal with fire', is the final message of the play. It evoked mixed and passionate audience response especially as it was picked up and echoed by the mother figure.

Language and language policy is a fraught issue in South Africa. The politics of language and translation has been a central issue both in the Junction Avenue Theatre Company workshops and in the plays. In a multilingual society, such as our own, the questions of language and power pervade every aspect of social life. At a more pragmatic level, English is the language of communication in the workshops; however, many members of the company only speak English as a second language. Other members of the group do not speak African languages so that the problems of meaning and communication become extremely important in the process of making a play.

The game of missed translation and misunderstanding in a multilingual society is a central and pervasive theme in South African Theatre. Junction Avenue Theatre Company has often experimented with language. One of the companies most powerful exercises involves a narrative workshop with imaginary languages and tongues. Our most successful realization so far of these concerns lies in the character of the Interpreter in *Tooth and Nail*. Half spirit, half man, he moves in and out of Sifiso's world of *realpolitik* and the world of the lost spirits, simplifying the complexity of the moment so that all can understand. Switching fluently from Tswana to Sotho to Zulu to English to the made-up language of the spirits, the Interpreter interprets events as well as providing the audience with access to the South African Tower of Babel.

Audience responses to the Activist/Interpreter couple were charged with both recognition and identification. Recognition of both the cumbersome and inadequate process of translation, and identification with the difficulties of communication and the burden of translation. Many great comic moments emerged from the brilliant rapport of Ramolao Makhene as Sifiso and Tale Motsepe as the interpreter.

Central to the question of language and meaning, it seems to me, are two speeches.

> SIFISO. In these cracked and bitter times
> caught as we are between the old and the new

In the other hold the hammer, in the other hold the nail
Learn to breathe beneath the waves
drown like rats or fly into the heart of the sun
Take these bitter times and learn from them
find gills grow wings
see in the dark
learn to see in the dark

These times are very complicated
it will not help us to ignore manyala, the rot,
We simplify at our cost.

This is everybody's war
It touches us all with its fire
some want the future, some want the past
understand the enemy and make him weak.
culture is a weapon.
We must be good readers of the signs.

INTERPRETER: Nothing is what it seems, everything must be
interpreted, learn to be good readers of the signs.

In Junction Avenue Theatre Company we are primarily committed to making a popular political theatre for the majority. But we
believe we have a responsibility to advance and constantly interrogate
the form of our work. Theatre makers debate with other theatre makers
via their work, and as I have argued earlier, theatre in South Africa
seems to have reached a major impasse. In retrospect, in spite of some
excellent critical reception, it is clear to me that *Tooth and Nail* was only
partially successful. The task we undertook seems enormous now. It
appears fairly impossible to grow a new language for our theatre in
one project. Narrative and character have a long and honourable history. Not without reason. I believe the way forward for us lies with
some kind of synthesis of the different styles we have developed over
the years, but good story-telling and rigorous work remain primary.

In the *Tooth and Nail* project, we were trying to find a way to
advance our theatre forms, make our content complex, deal with the
subtleties of the times and look towards a genuinely creative post-
apartheid theatre. All these tasks remain.

PHYSICAL IMAGES IN THE
SOUTH AFRICAN THEATRE

Mark Fleishman

The world-renowned teacher of theatre, Jacques Lecoq, performs a one-person performance piece as a demonstration of his ideas and theories on the theatre. This performance he calls *"Tout Bouge,"* everything moves. For Lecoq, the world is a theatre of incessant movement and to be true, the theatre, far from being simply an arena for recitation, must capture this movement complete with all its colour, rhythm and complexity. It is my belief that the theatre of South Africa is a striking example of such a moving theatre, packed full of dynamic physical imagery. Within the limitations of such a short article I hope to demonstrate this in some small way. What follows then is a series of evolving thoughts on the place of the physical image in the South African theatre.

I

The Word v The Gesture

At the climax of Athol Fugard's *My Children! My Africa!* there is a meeting in a deserted classroom between the teacher, Mr M, and his young pupil, Thami. A school boycott is raging outside. Stones have been thrown through the windows and lie amongst broken glass on the floor. Thami has come to convince Mr M to join the boycott but the teacher refuses. Mr M picks up one of the stones and holds it in his one hand. He picks up his dictionary and holds it in the other. He compares the two and comes to the conclusion that although they probably weigh about the same, the dictionary contains the whole English language while the stone is simply one word in that language. It seems to me that what is being implied here is a choice between the dictionary as a symbol of the word and the stone as a symbol of violence and destruction. Mr M would clearly have Thami choose the word; by staying on the side of the boycotters Thami seems to choose the stone. Behind this moment is a clear assumption on the part of Mr M, and I would argue Fugard himself, that the word is intrinsically better than the stone. After all, the stone is a base, inanimate object while words have the creative potential to fashion the most beautiful poetry.

It seems to me that this choice between the word and the stone symbolises a conflict at the root of the creative process in the South African theatre. What a writer like Fugard, steeped in a tradition of literary dramatic writing, fails to understand about this choice is that it is not the stone itself which is attractive to Thami and the generation he represents. What makes the stone attractive is its process of animation: the gesture of throwing; the physicalization of the object. It is the introduction of the physical body with its potential for dynamic action which motivates the choice. It frees Thami from the hegemony of the written word which presents itself as pre-ordained truth and as such forms part of a dominant culture which sets terms of high and low, included and excluded, and attempts to limit his freedom of action. At the same time it presents him with the possibility of other meaning-making processes such as the physical and the oral (itself a physical action) which have been marginalised by the dominant.

I would suggest that for most people making theatre in South Africa the written word on its own is woefully inadequate to portray or explain the full complexity of the reality they face. Ultimately, the choice between the word and the stone (word and gesture) is a false choice. Words and gestures are only two points in a plural field which includes many alternate positions that do not simply reduce to one or other side of such a binary opposition. A complex subject requires a complex treatment and gives rise to a complex text in which the written word, the spoken word and the transformative material body amongst others are in a constant state of dynamic dialogue. There is no essential hierarchy where one mode of expression, one process of making meaning can be seen as more important than another.

II

The Physical Body and Meaning

The physical body forms part of the meaning-making system of almost all theatre where human performers appear live in front of an audience. In Western theatre, however, most of the meaning is contained in the written text. The body provides secondary meaning, often quite unintentional and unplanned. The written text is given life when it is raised from the page and set inside the body of the actor. Much stress is laid on the clarity with which these words are spoken by the body but little attention is paid to the way in which that body moves in response to the words. In South African theatre, on the other hand, the body is not simply a vehicle for the embodiment of the text; it serves as part of the text in its own right. The physical body in South African theatre is a source of primary meaning which constantly challenges the hegemony of the written word in the meaning-making system.

Movement in South African theatre ranges from formal choreographed dance sequences: tribal dances, gumboot dances, *pantsula* dances or *toyi-toyi* sequences; to elaborate physical gesture existing alongside and interwoven with the words of the text; to more consciously conceived physical images created by the director and/or performers to replace words completely where words have become simply insufficient.

What are the origins of this increased importance of the physical in South African theatre? I can perhaps suggest a few. Firstly, many South African plays, certainly after 1976, have been workshopped rather than written. Text is created through improvisation, a physical process in which gesture exists before and alongside words as an independent sign system. In performance the workshop play exhibits a physical quality with a pronounced gestural component which runs alongside and interweaves with the words of the text.

Secondly, most black performers, at least, are influenced by an oral consciousness which as Walter Ong and others have shown differs fundamentally from a literary consciousness in a number of ways. One of the differences is that orality has a high somatic component. As Ong explains:

> The oral word never exists in a simply verbal context, as a written word does. Spoken words are always modifications of a total existential situation, which always engages the body. Bodily activity beyond mere vocalization is neither adventitious or contrived in oral communication, but is natural and even inevitable. In oral verbalization, particularly public verbalization, absolute motionless is itself a powerful physical gesture.[1]

[1] Walter Ong, *Orality and Literacy: The Technologizing of the Word* (London: Methuen, 1982), pp. 67–68.

Thirdly, if we follow Richard Schechner,[2] the theatre produced within a particular society mirrors the social drama of that society. In other words, the characteristic dynamics of everyday life in a particular culture influence the kinds of images one finds in the theatre of that culture. Life in South Africa, filled as it is with desperate struggles for change, for power and for simple survival, has a physically dynamic nature which feeds physically dynamic images on the stage.

Finally, the choice of the body as a language of communication helps overcome the vast language diversity of the South African audience. As Mbongeni Ngema comments with reference to *Asinamali*:

> I wanted to develop a style of theatre that would communicate with anyone anywhere in the world, that would bridge the barriers of language and culture, something in which the body tells the story much more than the words.[3]

In the sections that follow I will try to explore the body's primary meaning function in the South African theatre in a little more depth.

III

The Physical Body as a Site of Transformation

Barney Simon tells a story of the painter Georges Braque who is reported to have commented during the First World War that he understood the nature of art when he saw a batman turn a bucket which had previously carried water into a brazier for carrying fire. He tells this story in order to emphasise the importance of transformation in the art of the theatre.

I would like to examine two kinds of transformations that concern the physical body in South African theatre. In the first kind of transformation the body of the performer begins as neutral and changes in front of the spectator into a multiplicity of characters and images.

---

[2] See R. Schechner, *Performance Theory* (New York: Routledge, 1988).

[3] M. Ngema, "Bridging the Barriers: The Making of *Asinamali*," An interview with Mbongeni Ngema, by P. Stein, *South African Theatre Journal*, Vol. 4, no. 2, 99–105 (p. 103).

In plays like *Woza Albert!*, *Asinamali*, *Bopha!* and *You Strike the Woman, You Strike the Rock* a small group of performers appear as themselves to enact a particular story for the audience. The number of performers is small but the cast list is extremely long. Each performer plays a variety of parts as the story unfolds and as the streets of South Africa's cities and townships come to life on the stage. The transformations of the performers into this multiplicity of characters is not aided by complex make-up designs or elaborate costumes. Most transformations take place in front of the audience with perhaps a simple item of clothing, a hat, a coat, or a simple prop, a pipe, a newspaper, a pair of spectacles to aid the actor. It is the performer's body that changes most to suggest the age, the build and the essential quality of the character. In many of these plays, particularly where the casts are all male, the neutral costume of the performer is a pair of loose fitting pants with the upper body naked. This makes the physical transformation that much more visible to the spectator as the naked torso evolves from the neutral to a particular physical characterisation and back to the neutral again.

Andrew Buckland in his solo performance *The Ugly Noonoo* appears on an empty stage wearing only a pair of khaki shorts. He is mowing his lawn on a Saturday afternoon. Suddenly he hits a tough spot of grass and the earth opens up to swallow him into a fantastical world where he does battle with the infamous "Parktown Prawn"[4] or finds himself as a rebellious blood corpuscle inside a human body. At no stage is anything other than the body used to indicate environment or character; no props, no costumes, however simple. His body constantly changing and re-inventing itself is a separate stream of text running alongside and interweaving with the words he speaks.

The second kind of transformation involves a physical action or gesture which begins as one thing and metamorphoses into something else passing through a range of possibilities in between.

In John Matshikiza's *Prophets in a Black Sky* there is a scene where one of the prophets, a man who has lived in a rural environment all his life, arrives in the city for the first time. He is shocked by the noise, the colours and the pace of what he finds. He meets a city-wise night-watchman who proceeds to enlighten him about the city. The

---

[4] The "Parktown Prawn" is a large and particularly ugly looking type of cockroach which terrorises households in Johannesburg.

night-watchman lifts up his kierrie and tells the prophet it is a shovel.
He then tells the prophet to pick it up, to put it down, to start to dig,
over and over again, until the prophet becomes an automaton, slav-
ishly repeating actions in response to the watchman's barked com-
mands. The actions become faster and faster, more and more out of
control, a flailing dance in which the original image opens up to signify
far more than a man playing at digging: desperation, entrapment, a
manic will to please and much more.

In Chris Pretorius's *Weird Sex in Maputo* the two characters find
themselves together in a room in an old colonial hotel in Mozambique.
There is no explanation as to how they got there or even why they
are there. In fact they seem unsure themselves. There is very little in
the way of spoken dialogue. The action involves their difficult, often
confused and increasingly desperate attempts at sex. What begins as
sexual foreplay, in a jerky, almost haphazard fashion, slowly begins
to transform into a desperate, violent dance which at times includes
the knock-about humour of the wrestling match, at other times what
seems like highly serious violent intent. The simplicity of the verbal
text is overtaken by the complexity of the physical actions as they
transform from simple easy-to-understand images to far more complex, often almost surreal ones. Meanings proliferate and the end
product is a text of physical poetry which could not have been simply
composed in words.

Jazzart's dance/theatre piece *Abamanyani* begins with a scene
in which children play games with objects they have found on a
rubbish dump including old tyres. At first the games are played in an
almost idyllic spirit as the laughing children share both the objects they
are playing with and the experience of playing together. Soon, however, an element of competition is introduced. The atmosphere begins
to change. The children begin to break up into groups. The groups
begin to compete against each other. The competition becomes more
and more serious until it explodes into violence which grows as the
tyres which were being used as toys become weapons to be used
against others and finally as a blazing necklace to be slung around the
neck of one of the erstwhile playmates. There are extremely few, if any,
words used in this quite lengthy sequence. It is simply a transformation of actions and objects which constitutes a physical text with a
complex power beyond the written word.

What makes each of the above examples of transformation so
rich is not that there is a change from one thing into another, but that
the change involves a range of possibility between the beginning and

end points which opens up a plural field of meaning for the spectator. Each image is in this sense dialogical: a play of open-ended possibilities interacting between two fixed poles which exist in some form of dialogue with each other.

Beyond the essential richness these physical transformations lend to the theatre in South Africa they have a deeper political import which is twofold. Firstly, they demonstrate the possibility of change in an active way that affects the spectator on a more subliminal level than a simple slogan or verbal statement might. Secondly, and to my mind more importantly, they form part of what Mikhail Bakhtin would call the "grotesque realism" of the South African theatre.[5] By refashioning and re-inventing the material body into extraordinary, often grotesque forms they subvert and parody aspects of the society and the world. The transformed body contains its own logic which can unsettle "given" social positions and interrogate the rules of inclusion, exclusion and domination which structure the social body.

IV

The Physical Body and Metaphor

A metaphor involves the application of the attributes of one thing (A) onto another thing (B) in order to elucidate some quality of B. In other words we use the attributes of one thing to describe the qualities of another. However, unlike with a simile where the connection is explicit (one thing is like another), with a metaphor the connection between A and B is implicit and requires an imaginative response from the reader/ spectator.

In *The Show's Not Over 'til the Fat Lady Sings*, Jennie Reznek is Belinda, an overweight woman struggling to deal with a body and a life that is tying her down to the ground. Through the process of the performance she slowly learns to come to terms with her circumstance and finally achieves her dream of flight. The performance is full of physical transformations of the kind dealt with above but it is the overall image of Belinda's dreams of flight, her failed attempts to get off the ground and her eventual flying, presented as a circus

---

[5] See M. Bakhtin, *Rabelais and His Word*, trans. by H. Iswolsky, (Cambridge, Mass.: M.I.T. Press, 1968); and M. Bakhtin, *The Dialogic Imagination: Four Essays*, ed. by M. Holquist, trans. by C. Emerson and M. Holquist, (Austin: University of Texas Press, 1981).

11. Jenny Reznek in *The Show's Not Over 'Til The Fat Lady Sings.* Photo: Ruphin Coudyzer.

web act or single rope trapeze, which is most remarkable. It is a carefully constructed physical image packed full of possibility, a powerful metaphor of liberation which raises the performance from a rather mundane, simplistic base in the issue of obesity to something on a much grander scale. What is being dealt with in the performance is the notion of possibility, of potentiality, of liberation; the medium is a physical image of weight achieving flight. In this way physical metaphors allow meaning to operate on multiple levels, not simply existing on their separate levels in isolation but often in a state of dialogue with each other.

In Matsemela Manaka's *Egoli* there is a central image of the two actors chained together from collars around their necks. Every movement they make is inhibited by the chains. The action of one affects the other so as to make them completely inter-dependent. As Ian Steadman comments the chain signifies the manner in which "the men are chained in bondage to the economic system" and that their ultimate goal is the breaking of this chain.[6] In this way the breaking of the chain is clearly meant as a metaphor for the struggle for liberation. However, the physical metaphor resonates on other levels too. The chained men are at once Siamese-twins, a double-headed hydra, dogs, slaves, brothers, prisoners. These meanings in turn reflect back on the original meaning, strengthening it and challenging it so as to render it more complex.

The value of such physical metaphors is that they indicate the essential unity of all things. One thing can be another. Belinda can fly. Andrew Buckland is a Parktown prawn. And in a world in which we are constantly battling to find traces of that which binds us together, to re-connect that which feels so separated, such images are essential.

V

The Future

At the end of her life the Mexican artist Frida Kahlo bemoaned the fact that her contribution to the revolution had been so slight. She wished that she, like her husband Diego Rivera who painted murals with clear political themes, had done more to serve it. She lamented the fact that

---

[6] I.P. Steadman, *Drama and Social Conciousness*: *Themes in Black Theatre on the Witwatersrand until 1984*, unplublished PhD thesis, University of the Witwatersrand, 1985, f. 370.

her paintings seemed so personal, so idiosyncratic, so apparently opaque. And yet in the manner in which her images challenge and reconstitute perceived notions of the 'normal,' presenting imaginative alternatives which open up a dialogue on possibility, they are today considered some of the most powerfully political artistic statements ever made. Many of her paintings are self-portraits in which the body of the artist is re-imagined to challenge some aspect of her world. In *The Little Deer* her head is placed on the body of a deer which has been pierced by numerous arrows causing blood to flow down its flanks. In *Roots* Frida is lying on the parched earth with roots and leaves growing out of her body into the ground. In *The Broken Column* her fractured body, imaged as a broken architectural column, is held together with leather straps and nails. Even working in a two-dimensional medium she understood the power of the physical and of its imaginative trans-formations. However personal these images were for her when they were made they resonate on a much broader canvas for us all today. In a similar vein we in South Africa have to learn to re-invent ourselves in a most active way and the theatre has a part to play in this process. Our challenge is to present images of the body in various forms con-stantly re-invented and transformed.

The physical image is multi-valent, ambiguous, complex. It leads to a proliferation of meaning which demands an imaginative response from the spectator. There are those that would argue that such open-ended images are inappropriate for a country struggling to deal with the uncertainties of a changing reality. They would have clarity, single meanings, a narrowing down of options in a manner designed to appeal to the audience's need for stability and certainty. I would suggest this is a misguided opinion. The theatre in our country has often been guilty of simplicity as much in its condemnation as in its condoning of apartheid. What we need now is the opening up of alternatives and options, the promotion of dialogue in a desperate attempt to avoid the replacement of one monologistic absolutism with another. The physical images in South African theatre that I have discussed above are essential to this process. Each is essentially dialo-gical: a double-voiced play of opposites. They are ambiguous, ambiva-lent, often opaque but each demands an actively imaginative personal response from the spectator. Individual choices have to be made.

"I WILL REMAIN AN AFRICAN."[1]
AN INTERVIEW WITH MAISHE MAPONYA

Question: You are now a University Lecturer in Drama, how far has this changed your approach to drama?

Maponya: I'm not sure if it has changed my approach. What has changed is my process of creating, in that I no longer have enough time to actually create and to present things on stage. It has not changed the situation of the theatre in general in the country, my being here has not changed that, so things are just as normal as they were before, if ever they were normal. That's what the situation is like. One thing I would say, in terms of ideas, is that I think I am developing in the theatre quite a lot by being here, personally, but I do not know if it does very broadly address the issues on the ground, in terms of the practice of the theatre in this country.

Question: What do you think of the theatre which is being put on today in South Africa generally, at the Market Theatre, here at Wits and in the townships? What do you see as the most important developments?

Maponya: Well there are differences. Starting here at Wits, the one thing that one sees contributing, in a way, is that we are dealing with a wide range of genres, a wide range of material, and we are exposing the students to almost every facet of the theatre in the world. And therefore in that way it is very beneficial to actually continue and have some kind of experience and knowledge about the existence of all these kinds of cultures and histories and manners of performance.

Question: What is the proportion of black students at Wits in the Drama department?

Maponya: About 40% black and 60% white. We are moving radically to ensure that we represent the dynamics of this country and it's a very

[1] This interview with Maishe Maponya was given to Geoff Davis and Anne Fuchs at the University of the Witwatersrand, 10 September 1992.

12. Maishe Maponya in Paris, 1987. Photo: George Hallett.

difficult situation because we aim to take about 60% or 50% students being black. But we end up with a situation where students don't write exams at Matric level or they fail drastically and therefore you have very few numbers actually coming in for interviews and auditions and admissions. So we are disadvantaged at that level.

Question: In the townships are there any new names, new playwrights? How do you see the development of township theatre? Is there still a Black Consciousness element in township theatre or has it all become an imitation of *Sarafina*?

Maponya: That's a very heavy one. I know that the kind of Black Consciousness approach does not exist any more. If it does it's on the periphery. I somehow tend to think that there are no new names that are actually emerging. But that does not mean that they don't exist. I'm saying that there are no new names actually emerging, I mean such as ourselves (Matsemela,[2] myself), the Peter Ngwenyas in the townships; there have been one or two names like Job Kubatse and Ali Hlongwane, but in terms of writing new names are not actually coming up, and I think it has to do with the whole complexities of the nature of politics in this country, but also the issues of publication, publicity, the media. When plays take place in the township they don't get coverage now. And even in town where black journalists are supposed to be coming, it's very rare that they come to performances. I've just had a perform-ance of Lorraine Hansbury's *Raisin' in the Sun* and it was not reviewed by any black journalist. That's quite interesting and that means that if it takes place in town and black journalists don't even come to the city, they are even less likely to come to the township where there are no venues, where there's no comfort which they can enjoy. So that's the problem.

Question: What do you think about the Market Laboratory experi-ment?

Maponya: The Market Laboratory experiment is a good attempt but it has limitations in itself. The coordinators are making a very genuine and committed attempt to be able to draw people to come over. But because people have to come on their own volition, they are not bound

---

[2] Matsemela Manaka, Director of the Soyikwa Theatre Company.

by anything, they are not being supported even financially to actually get over to do works or to do exercises. That's what I seem to understand. It's very, very difficult for people to basically spend their whole time there. Unless people are from Natal as I've seen a number of other young fellows there that are learning the skills of acting. Difficult also because they have been disadvantaged educationally. That's some of the aspects we have to be talking about. But once they are disadvantaged educationally, then what we have to address is the issue of language and what languages do you use to be able to do those exercises that you are doing? And the performances that take place there are mainly "try-outs" where you have to bring your own cast, transport them over and then go there. The space is very bare, and the Laboratory doesn't do much to help you towards the creation of the set and all that so that you can be able to visualize things and relate to the props and the set on stage. You have to have that relationship as a character, as an actor with the costume, with the props, with the set. And therefore you find performances are still very, if one may use the term, 'amateurish'. Very often, you find that kind of performance taking place. And it's young people, probably trying to explore, trying to find ground for their own pieces and find an audience or a promoter for their own plays.

Question: Can I just ask you about English-language theatre? I know Matsemela wrote a play called *Koma* where he used many of the languages of South Africa. Do you see the future of English-language theatre in South Africa as changing in the near future?

Maponya: Well, I see yes, definitely changes in the theatre. It has always been changing. We have always used various languages, I mean I have used various languages in *Hungry Earth* and in a few other plays. Therefore the use of English in the theatre is definitely changing and also the use of English is slightly different from the formal use of the English language. Our use of English is filled with the African idiomatic expressions. It is used in a way that inspires us, in that we are inspired basically by our own cultural roots, by our heritage, and our languages are different and the word order is different; we find ourselves using English in that way but it always makes sense.

Question: But you don't see a greater development of theatre purely in African languages?

Maponya: Well that would depend on the activities of the practitioners in the respective regions, so that the Venda-speaking people in the Northern Transvaal or the Pedi-speaking in the Northern Transvaal would be able to develop those languages if they are exposed much to what is actually happening. And much of that is also going to depend on the cultural policy that is going to be implemented when the so-called and long-awaited new South Africa ever happens.

Question: Let's get back to your own work. The theatre in South Africa is in a state of transition and is going to depend on the future political situation. But even though you haven't got very much time at the moment, what kind of play would you like to write personally in the future? Have you any plans, projects? Which way do you think South African theatre should go? Or may go?

Maponya: I think the direction should basically be people doing theatre that speaks about them. Theatre that addresses issues that are related to them or affect them whether politically or otherwise. And those issues would actually affect us differently so we would actually express them very differently. I don't believe in the sense or notion of multiculturalism and non-racialism in the arts, in theatre; I definitely think that is just a myth that is being imposed upon us to be able to keep control over us or to make us lose ourselves in terms of our own identity. Yet at the same time it is for people to decide. If people feel they are non-racists or non-racialists it's up to them, let them get lost in their own way and I will remain an African, and that for me is what gives me strength. And in terms of addressing the issues in the theatre, I would then look at the subject matter that I'm going to be addressing in whatever play I would be doing; that would be based on my own personal experiences, my perception of life, my perception of the change that is taking place in this country. And therefore I would not lose myself because I have something that is very valuable that I would have to share with my children, would have to share with future generations. It's myself as an African. And that is very, very important.

Question: What about the form of your theatre? You have been using a Western, European form of theatre in the past. Does this mean that in the future you would use other forms of theatre rather?

Maponya: Obviously in the future and even now, other forms of theatre need to be considered. It depends on what is available, what we know about our own forms of theatre, about our own cultures. If one may say so here, the performance in the African concept, drama in the African concept, starts off with man's battle between nature and man. And if you deal with those aspects, you begin to deal with aspects of ritual. And from ritual you have an extension of the festival or celebration. And that continues on and on and you end up with what we would be calling theatre. It is our knowledge about the origins of those aspects of customs or rituals or ways of life that would influence our forms and the styles that we would be using in performance. The story-telling that we are dealing with (you know everyone keeps talking about story-telling), the oral traditions, we could fuse those with the Western, or, if you wish, other non-Western concepts of form, and that's how the Western tradition has always survived, it has also stolen from other cultures.

Question: What do you think about the Soweto dub poets, people who are using the oral tradition to give performances to large audiences today?

Maponya: What do I think about me? Because that's where I come from — some other poets actually copied from me.

Question: Do you consider this is theatre? I saw *Return the Drums* at Grahamstown in 1986 which was more or less the same thing, wasn't it?

Maponya: Except that in *Busang Meropa, Return the Drums*, the approach at that stage was slightly different from the dub poets. We tried to create a kind of theme around the renditions. We created situations within that whole performance and therefore in it was the whole element of drama as drama and, broadly, performance, and that's how *Busang Meropa* would actually differ from the other poets' work. The only problem with some young poets today, is that they lack a good sense of creativity, of the craft, of the use of language. We are obviously disadvantaged in that we are always reacting to the political situation, but we are also producing a kind of political rhetoric on stage. Largely because we are influenced by the political situation and therefore the creativity, the craft, suffers in this whole process. I think it's very important to bring that back.

Question: But if you think of the traditional oral poets they have always talked about politics, haven't they?

Maponya: But they have been very, very creative in their addressing of those issues. I can't think of an immediate example, but if I take five minutes I can draw you examples and indicate to you that this was always the case. And the poet in the traditional sense would be highly critical even if the poet was the chief's poet, or the nation's poet. They would also use innuendoes and they would use a language to be able to even criticize leadership in a way, and even comment on the way leadership is corrupt and all that. They would have that beauty of the language, without actually using political rhetoric and that is the difference between the poets then and the kind of poets now. We are influenced by the traditional poets; you will read that through one or two poems that I will give you that I have written recently.[3] You will pick those elements up: they are slightly rhetorical but there is a development here where I even become critical of the political strategies that we ourselves take. And in my writing now there's a sense of self-criticism so that I talk about "we" and if we are disadvantaged, I will say "we" are disadvantaged for these reasons, "we" are advantaged because of these reasons, "we" are insensible. I would not say "they" are insensible. I would use those terms.

Question: Over coffee you were talking about community theatre. About the development of theatre in the squatter camp situation. Could you perhaps say something about your involvement in that area?

Maponya: Yes, I have recently been involved in what is called "The Winterveld development programmes" out in the Winterveld in the Northern parts of Pretoria. The young people and the community there feel they need social recreation projects to relate to; amongst these would be drama or performance, and they had nothing immediately to relate to because they had not been exposed to drama or performance on stage. And a lot of them have actually lost the traditions which they don't know and don't understand. Whilst that's part of the rural area, it's also a squatter camp and they have lost that whole sense of their traditions of theatre and performance. So they are looking to

---

[3] See "Aimé Césaire" and "A New Chance" in: Geoffrey V. Davis (ed.) *Voyages and Explorations. South African Writing* (Amsterdam: Rodopi, 1994) *Matatu* 11, pp. 58 and 84–88.

people like myself and asking me to write plays for them or bring plays to them. There's a young group presently that's doing puppet shows; it is not a thing that they initiated themselves, they borrowed it or took the idea from what is called African Educational and Research Puppetry performance. They took that idea because they went to do some workshops with the leader, who is called Gary Friedman, and did some few performances and learned how to make masks and puppets. And so they've gone back to Winterveld and are trying to use that, I remember seeing that one of their proposals was that they become some kind of a puppet against Aids programme and I then said you can't say "puppet against Aids programme", because then you are limiting yourselves. You are saying you will be dealing with Aids and nothing else; so rather broaden it up and then deal with other things. So that's what's actually being done. We find that had to some extent disadvantages in that they are disadvantaged, but at least by doing performances and people appreciating their kind of engagement being able to create puppets, maybe people will learn and get inspired. Maybe that's important.

Question: What kind of people are members of such groups? Are they unemployed?

Maponya: Yes, they are all unemployed.

Question: I remember seeing years ago *Imfuduso* in Crossroads, in the squatter camp, which was a play developed by the women's committee and I think out of their own experience and not with outside help. Do you have groups that are putting something together without that kind of initiative being brought in from the outside?

Maponya: Yes, there are a number of groups that are doing that, but when we come to use our own judgment that's when we would say that some of them are not very much developed. You find lots of stereotypes in those performances. There's no development or even themes within the plays. Situations are not properly created contributing towards the broader theme. Largely because the people don't have the training. They don't have the skill, but at least it means there is something taking place. All it needs is for the policies of this country in the culture and arts to be able to address those imbalances and see how finally we can make contributions to develop those areas.

Question: That constitutes quite a good conclusion, but would you like to add something? To make a statement about theatre in South Africa at the moment or in the future?

Maponya: There is not much that I can say except that unless the disadvantaged black people, specifically black and Africans, realize their problems in this given situation in this country and begin to address those as Africans, or as black people, and deal with issues of identity, of definition of the self, rediscover themselves and deal with issues of critical consciousness and all those concepts, unless we get to that level, unless the young people get to that level, our future will always remain bleak in terms of how theatre and the arts and performance are going to develop — it will always be bleak, so it is a challenge for us. It does not help to basically make compromises even on issues which are a matter of life and death.

13. Zakes Mda in Paris (January 1993). Photo: George Hallett.

POLITICS AND THE THEATRE: CURRENT TRENDS IN SOUTH AFRICA

Zakes Mda

Art and Politics

When Albie Sachs (1990) made his controversial proposition that ANC members should be banned for five years from saying that culture is a weapon of struggle, he provoked a barrage of responses in the print media, and in seminars and conferences. This proposition, which stimulated so much unprecedented debate, was initially made by him in a paper titled "Preparing Ourselves for Freedom" which he presented at an in-house seminar on culture organized by the ANC in Lusaka in 1989. It reached South Africa through the pages of the *Weekly Mail*. His major concern was that the work of the artist had deteriorated to the levels of sloganeering, masquerading as art. He wrote:

> Instead of getting real criticism, we get solidarity criticism. Our artists are not pushed to improve the quality of their work, it is enough that it is politically correct. The more fists, and spears, and guns, the better. The range of themes is narrowed down so much that all that is funny or curious or genuinely tragic in the world is extruded.(20)

There were three strands that one could clearly observe in the responses that came, mostly from the artists themselves — or from cultural workers, as some artists prefer to be called — and from the critics. The first one, which articulated itself through the voices of such critics as Meintjies (1990), was in agreement with Sachs. Indeed, the voice said, sloganeering was a barrier to depth and genuine expression. Some other writers were cited, such as novelist Nadine Gordimer, Congress of South African Writers president Njabulo Ndebele and poet Chris van Wyk, who had on earlier occasions, long before Sachs's controversial paper, been crusading for an art that went beyond the knee-jerk responses to the hurt caused by apartheid. The voice went further to state that on the theatre-front practitioners such as actor/ director John Kani, worker-culture programmes director Ari Sitas, and arts editor Tyrone August, had long been complaining about the clichés and hackneyed approaches found in much of "protest" drama. Theatre practitioners who produced to a set formula were slammed for a lack of depth, since their work was "abounding in stereotypes, aimed more at overseas audiences than at the community at home." (34) A careful rider was added though that art could not "absolve itself from facing the ugly social realities of South Africa today." (31)

The second strand came from the militant cultural worker who insists that culture is a weapon of struggle, and as such it should be used. This artist does not apologize for sloganeering, for it is through slogans that the audiences are mobilized and rallied around a particular cause. The artist here does not pretend to be interested in creating works that will be of lasting value. He or she creates for the occasion, and the work may or may not live beyond the occasion. Indeed some writers got involved in a medium like theatre because they had a political agenda, and thought that theatre would be most effective in expressing their political ideas. We shall come back to this perspective when we examine the various categories of theatre that exist in South Africa.

The third strand was that of the "liberal" artist and critic, who read in Sachs's propositions a long-awaited admission from the saner ranks of the liberation movement that it had been detrimental to link art with politics. This was a position that asserted the autonomy and the permanence of the work of art, and the right of the artist as an individual to pursue his or her vision of the beautiful and the excellent without reference to ulterior ends (Brink 1991,1). This was an art for art's sake position, for it was emphatic in its assertion that the South African artist must create work that is not expected to, and indeed should not, be put to any practical use nor fulfil any ulterior function. Ahmed (1990) commented on this position and expressed the concerns of those who operated within cultural structures that espoused a different view, when he wrote:

> Liberals vociferously reaffirm their position — that they were right all along and that art must be divorced from politics. The paper [Sachs'] has caused some consternation within the mass-based progressive movement, where cultural workers (as Ari Sitas puts it) are worried that their work has been banal or even devoid of content (121).

It is clear that Sachs's concern in his original proposition was on quality, or lack of it, in the work of the constituency he was addressing. He had no intention of taking the "aesthetic position" in what Brink (1991, 1) calls "the immemorial debate between the aesthetic and the political." In an interview with a journal of South African cultural workers published in London Sachs says that he has been "praised for things I didn't say. I certainly don't believe you can ever separate art from politics, most definitely not in South Africa." (Langa 1990, 30).

The separation of art, and specifically of theatre, from politics is an illusive notion; and when one examines the different genres of theatre that exist in South Africa, it certainly has not been a factor in the production and enjoyment of the art in that country. It is generally taken for granted that the creator of theatre selects her or his material from life, and from his or her society. And of course South Africa is a society characterized by racial segregation, political oppression, and economic exploitation. South African theatre can never be abstracted from this particular context. The writer in South Africa, particularly the black writer, is not, to use Brink's (1991, 17) words, "writing about 'something out there' when he/she draws politics into the text: it is part and parcel of the most intimate experience of his/her daily life." Even an author like Athol Fugard, who is of a liberal tradition, and has on previous occasions incurred the wrath of the mass-based cultural movement when he stood as a lone voice that opposed the cultural boycott of South Africa, has unequivocally supported this view. In his graduation address on the receipt of an honorary degree at the University of the Witwatersrand he said that he was often inclined to forget just how politicized the South African environment was compared with most other "Western societies." He went further to say:

> When I am asked, for example, outside South Africa, about the relationship between politics and my play writing, I answer with total honesty that I don't really give the matter any thought. I point out that, as far as I am concerned, in the South African context the two are inseparable. I think of myself essentially as a story-teller, and as such, the notion that there could be such a thing as an apolitical South African story is a contradiction in terms. (Fugard 1992, 66)

I have said that art cannot be abstracted from its particular context, but the South African context is richer and more varied than the theatre has attempted to depict. For a long time now, a dominant trend in the types of theatre that exist in South Africa has been based on a unidimensional and prevaricated depiction of the South African reality. For example, the playwright wrote about those men who went to jail, and examined their sufferings and — in a later phase of his writing — their resistance. He told the story of those who laboured in the belly of the earth to make white South Africa rich. He clearly depicted their condition, their trials, their struggles, and in some cases their defiance and determination to change their situation. But he forgot to tell the story of those who did not follow them to jail or to the mines — the women and children who stayed at home and struggled to make the stubborn and barren soil yield.

The South Africa of this theatre was basically an urban and a male one. The observation that Ndebele (1984) made on South African literature in general, that the city had a tyrannical hold on the imagination of the average African writer, applied to theatre as well. Peasants and other rural dwellers were ignored as subjects of artistic attention. Once in a while, on very rare occasions, there would be a bright spark that would illuminate other aspects of the people's life, such as Gcina Mhlophe's (1988) *Have You Seen Zandile?*, an autobiographical two-hander that examined the life of a young woman growing up in rural South Africa. Other exceptions were *You Strike the Woman, You Strike the Rock* which examined the role that women played in the South African liberation struggle, and *Imfuduso*, which was on the question of forced removals, in this case at Crossroads squatter camp, Cape Town. It is significant that these plays were either wholly created (written, directed and performed) by women, as is the case with Mhlophe's play, or women played a major role in creating them.

Imfuduso was of special significance in that it was performed by the Crossroads women themselves, and depicted their own struggles in resisting forced removals. Generally the South African theatre practitioner shied away from depicting social and class conflicts among the oppressed themselves, and rarely did we see the family — even that one which has been broken down by the laws of apartheid — as a subject for his theatre.

It will be noted that I do not mention such plays as *Ipi Tombi* or *Kwa-Zulu*, which were set or partially set in the rural areas. These plays, conceived and produced by white entrepreneurs, never created or recreated any aspect of the South African reality, but were rooted in their own fantastical world. They were abortive attempts to glorify the government's Bantustan policies. As a result they never gained any popularity in South Africa, except with the white middle class and overseas tourists. One critic (Horn 1986, 213) referred to this as the Theatre of Exploitation, and has described it thus:

> A great emphasis was on spectacle and little on plot and character development; the values and mores of traditional African societies, often tempered by Christianity, are extolled, the material environments of such societies romanticized, and the rural setting demonstrated to be more congenial for blacks than that of the towns and cities.

This was a theatre of titillation, of the swinging pelvis and the tantalizing naked breast. It was a theatre of the perpetually happy native who sang and danced at the slightest provocation, particularly when he or she was in her or his natural idyllic rural environment. Love bloomed in these villages, birds sang, and maidens served their menfolk calabashes of beer against the background of bucolic sunsets and exotic lullabies. Rural poverty, unemployment, and sickness did not exist. The obvious conclusion that one was expected to draw was that apartheid or "separate development" with its Bantustan relocation policies was reasonable, humane and historically legitimate.

Alternative Theatre and Other Labels

South African theatre is not a homogenous monolith. It has trends and distinct categories whose social function is varied. What has been seen outside South Africa, touring European and American venues, represents only one or two categories of what makes South African theatre. Some scholars, such as Steadman (1984) and Angove (1992), have referred to the theatre that I will discuss in this paper as "alternative theatre."

It is a theatre, they say, which is revolutionary in nature, and challenges the established "white, heterosexual, culturally exclusive norms and values" (Angove 1992, 40). What this label implies is that in South Africa there are established theatrical traditions to which this theatre has emerged as an alternative. But we are not told what these established and acknowledged traditions are. There is an English South African theatre which has been, as Angove (1992, 41) points out, "characterized by a colonial mentality, still searching for and finding theatrical roots 'home' in England"; and a traditional Afrikaans theatre which has been rooted in the movement whose goal was to establish a body of Afrikaans literature that would enhance the Afrikaner identity. Both these two theatres were established and acknowledged in their respective communities. But this was by no means the theatre of the majority of the South African population. I certainly do not consider Gibson Kente's musical theatre, which for decades has enjoyed popular following throughout South Africa and has influenced at least two generations of theatre practitioners in that country, or Athol Fugard's erudite theatre, which also has its large following among the black intelligentsia and liberal white middle classes, as alternative to any other form of theatre that exists in South Africa today. The same applies to the pan-African theatre of Matsemela Manaka, the harrowing comedies and tragi-comedies of Paul Slabolepszy, the musicals of Mbongeni Ngema, the workshopped plays of Barney Simon, the political satires of Pieter-Dirk Uys, the work of the "young angry Afrikaners" such as Deon Opperman that holds the symbols of Afrikaner culture to ridicule, and the plays of Ronnie Govender that tell the story of the "Indian" people of South Africa. The work of all these playwrights and directors is not alternative, but representative of the different categories of the mainstream South African theatre.

The first category of South African theatre that I must briefly discuss is that of the indigenous modes of performance that are precolonial, but extant particularly in the rural areas of South Africa. These include praise performance poetry known as *dithoko* in Sesotho or *izibongo* in Zulu. It also includes dance performance modes such as *dipina tsa mokopu* in Sesotho which are performed at harvest time, and reflect the world in which girls and young women live, and the social relations in the village. Each ethnic group in South Africa has its own performance modes ranging from para-theatrical religious ritual to folk narratives that are performed by a single actor who assumes the roles of all the different characters in the play: the Zulu *inganekwane*, the Xhosa *intsomi*, and the Sotho *tŝomo*. All these modes have highly developed dramatic elements, and are gaining particular significance with the new popular theatre movement that I will discuss in the next section of this paper.

One major category of South African theatre that has been dominant for three decades, and has been popular throughout the country, is referred to by critics as Township Theatre. It is called that because it is rooted in the townships. It emanates from them and rarely emerges from township venues. The major practitioner in the genre is Gibson Kente who, since 1960, has created plays that have been performed by his traveling company even in the smallest towns of South Africa and neighbouring states such as Lesotho and Botswana. This theatre is characterized by the extensive use of music and dance. Kente is highly proficient in musical composition and in choreography. He is also credited with the invention of a peculiar style of acting which is full of energy and is spectacularly over-theatrical. It is a style characterized by bulging eyes, wide-open mouths, heavily punctuated dialogue, and exaggerated movements. Kente has been so much of a major force in South African theatre that many playwrights, actors and directors working in the theatre in South Africa today have at one stage worked under him. His method of acting has therefore diffused itself even in other categories of theatre that are not Township Theatre. One critic wrote:

> The approach worked well in the past when it had been creatively adapted for theatre and used in such plays as *Sarafina*, *Asinamali* and to an extent *Bopha!* Percy Mtwa, Mbongeni Ngema and even pop singer, Brenda Fassie, are all referred to as "Gibson [Kente's] Products". (Leshoai 1989, 6)

Township Theatre is very formulaic, and like the European and American melodrama of the 19th century it has its stock characters. In every play the audience would expect to see a dim-witted policeman, often brutal, a priest, a comical school teacher, a shebeen queen, a township gossip who is also a comic relief character, a diviner, a streetwise fast-talking hoodlum, and a beautiful "sexy" girl. The plot would involve a church service usually of the African independent churches known as Zionists, a wedding, a jail scene, and a funeral. There would be plenty of slapstick humour, and of weeping. The story would not be overtly political, except in rare cases such as in Kente's *Too Late*, *How Long*, and *I Believe*. Township Theatre dealt with the sensational side of life: prostitution, adultery, rape, and divorce. These themes were examined in a simplistic manner, which disregarded causality, and served on the whole to endorse and promote official values. Horn (1984) has this to say about this theatre:

> The narrowed and absolutist melodramatic vision also characterizes the plays of Gibson Kente, South Africa's most prominent black playwright-producer and one of the progenitors of the modern black urban theatre. In more than a score of plays for stage and television, Kente's argument has remained essentially the same: work within the system, get educated, reject temptation, maintain family cohesion, accumulate wealth through personal industry and, perhaps, encourage orderly reform — but never the radical revision of the existing scheme of things.

This critic has referred to this as the Theatre of Acceptance and Lament. It reached its peak of popularity throughout the 1970's, with long running productions by such playwrights as Sam Mhangwane (*Unfaithful Woman, Ma-in-Law*) and Boikie Mohlamme (*Mahlomola*) touring the townships throughout Southern Africa. Today the popularity of Township Theatre has tremendously waned, although its impact continues to be strong in the current trends.

Another category of South African theatre has been referred to, for want of a better name, as Town Theatre. It is called that because it is performed in purpose-built city venues, and rarely does it go to the townships. This is the kind of theatre whose main focus is on the production of a creative product, rather than on consumption. It is therefore an erudite theatre that employs theatrical codes that need a more intellectual interpretation than does Township Theatre. Town Theatre is created by both black and white intermediate classes, whereas Township Theatre is created solely by black practitioners who run commercial theatre companies. Town Theatre is based on traditional Western models in form, or on more experimental international modes, although the content is South African.

Township Theatre on the other hand is highly syncretic, using both popular indigenous African modes and Western ones. In most cases Town Theatre will deal with political themes, and when it does it becomes a "protest theatre". It is important to note how the phrase "protest theatre" is used here. There has been a tendency in the South African media to refer to any play that treats political themes as "protest." Not all political theatre is protest theatre. Least of all, agitprop cannot be protest. That would be a contradiction in terms. Protest theatre makes a statement of disapproval or disagreement, but does not go beyond that. It addresses itself to the oppressor, with the view of appealing to his conscience. It is a theatre of complaint, or sometimes even of weeping. It is variously a theatre of self- pity, of moralizing, of mourning, and of hopelessness. It never offers any solution beyond the depiction of the sad situation in which the people find themselves. An example of this category can be found in a number of Athol Fugard's plays, particularly his earlier works, including those he jointly created with black actors such as The Serpent Players, John Kani and Winston Ntshona. His plays have depicted various aspects of segregation in South Africa, such as the Immorality Act in *Statements*, racial classification in *The Blood Knot*, and the Group Areas Act in *Boesman and Lena*. These plays clearly protest against racial segregation by depicting its inhuman nature. But these works have some prevarications in their depiction of the South African reality. The oppressed suffer in silence and are not involved in any struggle against the oppression. Instead they are endowed with endless reservoirs of stoic endurance. The spirit of defiance that exists in the real life situation is non-existent in these works. When one has seen a play like *Boesman and Lena*, and one is not at all familiar with the situation in South Africa, and with the fact that people in South Africa have struggled and fought against oppression in different ways, one is left with the impression that the blacks really deserve to be oppressed, for they let oppression happen to them.

Fugard, like Kente, has had a big impact on South African theatre. His theatre, and that of a number of Town Theatre practitioners such as Barney Simon, has been seen a great deal in American and European venues. Inside South Africa a number of practitioners of all races were influenced by Fugard, and also by Simon.

Some theatre practitioners in South Africa went beyond protest, a position which began with the advent of the Black Consciousness movement in the 1970's. The case against protest theatre was that by its nature it attempted to reveal the blacks to the whites, and placed the onus on the blacks to prove their humanity. The theatre practitioner was no longer interested in creating a theatre of complaint. This position gained momentum in the early 1980's. It is during this period that the Theatre of Resistance, which was quite distinct from the protest of Town Theatre, gained a mass following and became the main genre with practitioners from all the ideological leanings in the South African liberation politics spectrum. Whereas protest theatre addressed itself to the oppressor, this new theatre addressed itself directly to the oppressed with the overt aim of rallying or of mobilizing the oppressed to explore ways and means of fighting against the oppression. It was agitprop, for it attempted to propagate a message, and agitate for action on the part of the oppressed to change their situation. It was a theatre which, at its best, served as a vehicle for sharing perceptions and insights among the oppressed themselves, and more importantly which attempted to alter perceptions. At its worst it became a litany of slogans that denounced the oppressor, and extolled the virtues and prowess of the leaders of the liberation struggle.

Matsemela Manaka was one of the more creative practitioners of Theatre of Resistance. His play, *Egoli* (1979), was well-received when it opened at the People's Space Theatre in Cape Town under the directorship of Rob Amato. The play is set in the hostel of a male workers' compound at a gold mine. It centres around the relationship between, and the experiences of, two migrant workers. It has sharp, short scenes, each, according to Larlham (1985, 86), "a heightened poetic image of the workers' experience, past and present." Larlham goes further to say:

> These sequences, metaphors for the plight of the Black man, contain little realistic dialogue. The violent ritual removal of the shackles, for example, is accompanied by a chant, "people share Egoli ["city of gold" (Johannesburg)], people die Egoli," and a song "How we fight for my freedom." Once they are freed, Hamilton [one of the characters] makes an invocation for positive action: "Now that you are free do not wait for life to happen to you — make it happen." This is followed by a song of hope. (87)

The setting of *Egoli* is stark, and the play depends very much on dream sequences, rôle-play, and flashbacks. It is highly stylized rather than naturalistic, and sets and props are sparsely used. It is a theatre that depends more on human resources rather than on the paraphernalia of the stage. This became the common method of staging with all the Theatre of Resistance that followed. Of course the stark and sparse stage was not Manaka's invention. Fugard used it. And so did Jerzy Grotowski in Europe. Another example of this genre is *Asinamali* by Mbongeni Ngema.

Whereas Township Theatre was confined to the townships and Town Theatre kept itself in the purpose-built city venues,[1] Theatre of Resistance — which has been called the Theatre of Criticism and Confrontation by Horn (1986, 213) — crossed barriers, and was seen at weddings and funerals, at political rallies, in church and school halls in the townships, and in city venues such as the Market Theatre. It even took over from Town Theatre as South Africa's main theatre export.

By the late 1980's Theatre of Resistance had become the dominant genre in South Africa, and very little was being heard of Township Theatre. A great number of the practitioners who used to produce Township Theatre adopted Theatre of Resistance. It became a powerful political weapon which was promoted by the mass-based political

---

[1] There are only two recorded occasions when Township Theatre plays were performed in the city venues before white audiences (Larlham 1985, 70). Kente's *How Long* was seen at the Lyric Theatre in Durban in 1975, and *Mama and the Load*, also by Kente, at the Market Theatre in Johannesburg in 1980.

movement that was active inside the country at the time. As Fugard (1992, 2) says: "the drama on the streets [was] being so immediately reflected by the drama on the stage." However the unfortunate development at this time, which continues to this day, was that the "resistance" in these plays was only in content, and not in function. With the opening of city venues to all races, there was a movement of theatre production away from the people in the township. In the heyday of Township Theatre people in the townships had access to theatre, for it was performed in their midst in township venues. It was not unusual for a labourer who had been digging trenches on the road all day to go and see a Kente play at Diepkloof Hall in the evening. Theatre was not an elitist activity as it has become in the Western world. The irony of it all was that the more the theatre became radical in South Africa, the more it became revolutionary in content, the more it moved away from the people. By 1990 almost all relevant theatre of the Theatre of Resistance category was performed only in city venues, and the audiences were white liberals and sprinklings of members of the black middle class who could afford to drive to these expensive venues. There were a few groups that would begin their work in the township. But even these aspired to be in the city venues, and would indeed end up there when they got the necessary recognition from the white managed theatre establishments. The establishments would then re-shape these productions, and add the essential slickness, in readiness for the export market. Those members of the working class who used to enjoy theatre were now deprived of it. They could not afford to travel to the city in the evenings to see a play. Besides transport problems, ticket prices were prohibitive. Politically committed groups like the Cape Flats Players, however, before they took their Theatre of Resistance plays to the Baxter Theatre in Cape Town, would tour some of the most marginalized areas in the Western Cape. Thamm (1989, 25) reports that over the years the group's productions, which include *Inkululeko Ngoku — Freedom Now!*, *Senzenina?*, *Aluta Continua*, *Dit Sal Die Blerrie Dag Wees*, and *What About De Lo*, have been seen by over 600,000 people from the remotest villages to major city centres. The Cape Flats Players were an exception rather than the rule. Other exceptions were groups like Gamakhulu Diniso's Busang-Takaneng; and other township community and youth club groups such as Nyanga Theatre Group in Cape Town and Sabata Sesiu's groups, which continued to create Theatre for Resistance in ill-equipped buildings in the townships.

A further irony was that the opening of city venues to all races took the theatre away from the people. In the heyday of apartheid, when these city venues were closed to black people, theatre was with the people in the townships. Today it is the ambition of most play-wrights to have a play at the Market Theatre, and then of course in Europe and America. Writers now write purely for export, and design their plays in a manner which they think will be acceptable to overseas audiences. A critic wrote of one of such plays:

> This brings one to the core of the problem in *Sarafina* [by Mbongeni Ngema]. With its bowler hats and designer glam-our, it is earmarked: export. While extremely informative to Broadway audiences, to local audiences it states the familiar and obvious, giving it a simplistic and superficial quality that demeans the events being dealt with. (le Roux 1989)

Although Ngema's work plays to full houses at the Market Theatre (I counted an audience that was 96% white at one perform-ance, and this was quite normal for this venue even for those plays that are regarded as "black"), the South African critics have not been kind to him. Barry Ronge (1990, 15) of the *Sunday Times* says Ngema's work, with the single exception of *Asinamali*, is trite. He says a play like *Township Fever*, for instance, lacks dramatic substance, effective char-acterization, intellectual complexity, and subtle acting: "It is so naively poor, yet so richly opportunistic that it simply outraged me." Another critic, Rina Minervini (1990, 8) says the play is likely to engender more critical enthusiasm on Broadway than in Johannesburg. Ngema, she says, uses images that have long lost their theatrical currency in South Africa because the *toyi-toyi*, the raised fist and "*Amandla!*" will still thrill a New York audience. If Ronge and Minervini are representative of the white liberal press, the black press is even more scathing. Nyantsumba (1991, 68) writes that commercialization and commercial-ism have reduced black South African theatre to a predictable and woefully disappointing parochial art. We are fast reaching a stage where there is no art in local black theatre, but an assemblage of familiar anti-apartheid signs, images and slogans which appeal only to one's emotions. These unfortunately are plays that go on to win award after award in Europe and the US, and all because they so predictably deliver that anti-apartheid message people overseas yearn to hear.

This critic goes further to say that *Sarafina* was a commercial success but certainly not an artistic success: the play was well-directed and meticulously choreographed, but lacked both plot and main theme.

One very significant factor about the work of Mbongeni Ngema is that it has successfully combined the elements of Township Theatre with those of Theatre of Resistance. He considers his work as falling into a new category which he calls Theatre of Liberation. He says that Theatre of Liberation is a more useful and inspirational alternative to protest theatre. Such theatre, he says, strives to free the audience from the psychological legacy of oppression; and the success of *Sarafina* was due to its accent on liberation (Wren 1990, 28). Alas, the audiences that were liberated from the "psychological legacy of oppression" were not those from the townships and rural areas who form the vast majority of the oppressed in South Africa, for they never saw the play.

I have often come across the question from overseas audiences, "If the South African regime is so oppressive, how come these plays are allowed to go on?" The answer, of course, is that although these plays are militant in content, they are quite harmless to the regime since they are performed at venues whose majority patronage is that of white liberals ("preaching to the converted" the saying goes in South Africa). They do not reach the real people who are capable of taking revolutionary action after being rallied and mobilized by the works. Theatre practitioners who operate at grassroots level are always harassed by the state, and even arrested. For quite some time the state machinery of censorship has been erratic and bungling. But even the censor was smart enough to realize that the fact that these works were confined to special venues in the city, and then were exported abroad, could actually do more good for the South African government than harm. For instance, they have created a false illusion of a democratic environment, with healthy dosages of freedom of expression, that supposedly exist in South Africa, where the government can be criticized so vehemently, yet the works continue to be staged. Whereas the government has not hesitated to take immediate and overt action against grassroots theatrical operations, covert action has been taken against targeted performers even in city venues. For instance Potgieter (1992, 5) of the *Sunday Times* uncovered a unit run jointly by the South African Defence Force and the Johannesburg City Council. Among its projects was to assault actors André-Jacques van der Merwe and André Lombard who were taking part in an anti-war play, *Somewhere on the Border*. All these plans were made at the SADF headquarters in Pretoria, at the time when the "anti-conscription fever" was mounting. The objective was to stop the production. This was the same covert unit which disrupted and teargassed a concert by singer Jennifer Fergusson at the Market Theatre.

Current Trends

The sudden changes that happened in 1990, the release of the political leaders from prison, the unbanning of the liberation movements, the negotiations, the rise and fall of CODESA (which, according to Karon (1992, 30), has achieved the comical status in South Africa which former Vice-President Dan Quayle enjoyed in the US, judging by the number of comic references to it), caught the Theatre of Resistance practitioner off-guard. These events happened so unexpectedly that he or she is at a loss for words. The type of practitioner who depended on sloganeering does not know yet what new slogans to shout. The situation that obtained before these drastic changes had provided him or her with all the ready-made plots, and even all the ready-made dialogue. There is now some silence, perhaps momentarily so, in the Theatre of Resistance front, until the practitioner finds a new voice with which to respond to the new situation.

   In 1992 a new type of informal theatre that is performed in the streets has emerged. This is in the form of mock trials that are staged at political rallies in Cape Town, Johannesburg and other cities. A courtroom situation is recreated, and actors assume roles of judges, prosecutors, accused, and witnesses. Sometimes they wear masks that are caricatural of the characters they portray. In the course of the trial there will be flashbacks, re-enacted by other actors, of the events that unfold in the evidence that is presented by the witnesses. There is always song and dance in these re-enactments. It must be noted that the performers of this drama are not professional actors at all, but ordinary members of the audience: that is, participants in the political rally. According to Rickard (1992, 5) of the *Weekly Mail* these mock trials feature on the mass action programme organized by the African National Congress and its allies in several regions. President F.W. de Klerk and KwaZulu Chief Minister Mangosuthu Buthelezi head the list of the most popular choice of "accused" to be tried. Inkatha has vehemently complained about these trials, and has referred one such trial in Pietermaritzburg to the National Peace Committee as a violation of the Peace Accord. They say that this theatre fuels the forces of confrontation rather than negotiation. ANC supporters, on the other hand, claim that such trials express people's anger that nothing is done to bring serious criminals to justice, and to stop the violence. Although the ANC insists that these trials are legitimate protest, it has however amended its mass action code of conduct by ruling it inappropriate for "death sentences, life sentences or any prison sentence to be passed at mock trials if the organization is to achieve its objectives of peace and democracy" (*Sunday Star*, 1992, 4).

While the "masses" are performing their theatre in the streets, the city venues that used to flourish with local productions have gone dry of both local plays and audiences. Another factor which has led to this drought is lack of funding. John Gaunt, a consultant of the Standard Bank, which has been one of the leading public sector corporations that have funded the arts, says that funding of the arts, whether from private or public sources, is under pressure. This is because of recession, and because social priorities have changed: the arts "would have to take a back seat to issues such as education and housing." (Daniel 1992a, 38). International donors as well have shifted their focus to "developmental" issues. Theatre, they say, served its purpose when the people did not have other channels for expressing themselves.

The city venues are now finding it more profitable to produce plays from the mainstream British and US theatres. Running in Cape Town at the time of writing this paper are *Educating Rita* at the Baxter Theatre, and *A Chorus Line* at the Nico Malan Theatre. The latter musical is lent "an air of Broadway authenticity" by its cast of American singers and dancers. The production attracts huge audiences, and according to one critic it is "as slick, glitzy and corny as you'd expect it to be". (Thamm 1992, 40) At the Market Theatre Ariel Dorfman's *Death and the Maiden*, set in post-Pinochet Chile and dealing with the theme of reconciliation, vengeance and justice, is running. The Dance Theatre of Harlem is performing at the Johannesburg Civic Theatre, with the endorsement of the ANC, the PAC, and the Performing Arts Workers' Equity (PAWE). However some artists have objected that vast amounts of money have been spent to make this tour possible. They consider the spending an iniquitous extravagance at the time when the entertainment industry in South Africa is in a crisis. A petition was drawn up to protest against the tour. The Dance Theatre of Harlem was endorsed by many organizations because of their "impressive outreach program" that would benefit South African dancers (Daniel 1992b, 22 & 24) The proliferation of overseas theatrical productions, either in the form of property (as in the case of Dorfman's play) or as a finished pre-packaged product (the Harlem dancers) is made possible by the fact that the ANC lifted the cultural boycott, even though AZAPO and the PAC have objected to that action.

In spite of all these problems, 1 do not agree with those who feel that South African theatre is now in the doldrums, or has breathed its last with the demise of the old order. The death of apartheid will also be the death of South African theatre only if your view of South African theatre is limited to that category of theatre that emanated from the Market Theatre and other similar venues: the Theatre of Resistance, or even the Town Theatre protest variety. But South African theatre is more varied than that. For instance, for a number of years now the Organic Workers Theatre has been gaining momentum. This came about as a cultural initiative of the labour movement. Worker plays are produced by the workers themselves, and in many cases deal with shop floor issues. When they do, they are usually created for specific in-house performances during meetings and workshops. However some plays are large-scale, and are created for a wider audience. They deal not only with labour issues, but with other related social and political themes. Both the performers and audiences are working class, and the plays themselves analyse the conditions of exploitation, and make the necessary connection between the work place and the community experiences. Ari Sitas, Nise Malange, Mi Hlatshwayo, and other activists from the Culture and Working Life Project in Natal have been very active in the promotion of the Organic Workers Theatre. Organizations like the Community Arts Project in Cape Town have conducted many courses and workshops on theatre skills for theatre workers from the Congress of South African Trade Unions.

Another movement is that of Theatre for Development. The concept is an old one in Latin America and in other parts of Africa, but in South Africa it is only just beginning. Basically the main objective is to use the people's own performance modes, such as those discussed earlier in this paper, to create community dialogue particularly in the rural areas (which have been ignored and neglected even by the liberation movements) and in the marginalized urban slums, so that participants may, through theatre, create their own messages on the issues that concern them, and possibly work out their own solutions. This type of theatre is anti-agitprop since its emphasis is on utilizing theatre as a vehicle for critical analysis, which in turn will result in critical awareness, or conscientization.

The process of conscientization involves the active participation of the people in transforming themselves by engaging in a dialogue through which they identify their problems, reflect on why the problems exist, and take action to solve the problems. Theatre practitioners, who are called catalysts in this process, do not create theatre for the people, but with the people. Catalysts go through the process of information gathering in the target communities, information analysis, story improvisation, rehearsals, community performances, community discussions, and follow-up action. Community members are involved throughout this process.

People are therefore able to identify their problems within the context of a particular social order, and the theatre provides the means to codify that social reality. This is the theatre that provides the "new language" that Meintjies (1990, 30) was concerned about when he wrote: "The priority [during the culture of resistance era] was to rouse and embolden the oppressed. Now we need a new language, one imbued with promotion of life, a celebration of democracy building on creative grassroots energy."

By 1974 Theatre for Development was wide-spread in neighbouring countries like Botswana. In South Africa, however, it has only become popular after the 1990 political changes. It must be mentioned, though, that for a number of years before that organizations such as the Afrika Cultural Centre under the leadership of Benjy Francis and the Soyikwa Institute of African Theatre have been exploring, and indeed utilizing, some of the methods of Theatre for Development. The subject was even included in their training programmes.

An earlier attempt at producing a Theatre for Development play, although the author did not call it that, was *Koma*, a dramatic and musical piece on literacy by the highly prolific and proficient playwright, Matsemela Manaka. However, unlike in Theatre for Development, the play did not give the target audiences the means of production of the theatre, since they were not involved in its creation, and therefore in the creation and distribution of the message. I will make a more detailed appraisal of this play — which I have not done for any other play discussed in this paper — because I place great import on the correct methodology of Theatre for Development and on the role this genre will play in a future South Africa.

The intention of *Koma* is not to use theatre as a methodology for teaching the target audiences the skills of reading and writing, but to motivate them to participate in literacy programmes. Manaka took his play into the rural areas, where it was performed under the trees at village meeting-posts, at the markets, and at village schools. In this respect it did what Theatre for Development is supposed to do.

The play opens with a poetic but romantic view of Africa

> When Africa was Africa
> Black was the only colour
> And all was perfect

This is followed by a beautiful song lamenting the lost culture. However right from the beginning the message of the poetry is lost to the rural audience since the linguistic codes he employs are not commonly shared by the performers and the audiences. Manaka is not unaware of the language problem, for Hadland (1988, 27) says:

> By using four languages in the play: Pedi, Southern Sotho, Zulu and English, Manaka believes he has to some extent adhered to Nigerian (sic) writer Ngugi wa Thiong'o's plea to write in indigenous African languages. "But the point has its limitations," he says. "In looking at post-apartheid society which language is non-racial?"

Indeed the play indicates that this question has not been resolved for the bulk of it is in English. Only a few phrases are in Pedi, Sotho or Zulu. The fact that most of the songs are in the three African languages does not contribute much in decoding the message since most of the messages are encoded in the English dialogue, and in other visual references that convey dramatic information.

The play proceeds to an exchange between two lovers, and this sets the conflict. The exchange is in English, and there is no doubt that Manaka is a proficient weaver of words who has also mastered the aesthetic staging techniques of the theatre. However here also it is doubtful if the codes he employs are shared by the target community. The aesthetic codes, for instance, are those that have elements that mystify theatre and put it beyond the realm of the rural community. Rural communities, it must be remembered, have their own codes that are highly aesthetic.

This scene is followed by a telephone conversation between Ntombefuthi (one of the lovers who is a major character in the play) and her uncle. He wants her to go home to the village to help him count his cattle. There is the intrapersonal conflict as to whether she should go count cattle in the village or teach literacy skills in the hostels. Her mother also does not understand what she is doing with books since she long finished school. People from the village come to fetch her to count her uncle's cattle; at the same time the local church minister also comes to persuade her through prayer. But she leaves in the middle of the hymn, and her mother remains weeping.

The scene moves to the hostel where enthusiastic inmates attend night school and learn to read and write from Ntombefuthi. They no longer stay idle during their leisure time, and can now also sign their names. However, it is a communal life in the hostel. While other men are busy reading and studying, there are those who are dancing, shouting, watching television, and playing their guitars. In spite of the din, those who are keen to learn persevere, and manage to write such words as UKUFUNDA (to read or to learn), due to Ntombefuthi's dedication. Later the hostel inmates are told that Ntombefuthi is going to leave them to count her uncle's cattle. However, she has founded a music group for them and they are going to learn to read and write through music. The band assembles and plays very good jazz. Ntombefuthi enters and works at her books while the band plays. Her hostel students enter to join the jazz band, but using their own instruments such as the *mbira* and an old acoustic guitar. Western musical instruments and indigenous ones all join together to produce music.

Throughout this performance the only active audience participation is when they clap hands to show their approval and enjoyment of the well-executed performances such as those of the hostel dancers during the joint music session. During this dance Ntombefuthi keeps her superior aloofness, then condescendingly joins the dance from the sidelines. She requests the band to play a particular song, and gives her hostel students papers from which they read the lyrics. They master these at once, throw away the papers, and sing in Sesotho that education is the wealth of the nation, and "forward with adult education."

Although *Koma* is a brilliant play in its mastery of the techniques of theatre, as Theatre for Development it is not effective since it needs an audience schooled in the modes of Western theatre to decode the messages. The target audiences, however, are the rural communities who are schooled in the ways of production and enjoyment of their own popular performance modes. The play itself is centred around the struggles of hostel dwellers in the city, and does not relate these to the life of the rural communities where the performances are targeted — besides the question of counting cattle.

Writing on Kenya's Kamiriithu Project, Ngugi wa Mirii (1980, 55) says:

> It is not possible to discuss any educational content without seeing it in the context of the social/economic structure which gives rise to it and which in turn it reflects. This is particularly true in adult literacy.

Koma does not examine literacy in the context of the rural people's experience. It is therefore doubtful if the creators of the play went through the information gathering stage in the target areas, nor did they assess the needs of these communities. As for the migrant workers in the hostels, it is not clear from what class position their needs were defined. The play does not reflect that they were defined at all, because the literacy content depicted in the play is not the needs and problems of the community people, and their everyday life struggles, but the poetry of intellectual authors such as Don Mattera, Njabulo Ndebele and Es'kia Mphahlele. Literacy is not only the acquisition of the skills of writing and reading, but the literacy content itself is part of education to mould a certain consciousness about people's struggle in society. Content by intellectuals who write in English, however relevant and politically "correct" it may be, becomes meaningless to people who cannot understand that language, and the theatrical codes employed to convey that content.

However, the major point is the lack of audience participation in the theatre of *Koma*. Although there is some follow-up action in that, according to Hadland (1988, 55), "wherever the play goes, it will be followed by a pile of cost-price books supplied by five South African publishers: AD Donker, Ravan Press, Skotaville, David Philip and Heinemann," its method lacks a participatory approach. At best it becomes diffusionist since it reflects a classic situation where an external superior agent goes out to persuade the rural communities to adopt innovations. In this case people become mere consumers of messages, since they are not involved in their creation. They are not involved in the process of a critical analysis of their problems, and of working out their own solutions. After the performance they remain without any critical awareness of their objective situation since conscientization did not happen. *Koma*, like a lot of Theatre for Development programmes in Africa today, is an example of an élitist concept of theatre rather than a democratic and participatory one.

There are two other projects that attempt to utilize the methods of Theatre for Development in Johannesburg. Both of them are works-in-progress at the time of writing this paper. One is operated by the

Department of Arts and Culture of the ANC, who invited an eminent director from Sweden, Teresa Devant, to hold workshops for their members who come from different regions of South Africa. Devant's workshops will result in a play created by the cast, the objective of which is to educate the communities on the meaning of elections and on voting procedures. Another project with a similar mission is sponsored by Matla Trust, an organization devoted to the promotion of democracy through education. Matla Trust commissioned three theatre practitioners, Peter Ngwenya, Doreen Mazibuko and Willie Tshaka to develop a play that will tour nationally and teach "the masses" about voting and democracy. But this effort is flawed in that it does not involve the target communities in any process of critical analysis. The same can be said of the ANC project if the group that is being trained by Devant will produce a play that will tour the communities as a finished product. However, if the participants return to their regions, and use the skills they have acquired from Devant's workshops to create plays with the active participation of community members, utilizing the communities' own performance modes, then a truly conscientizing theatre will be achieved. The Matla Trust project has been criticized for failing "to enlist the help of grassroots theatre groups, which could help play a vital role in entrenching democracy in communities." (*New Nation* 1992a, 10)

It would be wrong to leave the reader with the impression that with the advent of a new political dispensation there is absolutely no new South African theatre being produced at city venues. Manaka's work, for instance, has developed in a new direction which he calls Functional Theatre. Through it he attempts to promote African culture, and the products of that culture. His play, *Blues Afrika Café*, is set in a restaurant, and African food is actually served to the audience. This is not some variety of dinner theatre. The restaurant, the food, the people who serve it, and even the audience, are an integral part of the plot. Another play is *Ekhaya* which serves to promote the appreciation of visual arts. Here too the artists and the actual paintings in the play are an integral part of the plot. Although this theatre is performed at the Market Theatre, *Ekhaya* led to his opening a museum and art gallery of the same name in the township of Diepkloof.

Stalwarts like Ronnie Govender who have consistently produced works of quality continue to write. His play, *At the Edge*, was produced at the Baxter Theatre in Cape Town, and later performed at the 1991 Edinburgh Fringe Festival. It is a one-man play performed by Pat Pillai, and is set in Cato Manor where 180,000 people were moved to matchbox homes in make-shift ghettos when that township was declared a white group area in 1958. The play is a worthy addition to the "removals theatre"; those plays of varying merit that look nostalgically at life in the townships where people were forcibly removed. These include *Sophiatown* by the Junction Avenue Theatre Company, *Kofifi* by Sol Rachilo, *Buckingham Palace District Six* by Richard Rive, and *District Six the Musical* by David Kramer and Taliep Peterson.

Govender's work has gone unrecognized and unacknowledged in South Africa. The Edinburgh Fringe Festival programme notes of *At the Edge* claim that his relative obscurity has been largely self-imposed because of his refusal to export his work and to appear on South African television and national festivals in support of the cultural boycott. This may be so, although there are many theatre practitioners who have refused to appear on SABC but who are better known than Govender. So, that is not the main reason. The main reason is that Govender is too good to be famous. He does not follow a formula that is proven to "sell plays," but his style is highly creative and innovative. At the time when it was the popular thing to shout slogans, his theatre remained rhetoric-free. His is the same fate that befell another playwright, Dukuza ka Macu, who remains unknown in South Africa despite his highly talented and innovative work; and Saira Essa whose pioneering work at her Upstairs Theatre in Durban is known only to a small group of ardent followers.

In conclusion, I must discuss briefly the latest trend in South African theatre, that of Theatre of Reconciliation. Angove (1992, 44) says the Theatre of Reconciliation gives a perspective "in which the reality of a polarized society is defied to present human beings from all racial and cultural groups, communicating, sharing and understanding." She goes further to explain that this is not a theatre devoid of fear, insecurity and introspection. It, however, aims to depict that there are possible solutions to the status quo, "and transcends present reality to display to its audience a potential South Africa."

Fugard's (1992) play, *Playland*, falls in this category. The play was inspired by a picture of white soldiers dumping bodies of SWAPO guerrilla fighters into a mass grave. The play centres around a white ex-soldier who had participated in the "extermination" of SWAPO guerrillas, and a black night (and day) watchman who had also found that murder was the only option, after his dignity had been violated by the rape of his fiancee by her white master. The setting is a travelling amusement park.

According to *New Nation* (1992b, 13) *Playland* is "a play that strives to retrieve the humanity of a people for whom violence has become a way of life." Fugard says that as a white South African he had become increasingly aware of the need to address the violence of the past. He says, "The play states my innate faith in the fundamental goodness of human nature. If a man is honest enough to confront his soul and ask for forgiveness, I believe the miracle can happen." (*Tonight!* 1992, 1)

It may be interesting to note that whereas the play was received with great enthusiasm by white critics, it received mixed reviews from black critics. At the performance I attended I counted an audience of more than three hundred people, of whom only three were black. Barry Ronge (1992, 17) of the *Sunday Times* called the play a landmark in the history of South African theatre. It is, he said, the most significant work Fugard has done in decades, and it comes at a time when the South African playwright has been fumbling about looking for new structures and ideas to express a new society. He added: "It is a play about redemption and forgiveness, which in this time of hatred felt like a cool, healing balm." The unnamed critic of *New Nation* (1992c, 12) saw it differently. He said that the preoccupation with the issues of forgiveness and reconciliation in recent plays on the South African stage offered short-lived insights limited by sectarian interests. He listed a number of plays on reconciliation, including *Playland*, that do not appear to address the crucial issue that justice had to be the basis for any discussion of guilt and atonement. *Playland* particularly, he said, does not contribute to the national debate on justice. Fugard situates the debate at a personal level. It is for his personal peace that the SADF man who fought SWAPO and abused black people as a way of life needs forgiveness. "In telling contrast, the sympathetic black murderer was tried and sentenced for his crime — but there is no suggestion that the ex-soldier should face criminal procedures (sic)." This critic says the common feature of the Theatre of Reconciliation is its silence on history. He says:

> There is never an explanation why we need reconciliation. Instead of explaining how we got here, the accent is on South Africa being a polarized society. Silence on our history makes it impossible to answer the question: on whose terms must forgiveness be granted?

The critic from another black newspaper, *City Press*, was more concerned with the depiction of the Afrikaner in the play. While praising it as a "moving tragi-comedy," he complains that South African theatre is "filled with stereotypic images of Afrikaners," while English whites also enlist in the SADF. (Pemba 1992, 16)

It is clear from these comments that as long as the question of justice has not been addressed by the political structures, a true Theatre of Reconciliation will not emerge in South Africa.

A Final Thought

The theatre of the élites — and all the other performance modes that reflect South Africa's cultural diversity — should, by all means, continue in the city venues, for it services its particular audience. Also there is no doubt that some of the productions that were exported did serve the important function of keeping South Africa on the agenda, and of sensitizing the international community to the injustices in the country. I, however, find both the Organic Workers Theatre and the Theatre for Development movements the most relevant for a future South Africa, since this is theatre that is rooted with the people in the marginalized rural areas and urban slums. Theatre for Development is the theatre of the illiterate, since in it there is no dramatic text that acts as a referent for the performance text. Workers and peasants together form the vast majority of the population of South Africa. Of necessity a truly South African theatre will not be that which is the sole privilege of the dominant classes, but that in which peasants and workers are active participants in its production and enjoyment. A theatre of the majority will not pander to the tastes of West End and Broadway audiences.

REFERENCES

Ahmed, Junaid (1990) "Culture in South Africa: the challenge of transformation," *Spring is Rebellious* (eds. Ingrid de Kok and Karen Press) Cape Town: Buchu Books

Angove, Coleen (1992) "Alternative theater: reflecting a multi-racial South African society?" *Theater Research International* 17, 1

Brink, André (1991) "Towards a redefinition of aesthetics," unpublished paper presented at the *New Nation's* Writer's Conference, December

Daniel, Raeford (1992a) "Arts funding under pressure," *Weekly Mail*, March 13 to 19

Daniel, Raeford (1992b) "Chorus of approval for Harlem dancers," *Weekly Mail*, August 7 to 13

Fugard, Athol (1992) *Playland and other works*, Johannesburg: Witwatersrand University Press

Hadland, Adrian (1988) "Learning to read Africa's wisdom," *Weekly Mail*, March 25 to 30

Horn, Andrew (1986) "South African Theater: ideology and rebellion," *Research in African Literatures*, 17, 2

Karon, Tony (1992) "Laughing when it hurts most," *Weekly Mail*, July 17 to 23

Kavanagh, Robert (1985) *Theatre and Cultural Struggle in South Africa*, London: Zed Books

Langa, Mandla (1990) "Interview: Albie Sachs," *Rixaka* Issue 1

Larlham, Peter (1985) *Black Theater, Dance and Ritual in South Africa*, Ann Arbor: UMI Reseach Press

le Roux, Frans (1989) "Theater," *Weekly Mail*, January 13 to 19

Leshoai, Thabiso (1989) "Theater," *City Press*, April, 23

Manaka, Matsemela (1980) *Egoli: City of Gold*, Johannesburg: Soyikwa/ Ravan Press

Meintjies, Frank (1990) "Albie Sachs and the art of protest," in: *Spring is Rebellious* (eds. Ingrid de Kok and Karen Press) Cape Town: Buchu Books

Mhlophe, Gcina (1988) *Have You Seen Zandile?*, Braamfontein: Skotaville Publishers (also Portsmouth N.H. and London: Heinemann/Methuen)

Minervini, Rina (1990) "The heart is lost in the Fever," *Sunday Star*, April 1

Ndebele, Njabulo (1984) "Turkish tales and some thoughts on South African fiction," *Staffrider*, Vol 6, No 1

New Nation (1992a) "Lessons in democracy for the theatre world," *New Nation*, May 29 to June 4

New Nation (1992b) "Playland," *New Nation*, July 19 to 30

New Nation (1992c) "Forgiveness, reconciliation and JUSTICE," *New Nation* August 7 to 13

Ngugi wa Mirii (1980) "Literacy for and by the people," *Convergence* 13, 4

Nyatsumba, Kaizer (1991) "Theatre in a rut," *Tribute*, January

Pemba, Titus (1992) "Good, evil, cliché characters," *City Press*, July 26

Potgieter, De Wet (1992) "SADF hid suspects in Webster probe," *Sunday Times*, August 9

Rickard, Carmel (1992) "Are mock trials a mockery of peace?" *Weekly Mail*, July 31 to August 6

Ronge, Barry (1990) "All trite on the night," *Sunday Times*, August

Ronge, Barry (1992) "Fugard beacon for SA theatre's future," *Sunday Times*, July 19

Sachs, Albie (1990) "Preparing ourselves for freedom,"in: *Spring is Rebellious* (eds. Ingrid de Kok and Karen Press) Cape Town: Buchu Books

Steadman, Ian (1984) "Alternative theatre: fifty years of performance in Johannesburg," *Literature and Society in South Africa* (eds. L. White and T. Couzens) London & New York: Longman; Johannesburg: Maskew Miller Longman

Anon. (1992) "No death sentences allowed in mock trial," *Sunday Star*, August 2

Thamm, Marianne (1989) "16 years on, a new look at freedom," *Weekly Mail*, May 12 to 18

Thamm, Marianne (1992) "Theatre: *Educating Rita* (Baxter Theatre) *A Chorus Line* (Nico Malan Theatre)," *Weekly Mail*, June 24 to 30
Tonight! (1992) "*Playland* has its US premier," *The Star*, August 27
Wren, Celia (1990) "Theatre of liberation or protest? It's still a winner," *Weekly Mail*, January 26 to February 1

THEATRE: THE POLITICAL WEAPON IN SOUTH AFRICA

Doreen Mazibuko

Culture in South Africa

It is very important to note that culture in South Africa has been state-controlled all along. That contributed a lot into shaping it up. Black culture was never given a chance to develop. On the other hand, the white Afrikaners were organizing their culture because they were in power. An organisation called FAKU (*Federasie van Afrikaner Kultuur Unie*) or Federation of Afrikaner Culture Unions was formed. The aim of forming this organisation was to allow them to be able to develop their culture and empower the whites, meanwhile undermining the culture of the oppressed majority of the population of South Africa.

Results

Two parallel running cultures were formed in South Africa: the privileged white culture and the oppressed black culture. South Africa never experienced a uniform or united national culture. The following fields of culture were under the full control of the state: sports, education, the church, music, theatre and business. These were also government-sponsored.

Before 1910, the Afrikaner Nation was undermined by the British. They were relying on land and farming, just like Africans. The war of control over the Black Nation then broke out between the Afrikaner nation and the British. The Afrikaners were poor and unskilled. They then started coming to the city and competing for the same power with the Black people. After the war of control between the Afrikaners and the English in 1948, the National Party took over.

The National Party could not tolerate the situation and it started working on uplifting the standard of the whites. In 1948, a truce was formed between the English and the Afrikaners and diverted anger towards blacks. The Afrikaner nation developed their culture and also built a very strong Afrikaner nation.

The most important component structures of the society were fully controlled by the National Party. Rugby became their national sport. Education was under their control and Bantu Education was introduced for Black people. The N.G. Kerk (Dutch Reformed Church) was formed and was used as a moral weapon to unite the Afrikaners and to justify apartheid.

They were even following Calvinist teachings. Folk songs and music were introduced. The monument called *"Eike"* was built to celebrate the growing strength of the Afrikaners' language — Afrikaans. The dominating culture then was the Afrikaner or oppressing culture. The media and education were used as instruments to enforce oppression.

The People's Culture or Culture of the Oppressed
(a)   Protest Culture
(b)   Progressive Culture

Phase 1: Protest Culture:

In the 1950–1960's, people started to challenge education. In 1952, there was a Bantu Education strike. People had no other alternative but to strike. This was an era of Black African Consciousness. Being black and proud was the slogan of those years. In the years 1950–1965, African Nationalism came into being. That was unity amongst the Africans and blacks. This period was marked by protest theatre. Plays written by Gibson Kente and the others came into being. Music by Dolly Rathebe, Miriam Makeba and many more others came to power. At this point stage plays and songs were used to conscientise the black nation and to educate them about the sufferings.

Phase 2: Progressive Culture:

This was in the mid-80's up to the present time. The main objective is to prepare for one national, non-racial and democratic culture. This period reminds us of groups like Johnny Clegg and Sipho Mchunu, Junction Avenue Theatre Co., Pieter-Dirk Uys, Chicco and many others. The problems impeding or hindering the national culture are the following:

1. The Homelands: The state has used the homelands to divide the oppressed in order to have full control of everything.
2. Education: There are thirteen departments of education in South Africa. All these departments have got different types of education — the worst given to the oppressed class.
3. State Control of the Media: This has completely stopped the voice of the people from being heard locally and internationally. The media (press, radio and T.V) are used to spread the propaganda of the National Party.
4. Lack of One National Cultural Movement: The existence of so many cultural movements, some government-sponsored and some not, has brought about the undermining of those cultural movements that are not sponsored by the government.
5. Resources: Black people do not have access to resources; as a result they cannot promote or develop their culture without financial support.

The Role played by Theatre in South African Politics

Theatre has played a major role in South African politics in many respects.

Employment

Theatre provides employment to a big number of the population of South Africa, both to educated/skilled and non-skilled/non-educated people. When looking at theatre in a broader sense, this covers the field of drama, music, dance. Many black people especially cannot afford the university and college fees for theatre. These people are employed in theatre because of the natural talent they have.

Racial Barriers

Theatre has contributed so much in killing the long existing racial boundaries. This begins amongst artists themselves when blacks and whites share the stage. In order to be able to depict the true history of our country we need to have all races on stage. This also extends to the audiences, where people of different races come together and share the same auditorium for entertainment.

   The era whereby the theatre was divided into black and white has come to an end.

Educational Tool

It has been discovered how informative theatre is in this country. So
many millions of people are denied the chance of going to places where
they will be informed and educated, but through theatre, people are
entertained and educated at the same time. There's no reading culture
in the black community, but theatre has made it easy for people to
think. Also the culture of racism has prevented us all, black and white,
from knowing about each other and theatre has become the centre
stage of that damage. Theatre has made it possible for us to discover
the importance of sharing one thing, i.e. being human beings first
before the race issue comes in.

Moments

Moments, a voter education play that is done by (myself) Doreen
Mazibuko, Peter Ngwenya and Willie Tshaka, has proved to be a great
success in undoing the damage done by the racist regime by denying
the people their right to vote. The majority of South African black
people do not know how to vote. This is what is making the South
African racist regime proudly feel good in calling the elections for a
democratic government, because they know they will be going back
into power because of the mistakes that will be made by the population
which doesn't know how to vote. This play will help the majority of
the population remove the racist regime from power.

Through this play *Moments* the people are entertained and
educated at the same time. That is killing two birds with one stone.
People cannot always be put in a classroom situation in order to be
educated. Theatre is the best teacher. This play is written in a sense that
it allows even the actors in it to develop their skills in theatre. It is a
result of research on how elections are conducted internationally and
also on the previous non-democratic elections that had happened in
South Africa before.

Three playwrights — Doreen Mazibuko, Peter Ngwenya and
Willie Tshaka — commissioned by Matla Trust, a politically non-
aligned organisation, worked together in putting the information and
the facts of voting and elections together, and thereafter Doreen
Mazibuko (the artistic director of the play) scripted or compiled a
script. The play is written in four languages: Sotho, English, Zulu and
Xhosa. It is also performed in different languages. The language in
which a performance should happen is dictated by the dominating

language in the area. Also actors have an ongoing task of translating their dialogues into other different South African languages. This is done in order to allow the play to reach all South Africans.

Story Line

The play concentrates mainly on the following issues: The past experience of the black people with the elections whereby the progressive political organisations were stopping them from voting for the urban councillors; the importance of voting; what is democracy; and how to vote. It does not tell the people *who* they should vote for, but it only teaches them *how* to vote.

During the performance, the audience pays very good concentration and at the end, a question and answer session takes place. During this time, people are given a chance to ask questions on whatever they did not understand concerning the play. They can also give comments which they believe will help build and strengthen the play. From the questions and comments drawn from the audience, we are able to add on and even develop our information even further.

We do make some changes here and there in the play, but we are very cautious that we do not get influenced by the audience with their political ideologies and thus become the agents of certain political organisations. We do not want that at the end of the day, we find ourselves losing some people who should have been educated.

Violence

Presently our country South Africa is dying of violence. Day in day out, hundreds of people are dying. This arises from different political organisations and different political beliefs and background. Again the play *Moments* has proved — by remaining neutral and not siding with any organisation — that people can work together. Amongst the directors and actors there are different political beliefs, but because of one thing they want to achieve i.e. educating their nation, they have learnt to tolerate each other and are working together. Also the audiences from different political backgrounds always share the auditorium coming to learn about their rights. This has brought about political tolerance amongst people of different beliefs. They all want to learn and arm themselves with the knowledge of how to remove the oppressing regime from power. Voting and violence have recently taken the centre stage.

Public Addressing and Leadership

Theatre builds confidence in a human being. In this country, the white leadership gets proper training because they can afford it, meanwhile black people cannot do that. Many of the oppressed class leaders are the products of theatre. Through theatre and their natural talent, they have learnt to feel confident and be able to stand in front of the masses and speak to them with the language best understood by the masses.

Democracy

Democracy has never been practised in South Africa. This is because of the kind of regime in power. Through theatre, especially this voter education play, people are made to understand what is meant by democracy. This is helping prepare the people for a democratic future. People must contribute in the making of laws that will rule their lives, but if they do not have knowledge of democracy they won't see the importance of voting and elections. Theatre is succeeding in informing people about this. We know that white children are taught in their schools about democracy, the importance of voting and that it is their right and not a privilege. All these important things in our lives have been taken as a privilege in South Africa. They have been taken as a white privilege for that matter. Now we have taken the advantage of theatre to undo all that damage in the people's minds.

Lastly, theatre is a strong political weapon because everything in life eventually is politics. As long as there is colour and race discrimination, everything will remain politics.

"THIS COMPOST HEAP OF A COUNTRY."
AN INTERVIEW WITH BARNEY SIMON.[1]

Question: We have a few historical questions to ask you, questions about the future role of the Market, and questions about your personal work. How has the audience at the Market Theatre evolved over the years since 1976 in a country where there have been great sociological changes? How have you tried to attract new sectors of the public?

From "Mirror One" to the Market

Simon: I don't know about evolution but the audience has changed obviously, through the decades. For our first audience we were quite a radical alternative. We were nomads on the face of Jo'burg; this is before '76, before we found the Market, when we were a base without our own performance space. We played in store-fronts, we played in hotel dining rooms and we just made theatre. Before that, I was working independently in multi-racial theatre, doing theatre privately in backyards always to invited audiences. Once I played next door to a man under house arrest so he could watch over the fence in a backyard; it was quite agile, a sort of guerrilla theatre, as you might say. I had spent time in Harlem with the Young Lords, these Puerto Rican, gentler black panthers who were very socially conscious. This is what started me doing health education, in the Transkei and Zululand. I called the group before I got involved with Mannie and the Company "Mirror One", a reflecting surface in which we might find an image of ourselves. This was my personal commitment, and if I'm artistic director, that should have some kind of connection to the Market, but it's a bit like King Canute having a connection to the Ocean. The thing is that it has been very important to me at all times to create a mirror in which our community can see itself and watch each other. We had a growing audience in our nomadic days and when we started the Market there was obviously an enormous excitement. The first play I did was *The Seagull*. We planned that as the first show in the Upstairs

[1] Geoff Davis and Anne Fuchs interviewed Barney Simon at his home in Johannesburg, 6th September 1992.

Theatre, when the rest of the theatre was a ruin. I got top actors to work for forty rands a week, or rather Mannie did, and there was an excitement to that, and when we opened the big theatre there was an excitement to playing *Marat/Sade* in this extraordinarily appropriate space at a horrifyingly appropriate time. I would not have started the Upstairs Theatre with *The Seagull* had I known what was going to be happening in June 1976; we were pacing ourselves with some dignity at the time. So the audiences that came I think were very concerned people. They were interested in what we were doing and the *Marat/Sade* was very spectacular theatrically so that was worth seeing, but short of that I think a lot of our initial, most concerned audience has emigrated.

"A struggle for survival"

Among blacks there is not a great tradition in Western-style theatre so one has had to build that audience as best one can, and when you say 'build' it sounds as if we had our bricks and mortar and our trowels. It's never as simple as that. It has always been a struggle for survival. We haven't always been fortunate over the years. We have had accountants who embezzled money and the most terrible time was when we had a disastrous fire. I don't know whether you heard of that. I don't know how it happened. It's been suggested it was arson. I'm not even sure of that because there are hobos who live along the railway lines and next to our sheds was a waste-cloth shed and in the winter I'm sure those hobos were sleeping there and smoking and something might have happened there. There were also vigilante groups that petrol bomb hobos, so one doesn't know what happened. So we haven't been the luckiest of people. I'm working now with three black women singers having a wonderful time, a family from Durban, a mother and two daughters and they're wonderful, and one of the daughters was saying, if you work with God it will never be easy. I don't know about God, but it's not been easy! About audiences, there's not that mass of control: audiences come to what attracts them. I keep saying at the Market, the theatre today is like a human body. If work is the heart, then marketing has to be the lungs, and publicity has to be the liver. I cannot now begin to judge the effect of a performance, if it hasn't had some kind of publicity, some kind of backing, which we find hard to achieve with the salaries we pay our people. The main problem is we have existed all our time without subsidy which is impossible by any world standard, to run three theatres continuously through the year with no subsidy.

Question: But what about sponsorship? You haven't had subsidies, but you have had sponsorship from big business in the past.

Simon: We haven't had sponsorship for the work. We've had sponsorship for the buildings.

Question: Has there been a certain redistribution of the funding into other enterprises, other institutions, since 1990?

Simon: We have the Laboratory which exists since the 1990 sponsorship through the Rockefeller Foundation in America and for various projects.

Question: I meant the opposite. Hasn't that kind of funding gone down?

Simon: Yes, since the recession funding has gone down.

Question: Would you put it down to the recession rather than big business preferring to put the money in education or housing?

Simon: That's why I mentioned the Laboratory, because it has been possible to raise money for projects like school set works being toured. But there's no money. A radical change has happened in the Market since Mannie's departure. I mean while he was there, this chaos was there, it's just been a steady graph totally anticipated. When Mannie was there at a certain point in our history he suggested the Company should be a financial concern, and none of us but he had the means to put money into it and he became the sole financial proprietor. We all worked for very low salaries because we were concerned with the work, but I think that that drive, the fact that he was taking care of his interest is not a thing that I would judge ill because it gave an energy to what he did. I mean there's been an excellent example now of *Playland* playing at the same time as *Death and the Maiden*. The Company has now become, at my insistence, a non-profit-making organisation and so the same publicity and marketing people worked on *Playland* and *Death and the Maiden*,[1] but Mannie — I say this in total admiration — just bullied them into giving an excellent service and our

---

[1] *Playland* by Athol Fugard was presented by Mannie Manim Productions, and *Death and the Maiden* by Ariel Dorfman by the Market Theatre Company both at the Market Theatre in July 1992.

gentler approach was totally non-effective. So somewhere along the line there is a certain pragmatism you have to acknowledge now and attempt to employ if you want things to happen and your staff is not skilled.

The Market Theatre Laboratory or "the dignity of time in which to work"

Question: Perhaps we could come back to the creation of the Laboratory.

Simon: Well much of my work as you know has been the creation of texts with actors, sending them out into the streets as I once sent nurses out into the Transkei to come back and report. I did all of that under specific economic circumstances with Mannie. I usually did a play in four weeks. *Black Dog, Injenyama* was done in three, which was total agony. It always seemed to me that if one was going to work in that way (and I felt it was an important contribution from the Market to the community) there should be some way that people should be able to workshop longer. That's always the thing I have envied in Junction Avenue, I mean they were volunteers. Of course when you're creating work there should be a time of creation, but there should be a time of meditation, of digestion, of perspective; meeting twice a week to me is better than to go through this four weeks time. So one of the most important things that we coordinated for the Laboratory was budgets for people to have two months, to do what they liked, to experiment as they chose without any commercial or presentation obligation. It was also the phenomenon in the 70s: there was *Sizwe Bansi* and *The Island* that somehow happened in a kind of isolation in their time to inspire blacks into looking into new ways of making theatre about the world that they live in. *Woza Albert!* also became a very specific phenomenon, it became a model for a lot of people in the townships, for a lot of workers' plays were modelled on that style. *Bopha! Asinamali* were sons of *Woza*. And then I suppose there was the massive phenomenon of *Sarafina*. *Sarafina* in no way represents a South African venture, although there was South African blood, sweat and bodies involved. It could not happen in South Africa under present circumstances, you could not find the finance to train and rehearse for over a year, which is what happened because the Lincoln Centre saw the possibility with Mbongeni of a considerable financial investment and so they sent money, I don't know how much but it must have been over $100,000. I suppose it must have come close to a million rand to work. Now a lot of the kids in the townships began to see documentaries of the *Sarafina* kids buying leather jackets on Fifth Avenue. That became an inspiration. They ignored the fact that these kids were trained only to do *Sarafina* and the fact that it took a year to get it right, but that was not their concern, and one found there was less and less interest in the making of real relevant personal work in the townships. So it was those two things: the one to give people who were really experimenting the dignity of time in which to work, the other was to start to present training, to send field-workers to people who were struggling in the townships, to have showcases every Sunday, showcases which involved audience discussion and the input of professionals who were watching. And so all these things seem to me to be radically important at the time now to create a place that became a forum and opened minds.

Question: Could you describe how the Laboratory actually functions?

Simon: Our Laboratory is funded initially basically with a three-year Rockefeller grant. There is an administrator. The first one was Mark Fleishman, it is now Tale Motsepe, who's an excellent young man. What the administration involves is organising classes every day in various forms of theatre skills from acting improvisation, mime movement and consciousness-raising. There is an actual course in theatre and light. It has to do with setting up these projects; do I need repeat what they are? You send in a project proposal, for instance you want to do a play about conservation. You then are permitted to have four actors and a director and you do what is the basic structural work of the piece. You have two months, you have free tea, coffee and biscuits, you have the space from 10.30 in the morning until 5 in the afternoon. You do what you like with that space if your proposal has satisfied the board — it's a multi-racial board equal in gender, equal in race — which decides which are the best projects to fund. The only thing that the Market Company does is have its first option on the presentation of the work; we would prefer not to have it performed at Performing Arts Councils not simply for political reasons, but why subsidize people who are subsidized by the government?

Relations with PACT and the ANC

Question: Have there been changes in the relationship between the Market and PACT (the Performing Arts Council of the Transvaal) recently?

Simon: I think relations with PACT were always problematic as Mannie was once the head of PACT and I think that there were those tensions, certainly for me; at one point there was a very strong decision not to work there until there was a change of government. I met Mannie when I was working at the Arena (a PACT theatre) which he set up in 1971 when there was a strong Black-Consciousness movement. It was suggested to me by friends to work on white-consciousness and I went deliberately to work at the Arena for a year. The frustration of working in that bureaucracy led to the formation of the Company. We and the actors who were under contract to PACT chose to leave it and form the Company and we went into the Market adventure.

Question: And you don't think that PACT has changed today?

Simon: I don't think it's an issue any more. I think by the time you publish this book PACT might be a totally different structure. I think years ago someone said to a member of the ANC in Mozambique that they didn't really need to send guerrillas any more (this was in the mid-eighties) because the country was like an overcooked chicken, the flesh was leaving the bones, you just had to wait. I feel that PACT whatever they are doing, whatever they are kicking, their days are numbered as they stand. I don't feel any particular antagonism. I know what the struggle is. I mean if I do a play I've got a longer list of things wrong with it than anybody else can tell me, I swear, so I know where one's focus has to go. PACT isn't a concern of mine. I'd like to get some of the money they get to help us a bit, but I feel it's all so complicated anyway. It's like a tangle of wool the country at this time. I've compared it to a compost heap. You know the waste that is fermenting. This terrible aberration of human dignity. Though somehow it's as aromatic and alive and unpredictable as a compost heap and so I can't pretend that I see things in any other way. PACT now gets money from people who are related to our members, our trustees, the bank, they get money from banks at this time. The point about it is if you can have your sign flashing in the State theatre you are going to get more positive investors than if you are playing in the Mofolo Hall, so it's business. Nicholas Ellenbogen, for instance, has never been without substantial financial backing whereas I can hardly get together a four-week rehearsal period but the fact that they know how to get the money is a measure of our organisation anyway.

Question: Well perhaps not entirely. Have you any links with the Cultural Desk and the ANC? What do you think about their policies? Does that concern you at all?

Simon: Sure, because of our history. When we were invited abroad, initially with *Woza Albert!*, we didn't consult and we were told we should have consulted. We were told that as they approved of the work, they would not picket us, but that we should have consulted and from then on whenever anybody has invited us, we have asked them to clear it with the ANC. I mean that's out of respect for the struggle.

A major change in audiences

Question: What about your own work now?

Simon: Have you got enough about the audiences? I believe there's a major change happening, that's why I am so excited about the place; I'm terrified in many ways, such phenomenal transition is going on now. You look at Hillbrow, the centre of the city where the most exclusive men's outfitters were, there are now stalls selling paper bags, soap and mealie-meal in the heart of the city. I was just sitting outside the Jo'burg Hotel and the number, the mass of well-dressed blacks moving in and out! Across the road very well-dressed young women emerged from an apartment house and went across to the lounge. I sat there for twenty minutes and must have counted (and many, many people went past me) about ten white faces, so we are going through massive transitions. The fact that blacks do not have a history in straight theatre but do have a history in performance, and a history in music as audiences, means that what you have to do is present something which touches on their nerves, meaning on the nerve-centre. A thing like *Woza Albert!* did that, *Sophiatown* did that, so that's hit and miss in drawing an audience particularly in these times. These times you know are hard financially and if you can rent a video for five rand and entertain your whole family, it is easier than seventeen or twenty rand a ticket.

Question: Is, in a sense, this development bringing a potential black audience into the City?

Simon: That's very much potential audience. On the other hand there is the problem of the Northern suburbs whites. I have a friend from

Barbados, a very good friend, she was only here a few days; she came up from Cape Town and she was staying with a friend in Parkwood and I said look I'm previewing *Death and the Maiden*, I'm working during the day, I'm working at night. Come and see the show and we'll have a drink afterwards and the friend refused to come into town. In other words, the Northern suburbs are not coming. The interesting thing is that when I did *Born in the RSA* in Boston in '86 in an area called Dorchester which is a mixed area, predominantly black, a lot of people from the richer suburbs of Boston did not want to come to Dorchester. If they came, they came in their third car rather than in the big one — so it's not simply South African.

Question: Have you done much of that here? Have you gone out into the townships or other venues? I remember in Bochum, Germany, they went and put on *King Lear* in the local cinema. You know they thought people would come and see it on the stage of the cinema rather than going to the theatre itself.

Simon: We have in the past. We have at the moment a company of *Romeo and Juliet* touring all over the townships, way across the Transvaal, that's the Laboratory. This is something I didn't mention about the Laboratory: making accessible to schools the dramatization of school set-books. I have never described that, I should describe it to you, because it's extraordinary. So we've also toured plays in the townships when it's been possible but at present it's not possible. People don't want to park their cars outside the township venue. Beyond the violence which exists the *Romeo and Juliet* combi was hijacked. We couldn't get a replacement. We've just only now been able to rent another one. It was hijacked, I mean the guy, the driver, was made to leave by two kids in their teens with guns, so it's not simple to tour the townships at present. But *Romeo and Juliet* is an example of the kind of work that I see as part of a future, when I talk about my sense of the future and the Market's role. A lot of it is based in the Laboratory and my feelings about the Laboratory. For instance what has been touring is a *Romeo and Juliet* directed by Vanessa Cooke. What we did, we got five young blacks who in their rehearsal period were also discussing the polemics of the play. It was a wide consciousness. It's not great Shakespeare as performed. I mean when I listened initially, it took me time to decipher what they were saying, but it was wonderful for the kids, young blacks acting the parts in central scenes with connecting narrative.

Romeo and Juliet in Sebokeng

And I went to a performance in Sebokeng, really a devastated area, I mean it's devastated now but then it was like hell; our landmark was a petrol station and you couldn't tell which petrol-station was which, they were totally gutted. There were these pumps stripped, you just had this coloured interior wire, the school itself was half-burnt out and on a truly windy, dust-blasted plain. And my hope was that we'd be able to do slide-shows showing what Elizabethan England was like so that you covered the whole context, but there were no curtains so you couldn't show any slides. The performance happened for kids many of whom didn't have books; on one occasion one of the actors that played in a High School where people were matriculating, found himself performing before one of his teachers who still had not matriculated and was now beginning to matriculate. So these were the circumstances we went out into, and what was wonderful on this particular occasion was the discussion afterwards: the girl, a very fiery young woman who played Juliet, said O.K. whose fault is the tragedy? And one kid said it was the nurse's fault, she should have been more strict with Juliet. Somebody else said no, it was Romeo. Romeo had messed around with girls before, he should have known better. Somebody else said no, it was the priest that shouldn't have been messing around with human life like that and somebody else said no, it was the other priest who had to take the message to Romeo. If he would have gone on a horse and not on a mule he would have got there on time. So that kind of discussion happened and one young man, he might have been a student leader, said no, the problem is not that, the problem is the parents who didn't know how to trust or forgive; and this had so many ramifications for the country at the time, to do with Buthelezi.

The survival of performance as a living force

So these were quite extraordinary events and that for me symbolizes why one loves to be here, it's so rich, the references are life always; when I work with black actors they go home in taxis, they live in the townships with all the dangers, and God knows what a hell Soweto must be. And I can still say my work has always got to do with a reference to life, and it makes it exciting for me as a multi-racial cast and I start to share these energies. So that to me is one of the futures I look into with almost total confidence: the survival of performance as a living force. The other thing I want to do through the Laboratory: we do send field-workers out to help companies that are working when they want help, we do have play-readings of new plays presented by professionals, we do have a lot of these services, but to me one of the things that I find would be wonderful — if I were free just to work on that I would be delighted — is setting up in the townships, the recruiting of theatre groups, the recruiting of young people interested in making theatre, setting up local theatre groups doing plays about the life that surrounds them in their own area. It could be didactic about the need for better sanitation, better education or the forming of food co-ops or whatever. For these plays to interchange, this is all. But anything in this country that calls itself a plan is an hypothesis you know, because the movement is so powerful, the ferment is so powerful.

Question: Do you see any grassroots theatre groups beginning to do what you are talking about in the townships?

Simon: Yes, we have had festivals that develop, we have plays on AIDS, all these subjects are being addressed. I think it would also be nice to set up maybe a trained field-worker as a catalyst or even as a director and start making people aware of focus, because to me the way out always, in the times which we are living, is the power of focus. If you learn to focus on your hand you begin to understand the meaning of focus and you can apply it to other places: so focused experience rather than competition. Often in black theatre, in my experience, there has always been this strong rivalry and jealousy and people are still not sure of what. There are some companies that are extraordinary but, as a whole, understanding what the meaning of work is, what an ensemble is, and the potential of it, is lacking. People like Gibson Kente have done it, but bullied people into that; it would be nice if you could create groups which are totally committed.

Death and the Maiden

Question: *Death and the Maiden* was a recent play you directed at the Market. Could you give some account of how you came to choose the play?

Simon: I was working with *Starbrites* last year as part of the Lift Festival in London and as part of the Lift Festival too at the Royal

Court, they were doing sort of workshop presentations of new work. I helped Gcina Mhlophe do a kind of one-woman dissertation. In fact she was at one point on a double-bill with *Death and the Maiden*. Apparently the Royal Court had commissioned I think it was Michael Hastings to anglicise the text. Dorfman had written it in English as a Chilean but both he and Hastings had been in America for a number of years and he was unhappy with the adaptation. Somehow I suppose the anglicisation had also changed its context in so far as he was concerned and he came over to readdress the script while they were working on it.

Question: Ariel Dorfman came over?

Simon: Yes, and he phoned me and asked me to meet him and he invited me to watch what was a pretty crude run-through and then I had dinner with him and he asked me to do the play. There is an interview with him which exists, that was in the *Star*, that maybe you should look at, it's interesting. It's not simply the fact that the play was relevant: I find the character, Paulina, the woman, extraordinary! I mean it's one of the most powerful female roles written for a long time. There is one interview with me where I indicate that when I fall in love with the heroine then I know that the work's going to be O.K. I became passionately concerned with Paulina, she interested me enormously and moved me, it's a woman in politics and a woman in history — in some ways it has a relationship to James Joyce's *The Dead*, and it reminded me of a film also by John Huston. It was a wonderful film and had this thing of the woman, of a relationship between people and the secrets which sometimes we carry inside ourselves, and are even secret from those whom we love: the mystery of another human being. There is one line in the play that blows my mind: at a certain point when they are talking about the fact that when she was in jail he was having sex with another woman, and this point, when she suddenly cries out , "beyond redemption", came from her own experience. The amnesty had to do with only those crimes in the past which had ended in being crimes which were beyond redemption. And this cry for me bonded the person and the politics of "beyond redemption"; the personal betrayal was also "betrayal".

Some years ago, I don't know if you were around at the time, I did a play called *Score me the Ages*, which is street-slang for "Tell me the Time", which was about male hustlers. When I was doing that work we were discussing the meaning or the adventure, or the experience of sexuality. There were only one or two gay people in the cast and I didn't want it to be about being gay but about the frontiers of loneliness for the men that hunt down the male hustlers, the danger and the loneliness of it. When I was working with the actors I would say, what is the shape of sex? When you are making love what is the shape of your body? How does it conjoin with the other? When you close your eyes, where does it stop? What space does it fill? What is this cave of sensuality? And when you close your eyes and are making love to one body, are you thinking of someone else? These are extraordinary adventures, to me, of the soul. When you jerk off, you masturbate, what makes you come? Is it one of your tenderest memories or the one where you were most lost, an animal? To get people to feel these things, to understand, you cannot, if you investigate in that way, you cannot begin to judge. And then if you look at Paulina who was blindfolded, masked, who was molested by brutes, and then a man came and plays this beautiful music to her and caressed her gently after God knows how many weeks of this other thing, she must have known that cave, the sides of that cave, that advent in her life that had separated her from all that was real. And how she must have loved this man, how she must have given herself to him, and then to have been betrayed by that! And I think that that betrayal to me was one of the most interesting things in the whole piece. That she had these two men, who betrayed, had betrayed her. I worked with the actors on these things, these were things of great interest to me. So beyond the relevance — and I cast Ramolao [Makhene], I cast a black man as the husband — I think I mentioned that to you) I was very interested in the assault of a western woman by a man who comes from a black culture, who was obviously a black South African. So these were the reasons that I chose to do it. It went beyond political relevancy. I think that the play is flawed, there is no question about it, it's like the Fugard, you have to begin with an hypothesis, you have to accept the fact that they couldn't overpower her. There is no way that she could have been in that room for that long unless imbued with a fantastic fury: she must have overpowered him, dragged him and lifted him on to a chair to tie him up. Do you know what I mean? If she's holding a gun (if she doesn't hold a gun, they'd overpower her immediately) but if she is a woman who's not used to holding a gun how's she going to handle a gun? Do you know what I mean?

Other dramatists

Question: What new dramatists are there today either in South Africa or in the world you would like to put on, or you admire or you are interested in?

Simon: Last night I went to see *Mooi Street Moves*. The best, that Paul [Slabolepszy] has done. Although my problem with him is I often see where the germ comes from, from some other piece of work, you know; *Saturday Night at the Palace* relates to *The Indian waits at the Bronx* and I'm still waiting for something to come out of a totally personal impulse, but I think it was a very nice play about now. It needs more work, but it's about Hillbrow *now* and that's interesting. It captures some of the anarchy and devastation and humanity. It needs more work. A person who really interests me enormously amongst South African playwrights, that I love to work with, is Fatima.

Question: Fatima Dike?

Simon: Fatima Dike. Apart from that I'm also very interested in workshopping and in doing classics. If I have any desire now, it's for some kind of sabbatical (which is impossible) when I can go around the world and look at other work. Somehow I've never been fortunate whenever I've been working in another country, I'm working, and I have to rush back to the Market. So I never have time if I'm part of a Festival to see it, and the timing has been unfortunate. We played in Zurich once and all the plays were Market Theatre presentations. By the time we came we were the climax of the Festival. So I'm not lucky that way. Something about Fatima, — she has this true anarchy; I think we relate the same way that I related to Percy [Mtwa] and Mbongeni [Ngema]; it's a wild thing the way I'm relating to these women now, there is some very instinctive thing in me that relates to certain energies. If I were to say why Percy and Mbongeni and I were a good combination, it had to do with our senses of humour as much as our concerns (which were not always coincidental) combined; I feel that sympathy for Fatima. And I'd like to do Chekhov for instance. I've done only one in my life and I love it. I'd like to do some Jacobean drama. I'm afraid, because of my training at Dorkay House and my training which was self-training ultimately in the poverty of the Market Theatre, I always think frugally. I've been forced to be a sort of minimalist, miniaturist, I've been forced to work from the inside out, something that has to do with pinpointing human beings under certain circumstances. People talk about the Brechtian approach, the alienation. I was living in London when in 1957 I saw the Brecht ensemble. They came just after his death and nothing moved me more than Helena Weigel in *Mother Courage*, but you also had a sense of history; it's nonsense to say that people are not moved. You mustn't get lost in the emotion and you don't if the work is fine enough and with the amount of time it took to make this work it was deeply textured. If I'm concerned it's almost in reverse, it's like finding the human being and creating the context which then tells us something about what is happening now.

Question: And would you be interested in putting on a playwright such as Heiner Müller?

Simon: I've never had access to good translations, you know — I wanted to do *Through the Leaves* — but that's not Heiner Müller. The one I'm interested in, I've forgotten who the author is now, it's about a woman who is a butcher of meat for animals and her love affair with this gross labourer. It's very beautiful.

Question: Franz Xaver Kroetz, he's Bavarian.

Simon: Beautiful.

"Now the concerns are much more complex"

Question: South African theatre has achieved a certain status on the international theatre scene. How can you reconcile this with people from outside coming in to teach South Africans how to perform?

Simon: First of all — part of what made South African work appealing was its passion, its concern for human rights, its concern for human dignity, its energy which comes with passionate concern. For instance *So What's New?* is not *Woza Albert!* delineating the problems; it's to me almost like a counterpart for the new South Africa because its a play about women and their concerns, it's realistic, but it covers all the paradoxes that make this country so fascinating. That might not be as instantly recognisable abroad as say *Woza* was, which is also a question of style, *Woza* was unique in its style at the time. Now in terms of overseas practitioners there is a change as we start to deal with problems that are problems. You know this thing of the Brecht quotation "Sometimes it's a crime to write a poem about a tree"? When apartheid was there what else was there truly to write about? There's no question of it. So now the concerns are much more complex. I mean Rose who lives here has had her house burnt down by stupid hooligans, no third force. How do we begin to address some of these things? She's lost her whole life in her late 50s, her whole life; she's lost her wedding certificate, she's lost all her records — she's not literate so it's hard to retrieve these things. She's lost everything she owns!

Question: This wasn't political violence.

Simon: No, this is what I'm trying to say to you. So for people abroad it's hard to begin to understand the complexity of this when they need the simplistics to happen. If they were really to go into this compost heap of a country, you know, it would take a long time for them to recognise the themes, to become literate in our themes, in our true themes. So I think that these visitors are important. I think it's the whole question of choice: to be able to go to the classes of these people, it has never occurred before, for decades before, so it's important that one has that dignity. I wouldn't question it at all. If the people who come, I would almost venture to say, have the *merit* to reassess their preconceptions and learn from the complexity and the paradoxes and the ironies of here, I think that would be terribly important for world theatre, for there's so much to learn from the way that life is confronted in this place. There was the case of a German Kafka; they came to do a Kafka piece and to me one of the cores, one of the most attractive aspects of Kafka is his irony and there was no sense of that. They did a very heavy *"Sturm und Drang"* thing about oppression which is sure there, but is not the arc of the whole story. The man who created it had skill and I'm glad the actors had the opportunity to work with a man who has skill but what its merits finally are for here, I'm not quite sure.

Question: I wanted to ask about films. I saw that *Bopha!* is being filmed in Zimbabwe, is that right? Is the Market involved?

Simon: *Bopha!* is an American production, there has been a total rewrite by American writers of the play. I mean the play as it stands couldn't be a naturalistic film; the play depended a lot on style, that of Percy [Mtwa] as director, major author and his very specific vision. And they've just taken the theme of the father who is a policeman and the son who is an activist. In fact they asked me to read through the script, they asked John Kani to look at all the Xhosa-speaking people. When I started to look through it I recognised that it's an idea about here, but it's not finally about here in a way that I understand. And if I were to start to correct speech patterns or something I would start to find a whole lot of other problems and I never had the time. I have had experience of working as a script-writer with overseas versions of South African reality. It can be financially interesting but ultimately they look for reassurance of what they have decided is happening here, validation rather than anything else. I was involved with *Dry White Season* which is essentially about the raising of a dinosaur, an Afrikaner, into consciousness (I coined a word for myself "conscientiously") and it really became a film about police brutality. But that was a decision and I admired many of the people involved including Euzhan Palcy the director; however what was really fascinating about the potential of the story was not finally addressed.

Question: But it's not in a sense a theme for a film for an international audience, that they quite relate to.

Simon: Well fine, but then they mustn't get South Africans to work on it.

A metaphor for what is so extraordinary here.

Question: Nadine Gordimer once asked if she could reply to a "non-question" — perhaps you would like to answer a non-question?

Simon: An interview with me — I'm not sure how much it is about South African theatre, as much as about my own concerns and I suppose if I think about myself, being here (and I do have other choices, much more comfortable and much more lucrative) — has got to do with the grace of being in love. I mean I'm just totally committed and just totally fascinated. Maybe had Rose burnt alive with her house, I would leave the country, but it hasn't happened yet and all the things we've touched on are things that move me into needing to work. I mean, maybe all our trustees at the Market are finally going to tell me to bugger off because we're not making money, what we're doing isn't enough or whatever. I certainly can't see myself stopping working and stopping wanting to work here. If I talk about wanting to work with Fats that's a very problematic decision because she's so unpredictable but that's in a sense a metaphor for what is so extraordinary here.

Geoff and Anne: Thank you very much Barney.

SO WHAT'S NEW?
THE STORY BEHIND THE PLAY[1]

FATIMA DIKE

We started working in October of 1990. I remember preparing for the workshop and feeling totally disorientated, because it was my first time starting work on a play in Johannesburg. I didn't really know a lot of people, most of my friends and acquaintances are people who are already established, with their own theatre companies, or working in established theatres in Jo'burg so that it was impossible to invite them to come and work on my programme. My lifeline was Gcina Mhlophe. She threw a few names my way, then Doris Sihula met me and told me she would be available to work when I was ready, so that more or less set the ball rolling.

I'd been in Jo'burg for two months when the violence broke out in the townships. At that time I was living in the suburbs and the whole thing was happening far away from me. Then I went to stay with a friend in Vosloorus. She lived on the better side of the township where people bought their houses. My friend also ran a shebeen in her house amongst other things. The shebeen was for blue collar people mostly, and no children, skollies and other undesirable characters were allowed in.

I hadn't been there long when fighting broke out between the hostel dwellers in Katlehong. Within hours several people lay dead, the fire of violence caught and within a week it had spread to the hostel in Vosloorus. Because hostels are homes to migrant workers, people tend to look out for each other. It may be people from the same area and they may come from different ethnic groups but the fact that they come from the same area binds them. In this case, it was Zulus versus Xhosas. All along the real reasons for these ethnic wars were not

---

[1] Fatima Dike's play *So What's New?* was workshopped in the Market Theatre Laboratory in 1990 and played at the Market Theatre in 1991.

known, I think two weeks later there was an article in the black press revealing the cause behind the fighting at the Katlehong hostel. It was a gambling quarrel between a Xhosa and a Zulu. Even as I read the article I could not bring myself to believe it.

Gambling quarrels have never created an ethnic war. People cheat when gambling, that is common knowledge. Other people, when they are on a winning streak, may decide they want to go home, thus depriving the losers of the chance of regaining their losses, that causes a quarrel which might even break out into a fight but it has never left tens of people dead or spread to other areas for that matter. So, very slowly the war changed the people's life styles. The first gunshots would go off at ten in the evening, the fighting would go on all night till six in the morning. Sometimes it would stop around two or three in the morning. One night, around 1 a.m. we heard the rumble of trucks driving down the main road, we peeped through our window. We saw truck after truck of the SADF. We cheered, because we thought that with the coming of the army the shooting would stop, Instead, that night we had the longest battle. It lasted till 6 the following morning.

The following morning people were telling stories of white men with blackened faces who were seen helping the Zulus fight the Xhosas. At that point the ANC youth joined forces with the Xhosas at the hostel and fought off the Zulus and their South African Defence Force allies, they even claimed to have shot and killed a white soldier at the hostel. In retaliation, the Zulus and SADF did a house-to-house search in the township, they killed women and raped women, they stole, killed many husbands and fathers. The government imposed a curfew between 10 p.m. and 4 a.m. in the townships. Our customers started leaving the shebeen at 9 not because they were observing the curfew but rather wanting to be home when the battle started at 10.

All this was happening on the other side of the township. We heard the gunshots from a distance, watched the killings on T.V. or saw people moving out with whatever was left of their homes loaded on wheelbarrows. It was real, yet it was unreal at the same time because it was not happening to us. It was like watching a scene from the *Ten Commandments*. One afternoon, my friend and I decided we'd had enough, we drove to Jo'burg to see a movie, we had something to eat before the film. On our way home, at about 9, somewhere between Jo'burg and Vosloorus we drove into a battalion of the South African Defence Force. It was made up of black men mostly. Some were on motor cycles, others were on motor cycles with side-cars. The ones on the motor cycles were wearing things that looked like gas masks over their faces. There were vans with glass sides. Inside there were men, 4 or 6 on each side, sitting with rifles between their legs.

At intervals there would be private cars driven by whites, then a few tanks and a truck with numerous headlights in front warning on-coming traffic of the cumbersome load behind. My mind raced around in my skull like a trapped rat. Would they kill us once they've discov-ered that we were two black women travelling on our own. Maybe they'll just drive us off the road and have the boys rape us. Maybe the battle had already started in Vosloorus, in that case what was the point of going home? Even if we did turn back where would we go, Soweto was in the same mess. We pushed on. To our relief, the house was still standing. That night we waited for the battle royal, but nothing happened. The following day we asked our neighbours, friends and customers if they'd seen that battalion passing through; no one had seen it.

One day at about 6 in the evening, we were sitting with one customer who was brave enough to come out and enjoy a beer at our place when a single gunshot went off. At first we couldn't believe that it was a gunshot, but he did. He stood up, opened his mouth wide and poured the beer down his throat. After he left, all hell broke loose.

For the next three nights we slept in fits as the worst battle raged in our township. People left their homes and sought asylum on our side of the township. A friend of ours who owns a house on the edge of lower middle class Vosloorus and upper middle class Vosloorus moved in with us. She was 8 months pregnant at the time. One night we sat in the dark listening to people from the other side running through our yard. Some people tried to hide in the car that was parked under our bedroom window. We were scared that they might break our door down if they were really desperate. On other occasions we were worried that all this violence might induce our girlfriend into labour in the middle of the night while the fighting was at its worst. Each morning came as a great relief. On the fourth day we could not take the pressure anymore, we decided to move to Daveyton till the fighting was over, later that morning, a friend who usually drinks at our place came by; he too was going away for a few days with his wife.

He had a funny story to tell. Apparently he was chased by Zulus, but he outran them. He got to his house, ran to the bathroom, removed the trap door in the ceiling and hid behind the geyser. The Zulus entered his house, looked for him and found his kids in the bathroom looking up at the ceiling. When they asked the children where their father was, the kids carried on looking up at the ceiling;

as they left, one of the Zulus told the kids to tell their father to come out now.

So, what's new? Our leaders are out of prison, people are still being shuttled from squatter camp to squatter camp.

After we came back from Daveyton, our side of the township held a meeting. After all the problem was no longer there, it was here. We had a lot to lose because everybody had a mortgage to pay, and if the people's war was coming our way we had to stand up and be counted. The men came to a decision, they should approach the police and let them know that they wanted to go to the hostel and disarm the hostel residents. When they got to the police, the police disarmed them first, then allowed them to go to the hostel. At the hostels they walked into an ambush. A guy who lived a few houses from ours was one of the victims.

What made his story more tragic was that he and his wife had just married and had moved into their house not so very long ago, in fact we didn't know them that well because they kept to themselves since they had just gotten married. The men who delivered the news to the dead man's wife found her outside in the yard doing washing. There was nothing to identify the dead man with except for an envelope in his pocket which happened to have his wife's name and address on it. They asked her if she knew the name of the person on the envelope. Her first instinct was to ask for her husband, but before they could tell her the bad news she knew, she told them that he was dead and fainted on the spot.

So, what's new? The passbook is dead, but so are thousands of our people. There's an invisible hand that kills at night behind a balaclava, with a petrol bomb, a tyre, fires an A.K. 47. People keep asking who is killing our people? They call it black on black violence. They know that we do not accept Buthelezi as a true leader. So, the A.N.C. is killing members of the Inkatha Freedom Party. And vice versa. All this violence boils down to two things. As long as we are fighting, the National Party can stay in power. When we are sick and tired of fighting and there's nobody left to speak on our behalf, we will have to accept their terms of reconciliation.

As long as there's chaos in Angola and Mozambique, Malawi and Zaire the A.K. 47s will keep on flowing to South Africa. The South African Police will offer huge rewards for information leading to the recovery of these weapons so that they may be used to bring down another black country in Africa that is on the eve of freedom. So, What's New?

PACT: CAN THE LEOPARD CHANGE ITS SPOTS?

Carol Steinberg

South Africa is in a difficult transition to democracy. What of the state-funded performing arts councils: are they singing the changes? If we are to believe the culture-crats of the old order, the councils have transformed themselves, become non-racial and adapted to the changing times. It will be argued here, however, that the performing arts councils have changed very little and that the legacy of white supremacy remains largely intact.

The performing arts in South Africa have been state-funded for many decades. The exclusive recipients are the four statutory performing arts councils (PACs) — one in each province. The largest of these is the Performing Arts Council of the Transvaal (Pact). Of the R70 million distributed to the PACs in 1991, Pact received about R30 million. Pact employs about 2,400 people and is situated in the heart of Pretoria in a modern, twelve-storey building.

This article explores Pact's origins and current strategies of democratisation. It argues that Pact's fundamental features — racism and Eurocentrism — have remained largely unchanged over the decades. It will suggest that radical restructuring — and not limp reform — is required to decolonise the performing arts in South Africa.

A legacy of racism

> Pact attempts to satisfy all tastes and to provide constant opportunities for people of all levels of the white population to attend stage performances.
>
> *Pact Annual Report 1972*

Pact (in Afrikaans, *Truk*) was established in 1963, the heyday of Verwoerdian grand apartheid, to serve the cultural interests of the white population. As an ideology production centre for the newly constituted Republic of South Africa, Pact's (unstated) task was to institutionalise and promote *volkskultuur*. While Pact officially catered for both English and Afrikaans speaking white South Africans, at its inception English was clearly the poor relative. In the spirit of Afrikaner Nationalism, Pact actively centred Afrikaner interests. Pact's State Theatre is a tell-tale sign: located on Strijdom Square in Pretoria, it is watched over by an over-scaled bust of J.G. Strijdom — the architect of apartheid — framed by a towering arc of concrete. The State Theatre is a monument to the culture of Afrikanerdom.[1]

Pact's defining feature is its racial exclusivity. To qualify for government subsidy — its lifeblood — Pact had to be "whites only." Government aid was conditional on Pact refraining from performing to racially mixed audiences, and from putting black actors on stage.

In the late 1970s, fifteen years after its inception, Pact's first shift in racial policy occurred. It began to apply to various city councils for occasional special permission to play to mixed audiences. This was, arguably, a response to the pressure of the 1976 Soweto uprisings and South Africa finding itself under the international spotlight. In any case, its multi-racialism was token and its mixed gatherings sporadic. Mixed audiences were not even path-breaking: multi-racial theatres in Johannesburg were already a *fait accompli*, thanks to the courageous struggles of the newly established Market Theatre.

A statement by Pact's chief director offers an insight into the organisation's thinking at this turbulent time:

> We believe it is essential for the future of South Africa not only to be physically and materially prepared for the onslaughts[2] of a world in political turmoil, but to enhance and stimulate its spiritual well-being at an ever-increasing momentum.

---

[1] "Nowhere does the iconography of power emerge in a South African context with greater clarity than in the piazza of the State Theatre in Pretoria . . . Steynberg's over-scaled Strydom [sic] head with its sundial shadow must surely be one of the most naked and banal expressions of political power to dominate any public place." (Dubow, N. 1984: 117)

[2] Note the "total onslaught" language popular in government circles at the time.

> ... Our country ... seems to be calling for a greater soul. It
> will achieve this only if it intensifies its cultural life, feeding
> its main cultural streams and getting them to meet more
> often. The performing arts could and should be instrumental
> in creating this greater soul. (*Pact Annual Report 1978*, no page
> number)

The sharp irony of this call is that in 1978, Pact was still serving
only the cultural interests of whites. If Pact was suggesting, as it
seemed to be, that its racial policy be amended, then its oblique and
cautious language is revealing. It suggests that Pact was so subservient
to the National Party that it did not dare, overtly, advocate a policy of
racial integration.

In 1981, almost two decades after its inception, an all-black cast
took to a Pact stage. Pact heralded the production of *Kanna hy ko' hystoe*,
using coloured[3] actors, as a momentous event that

> triumphantly reaffirmed that the [State] Theatre has one sole
> and sacred task, namely to open the hearts and minds of men
> to the dilemma of mankind. A task that transcends colour,
> creed and petty politics. (*Pact Annual Report 1981*:6)

In reality, Pact was still a whites-only organisation that tran-
scended neither colour nor apartheid politics: its founding charter was
unchanged, its board of directors and management remained exclusively white.

Pact's second shift in racial policy accompanied the 1983
Tricameral constitution. In response to popular pressure, and hoping
to increase its support base, the apartheid government brought
coloureds and Indians into separate parliaments with explicit junior
status.[4] The Tricameral constitution defined "own affairs" — to be
dealt with by the relevant ethnic parliament — and "general affairs,"
to be handled jointly, but in practice, under white control. The change
meant that many state institutions, like the PACs, now had to accommodate coloured and Indian people. The performing arts were classified as a "general affair".

---

[3] I use the term "coloured" in the South African sense: an officially classified,
mixed-race, ethnic group.

[4] Most coloured and Indian South Africans rejected this dispensation and
boycotted elections associated with it.

One might have expected the performing arts to be classified as "own affairs" institutions, which "specially or differentially affect a population group in relation to the maintenance of its identity and the upholding and furtherance of its way of life, culture, traditions and customs" (section 14 of the Republic of South Africa Constitution Act, 1983). Their apparently anomalous "general affair" classification was clearly aimed at avoiding setting up separate cultural institutions for coloureds and Indians, as the "own affairs" logic implied. There was never any serious intention, on the part of both the government and the PACs, to cater for the population as a whole.

A few examples illustrate this point. In 1983 it became the policy of each of the PACs to perform only in multi-racial venues. However this involved simply removing official racial barriers. Minimal attempts were made to actively encourage black audiences to attend: to broaden the spectrum of productions, to employ different marketing strategies, and to use venues more accessible to black people. As Pact's chief director said at the time, attempts to assist "other" groups — such as "Indian dance groups, black choirs, black drama groups and coloured impresarios" — must occur on a "secondary level" (*Pact Annual Report, 1987–1988*: 18).

Pact made provision for a multi-racial board of directors. Its board subsequently co-opted black members, but they were few and drawn from that narrow band of Indians and coloureds who were prepared to co-operate with Tricameral institutions. They were, comments Louw (1989), in an analysis of the PACs,

> selected in terms of a "Tricameral logic": i.e. they are selected to be supportive of the Tricameral constitutional "reforms" and will not challenge the de facto maintenance of white hegemony. (107)

The Tricameral vision with regard to the performing arts reaffirmed the apartheid notion of "separate cultures" and preserved white privilege and domination. It essentially involved implementing minor reforms in order to (inadequately) accommodate black — mainly coloured and Indian — people in a previously "whites only" structure. While racial policy was amended and a few token measures adopted, Pact quietly pursued its original mandate to address the cultural interests of the white population.

In 1993, not only is Pact's official charter still the Tricameral one, but, it will be argued here, its practice continues to entrench white domination.

Non-racial or multi-racial?

> The ANC alliance launched a concerted attack on Pact during
> the latter part of this year . . . Their demands concerning a
> non-racial organisation are ridiculous as Pact was a non-racial
> organisation long before any of the current advocators of
> equal rights had even thought of it.
>
> Louis Bezuidenhout
Pact Executive Officer
1992

In a way, Bezuidenhout is expressing the ultimate arrogance: that the
coloniser liberated the colonised long before the latter even considered
it. In reality, Pact's talk of non-racialism is recent. As late as 1988 it was
referring to blacks as "other groups" with "secondary" interests.

There is, in South Africa in the 1990s, an ideological contesta-
tion over the term "non-racialism." Ideological state apparatuses
(Althusser's term), like Pact, are attempting to drain "non-racialism"
of its more radical connotations so that it comes to signify "multi-
racialism". It is an attempt to co-opt and defuse a word, and with it,
a conceptual terrain.

For Pact "non-racialism" denotes "bringing together all races
in the theatre" (*Truk/Pact Info 3*, 1992: 3); "non-racialism" is synonymous with "multi-racialism": the mere fact of being racially inclusive.
By this definition, Pact is indeed "non-racial".

To define "non-racialism" as the simple absence of racial barriers is absurd. When Pact's critics call for "non-racialism" they are
demanding something more than the simple removal of "whites only"
signs and the incorporation of blacks into a "whites only" organisation.

This is not to say that "non-racialism" means the same thing
to all of Pact's critics — who span a wide range of views. "Non-
racialism" signifies, on the one end of this spectrum, colour blindness;
and on the other, an Africanist conception of "the democratic rule of
an African majority" (*Azania News*, 26, 3, 1989, cited in Frederikse, 1990:
249).

But despite its polysemy, "non-racialism" signifies a shared
and crucial meaning for all of Pact's critics: it entails "a completely
restructured society" (Frederikse, 1990: 3–4). With regard to Pact, the
primary goal of non-racialism is the active centring of black interests
within the organisation — both conceptually and in ways that reflect
the composition of South African society as a whole.

The battle over the interpretation of "non-racialism" in transitional South Africa has important consequences for the future. Pact's

critics are not convinced that the organisation's racial reforms amount to "non-racialism."[5]

Pact's racial bias remains glaring. Its audiences remain overwhelmingly (about 95%) white[6] and it has yet to build a venue in a "non-white" residential area. While Pact's companies may be multiracial in that they include some black artists, the control of Pact remains in white hands. There are still no black managing or artistic heads of department — in fact, of Pact's twenty-one senior officials as at 31 March 1991, none are black (*Pact Annual Report 1990–1991*: 18–9). Of the fifteen person Board of Directors of 1992, only one is black. The racial profile of Pact's key decision-makers has not changed since 1963. Nothing — not a multi-racial drama company, nor an outreach programme, nor a Soyinka play — can soften or obscure the fact that Pact is controlled and directed almost exclusively by whites.

The worship of Europe

> If all Eurocentric art is to be removed from South Africa, there will be precious little left on which a new cultural form or image can be built in a new South Africa.
>
> Dennis Reinecke
> Pact General Director
> 1991

This recent comment is staggering in its implications. Pact's chief is betraying his utter contempt for (ignorance of?) the full rich history of South African culture: from the traditional Sotho dancers of Sekekune to the musical extravaganza that is *Sarafina*, from the worker plays in Mphophomeni to the township theatre of Gibson Kente; from jive to *mbaqanga*. The end point of Pact's Eurocentrism is a radical disavowal and undermining of South African performance traditions.[7]

Pact's aspiration towards creating perfect imitations of European "high art" has always been central to its artistic endeavour. It has

---

[5] See, for example, *DAC: Department of Arts and Culture Bulletin 1*, June 1992; de Beer, D. 1992: 2; Accone, D. 1992: 2.

[6] This is in the estimation of Pierre van Pletzen, artistic director of Pact Drama. (Author interview, Pretoria, 13/11/1991).

[7] This article draws mainly on drama for its examples. The argument, however, can be extended to the other art forms.

used public money to encourage the European "high arts" to the detriment of indigenous South African drama.

In this article, "Eurocentric" and "indigenous" are polarised for conceptual clarity. In practice, however, the two categories are often blurred. "Indigenous" signifies locally written/workshopped/choreographed/conceived, rather than non-Western. It is not a purist concept. Hence, *Sarafina* is "indigenous", even though it is derived from the Broadway musical genre and may play in a proscenium arch theatre.[8] The point is that *Sarafina* was made by South Africans and represents an aspect of South African experience. "Eurocentrism" signifies, by contrast, the mimicry of European art forms and aesthetic standards, and the resulting marginalisation of the indigenous.

In practice Pact tends to allocate the largest proportion of its budget to the European "high arts" — opera, ballet and orchestra. In the 1970s, its orchestra received a larger slice of the subsidy cake than any other department. In the last few years, the opera department has consistently received the largest budget

Over the decades, Pact has spent large amounts of money on the costly importation of foreign artists. In 1977 the Niemand Commission expressed a "debt of gratitude to immigrants, who at present constitute 80 per cent of the members of our professional orchestras" (*Report of the Commission of Inquiry into the Performing Arts*, hereafter *Niemand Commission*: 49). Today this has hardly changed. In 1992, only 27% of the current Transvaal Philharmonic Orchestra were South African citizens ("Pact Press Release: Progressive Cultural Workers pamphlet", 06/08/1992, no page number). As recently as 1990, Pact imported the entire Baden-Baden Symphony Orchestra at an enormous (undisclosed) cost. In 1992 four international artists were imported simply for Pact's production of Verdi's opera *Attila*.

Pact has justified this approach on commercial grounds. There are, it has argued,

> various art disciplines which cannot be viably presented by commercial managements. The drama classics, opera, ballet, symphony orchestra and serious music programmes are all art forms which require subsidy. (*Pact Annual Report 1989–1990*, p. 2)

---

[8] Much like the European Cubist movement derives its inspiration and style from African art.

However, there are a myriad art disciplines in South Africa that may not be commercially viable — including traditional African dance and music, and experimental and avant-garde drama. Pact's interpretation of its mandate is highly specific and ideologically charged.

The language of universalism is employed to reinforce European aesthetics and standards as the norm and other traditions as deviant. One of Pact's major assumptions is that art has the capacity — "integral to civilizations and cultures" (*Truk/Pact Info 3*, 1992: 1) — to enrich the human spirit on a universal basis. As Reinecke expresses it;

> The performing arts do not differentiate. Barriers and cultural differences — whatever these may be — are of no consequence. Members of an audience are united by the "soul enriching" experience of production regardless of political persuasion, creed or race. (*Truk/Pact Info 1*, 1992: 2)

There is nothing universal about the Eurocentric "high arts". As Pact's audience demographics reveal, they are enjoyed by a small narrow band of South Africans — upper middle class whites.[9] Pact's frequent attempts to defend the Eurocentric art forms as universally appreciated — and these defences are more prolific of late[10] — effectively continue to exclude black South Africans from full participation in Pact — as audience members, artists and administrators.

If "no amount of marketing in the world is going to convert 25 million non-white South Africans to appreciate opera" (Anon, 1988, p. 5) — as the head of NAPAC, a sister PAC, lamented in 1988 — then the decision to fund opera more generously than drama, for example, reeks of racial exclusivity. To use the ostensibly race and class-blind discourse of universalism in this way is simply to preserve the status quo.

By the same token, the language of universality is used to assert political neutrality. If the European "high arts" are bearers of

---

[9] I am referring here to the 1977 Human Sciences Research Council (HSRC) survey of PACT audiences; the discussion of audience demographics in "PACT Drama in the 90's — A Decade of Development"; and Pierre van Pletzen's observation that 95% of Drama Department audiences are white (Author Interview, Pretoria, 13/11/1991).

[10] See, for example, *Truk/Pact Info*, editions 1, 2 and 3; *Pact Annual Report 1990–1*, p. 3; Geralt MacLiam, 1991: 1

universal truths, then Pact can argue that it "has always distanced itself from politics", and that it is "political organisations and certain of their leaders"[11] who, in criticising the elitist nature of the Eurocentric arts, "are trying to coax Pact into the political arena" (*Truk/Pact Info 3*, 1992: 2).

These organisations, Pact argues, are anti-art — or are prepared to let their political ambitions destroy art. If Eurocentric culture is Culture and the "high arts" are Art itself, then the appeal of these organisations to reduce the amount of public money spent on the Eurocentric "high arts" is tantamount to a request to spend less money on art. This is in keeping, argues Bezuidenhout (*Truk/Pact Info 3*, 1992: 2), with their earlier attempts to politicise and undermine art with the cultural boycott and international cultural exchange regulations ("sinking the opening production of the Johannesburg Civic Theatre"). It is the perverse logic generated by the Eurocentricity/universality/civilisation nexus of concepts, that can lead Bezuidenhout to ask (rhetorically),

> Do these groups actually have the promotion of the performing arts at heart or are they simply trying to further their own interests in the new South Africa? (*ibid*)

This approach is ironic. For it was the government of the hardline Afrikaner Nationalist, Verwoerd, that gave the newly formed PACs two contradictory, and highly political, tasks. On the one hand, they were to encourage the "decolonisation" and "indigenisation" of the performing arts (*Niemand Commission*, 1977: 80). They were expected "to establish and sustain language, national sentiment, religion — the entire life of the [Afrikaner] nation . . ." (Ibid: 19). On the other hand, they were to ensure that foreign art forms — the European "high arts" — were integrated into white South African culture.

These two goals reflect the contradictions of an internal colonialist[12] culture—of a people in, but not of, Africa. Afrikanerdom, in attempting to define itself as "a distinct and separate nation with its own history, traditions, religion, philosophy, language and culture" (de Villiers, 1971: 367), had to distinguish itself from the imperial

---

[11] In context, Pact is referring to the ANC and the Performing Arts Workers Equity (Pawe).

[12] Internal colonialism is a "special type" of colonialism since both the coloniser and colonised occupy the same territory. In other words, the typical features of colonialism exist, but there is not the geographical separation of metropolis and colony.

culture of the mother continent without identifying with the indigenous culture of the colonised.

Post-colonial theorists[13] assert that as one of the processes of colonisation, the imperial culture is instituted as the norm while the culture of the colonised is marginalised. This normative culture is imbued with value — civilisation, linguistic and aesthetic superiority — in the process of constructing the culture of the colonised as its inferior, savage "other." The imperial culture denigrates the indigenous culture to justify its conquest and subsequent rule of the colony.

But the Afrikaner nation was both coloniser and colonised (by the British). Afrikaner culture, in establishing its hegemony, had to undermine African culture in order to assert itself as civilised. But, in the same movement, it had to establish itself as "indigenous." In this lay its contradiction.

Because it had no other cultural foundation from which to draw, the art forms it adopted were European. But because it was alienated from modern Europe, it adopted the remnants of another era, of a Europe before its perversion by post-war liberalism. Even in contemporary Europe, the "high arts" are strands from the past, rarely living cultural forms. For the Afrikaner Nationalists who adopted them, the "high arts" represent an "imagined" (in Benedict Anderson's sense) culture: an image of a long past phantom civilisation that is and is not European; is and is not African.

The European "high arts" directly privilege white cultural interests in that they are performed and patronised largely by whites. But the indirect, symbolic role they play is perhaps more significant. The "high arts" are emblematic of the "first world" — white — culture that Pact wants to preserve in a future South Africa. That fragment of imagined nineteenth-century European civilisation is the symbolic last outpost of the ruling order.

Outreach: the final solution?

> In addition to the productions that already form part of this organisation's planning, serious consideration has to be given to . . . the development of marginal audiences . . .
>
> Dennis Reinecke
> Pact General Director
> 1992

---

[13] See Ashcroft et al, 1989, for a summary of the major post-colonial cultural theorists.

In the 1990s, Pact's claims to multi-racialism (or non-racial-ism)[14] rest on two major legs: the inclusion of black people in its permanent companies and its outreach programmes. The concept of "outreach" is a "New South African" vogue in which previously "whites-only" organisations "reach out" to black communities. In Pact's case, outreach involves playing to audiences who, historically, have had little opportunity of seeing Pact productions.

The outreach programmes are held up as proof of Pact's commitment to — and success in — presenting a wide spectrum of the performing arts to all of South Africa's societies. They credit themselves with

> ensuring our entire population [has] the opportunity of experiencing the joys and wonders the performing arts have to offer. (*Pact/Truk Info* 2 1992: 3)

Pact now acknowledges that apartheid's "socio-economic legacies" means that

> most black people live very far from the theatres, and the fact that they tend to have lower-income jobs also means that theatre is a rather inaccessible luxury. ("Pact Drama in the 90's: a decade of development", n/d: no page numbers)

Pact's outreach programmes attempt, among other things, to facilitate the development of black theatre. This has entailed either bringing black audiences to established theatres, or taking the productions to black communities. The content of the outreach programmes is usually educational — in the case of the schools' programmes, dramatisations of the prescribed Shakespeare; in the case of the wider community, productions about the performing arts themselves or plays addressing social issues such as child abuse.

The tours of the "Truck Theatre" — a pantechnicon that unfolds into a small stage, thereby functioning as a mobile theatre — were instituted in November 1991 and constitute Pact's most publicised outreach programme. Others include the black schools' tours and the

---

[14] See, for example, "Pact Drama in the 90's: a decade of development", n/d: no page number.

transport and ticket subsidisation scheme for black pupils (*Pact/Truk Info 3*, 1992: 2).

At one level the outreach programme is an attempt to deal with the need for change. But, examined more carefully, it is clearly inadequate and, even, misconceived.

The target communities comprise the vast majority of the South African population. Yet the proportion of Pact's budget and resources that are allocated to these programmes is very small. Pact does not directly use its annual government grant to fund its outreach programmes, relying instead on private sector assistance. The "Truck", for example, was donated by Transnet, and its tours are sponsored primarily by Nedbank. The Department of Education and Training (DET) sponsors the black school tours. Spending on outreach constitutes a tiny percentage of Pact's annual budget.

Perhaps more importantly, in prioritising what it calls the "mainstream" productions, and appealing to private funders to sponsor "the project aimed at marginal audience development" (*Truk/Pact 4*, 1992: 2), Pact reveals its primary focus: the outreach programmes are an optional extra, existing precisely on the "margins".

The concept of "outreach", as interpreted by Pact, is inherently conservative. It allows for existing practices to remain intact by creating a relatively small "marginalised" programme that ostensibly — and with maximum publicity — addresses developmental needs.

As with the Tricameral modifications of the mid 1980s, the outreach concept of the 1990s entails the inadequate accommodation of blacks into a structure that continues to serve the cultural interests of whites. There is a difference between an outreach approach and a developmental approach. A developmental approach would mainstream that which the outreach programmes marginalise. It would define the *raison d'être* of Pact as the development of the Transvaal's historically neglected majority communities, and would re-orient Pact's resources and infrastructure in that direction. To the extent that it continued to serve minority interests, these would exist on the margins.

A new Pact?

> The FIA [Federation of International Actors] condemns the reticence of the South African Performing Arts Councils to democratic change . . .
>
> FIA International Conference resolution
> 1992

For Pact to be non-racial, it must place majority interests at the centre. One mark of success will be when the board of directors, senior management, casts and audiences more accurately reflect the composition of South Africa's population. Another will be when Pact is finally at the cutting edge of cultural innovation, vigorously promoting the diverse spectrum of South African theatre, music and dance.

Only fundamental restructuring can achieve this. A change of policy and key personnel would be insufficient. For Pact's artistic and political character is matched by its infrastructure — geared to facilitate the production of the "high arts" in white residential areas. Pact's highly centralised structure — most of its artistic and administrative activities take place in one building — needs to be radically devolved if the full range of artists and audiences in the Transvaal is to be served.

Current Pact management has neither the will nor the vision to democratise Pact. It refuses to participate in public debates on the issue, even ducking out of scheduled radio and television panel discussions. As late as 1992, it chose to deal with critics trying to submit a memorandum by having them arrested for trespass and thrown into prison. Despite Pacts apartheid legacy, no self-critical remark, no apology for its past, has emerged.

In this transition period in which South Africans' identities are confused and fluid, Pact's potential role is crucial. It could provide the Transvaal's societies with the means to represent themselves — their lives and ideas — on the stage. Instead of bringing the odd township school to *Lucia di Lammermoor* or *Attila*, Pact could be facilitating a process of self-reflection and debate contributing to the effort to build democracy.

REFERENCES

Accone, D. 1992. "International Actors' body lashes Pact," *Star Tonight!* 7 October, p. 2.
ANC/DAC. 1992. *DAC Department of Arts and Culture Bulletin 1*, June.
Anon. 1987. Interview with Mr Justice J.J. Kriek. *Scenaria* 81, October.
Anon. 1988. Interview with Rodney Phillips. *Scenaria* 88, May.
Ashcroft, B. et al. 1989. *The empire writes back: theory and practice in post-colonial literatures*. London and New York: Routledge.
de Beer, D. 1992. "Pawe and Pact in confrontation," *Star Tonight!* 4 September, p. 2.
de Villiers, R. 1971. "Afrikaner Nationalism" in Thompson, L. and Wilson, M. *The Oxford History of South Africa Vol. II 1870–1966*. London: Oxford University Press.

Dubow, N. 1984. "Art and edict," *Leadership South Africa* 3(4), fourth quarter.

Frederikse, J. 1990. *The unbreakable thread: non-racialism in South Africa.* Johannesburg: Ravan Press.

Kriek, J.J. 1987. "The future of the performing arts in South Africa." *Scenaria* 81, October.

Louw, P.E. 1989. "State-subsidised theatre following the September 1984 Vaal Uprising," *South African Theatre Journal (SATJ)* 3(2) September.

MacLiam, G. 1991 "Pact's bold defence of Eurocentric Art," *Star Tonight!* 20 November, p. 1.

Pact Annual Report 1970

Pact Annual Report 1978

Pact Annual Report 1987–1988

Pact Annual Report 1989–1980

Pact Annual Report 1990–1991

Pact. 1992. "Pact press release: progressive cultural workers' pamphlet."

Pact Drama. n/d. "Pact Drama in the 90's: a decade of development."

Pawe. n/d. "Pawe discussion paper on performing arts councils (PACs) policy."

"Report of the Commission of Inquiry into the performing arts". 1977. Pretoria: Government Publisher.

Truk/Pact Info 1. 1991. November, December 1991, January 1992.

Truk/Pact Info 2. 1992. February, March, April.

Truk/Pact Info 3. 1992. May, June, July.

Truk/Pact Info 4. 1992. August, September, October.

Truk/Pact Info 5. 1992. November, December 1992, January 1993.

van Pletzen, P, van der Spuy, M. and Terry, P. Interview conducted by author 13/11/1991, Pretoria.

THE FUTURE OF THE PERFORMING ARTS COUNCILS IN A NEW SOUTH AFRICA

ARNOLD BLUMER

Towards the end of 1990 the Theatre Action Group (TAG)[1] was formed in the Cape. The following policy statement and correspondence is quoted in its entirety, because it highlights parts of the history of the Cape Performing Arts Board (CAPAB) and points to some issues which CAPAB — and for that matter also the other three Performing Arts Boards — will have to address if there is to be a future for them. TAG states:

> The Theatre Action Group comprises a broad range of individuals involved in conventional theatre institutions and community theatre groups who have come together to pool their material, technical and human resources for the development of theatre in the Western Cape.
>
> TAG's co-ordinating committee was elected to be as representative as possible and consists of Mike van Graan (Director of CAP and TAG's chairperson),[2] Johan Esterhuizen (Stellenbosch University drama department and TAG's secretary), Charlton George (Action Workshop), Professor Mavis Taylor (Head of the University of Cape Town drama department), Dumile Makgodla (New Africa Theatre Project — NATP), Bo Petersen (CAP Theatre Company), Jay Pather (Jazzart), Janis Merand (freelancer), Mike Cloete (former director of audience development at CAPAB), Mwzandile Sangile (graduate of NATP), Liz Mills (University of Cape Town drama department), Ivan Sylvester (Cape Flats Players) and Claire Slingers (SA Domestic Workers' Union Cultural Group).

---

[1] For a variety of reasons TAG has since dissolved and merged with the Performing Arts Workers Equity (PAWE).

[2] CAP is the acronym for Community Arts Project.

It is the intention of TAG to draw together as many theatre groups and practitioners as possible to co-ordinate the development of theatre in the region effectively. Accordingly, while TAG noted that CAPAB has been boycotted by a large section of the community for a long period of time because of its apartheid legacy, it recognised that changing political conditions favoured a more constructive engagement with CAPAB to help transform it into an institution which served the performing arts' needs and aspirations of all the people of the Cape. Furthermore, it was in TAG's and CAPAB's mutual interest to develop a relationship, since TAG would have access to CAPAB's significant resources while CAPAB would gain increasing credibility by having access to TAG's broader constituency.

However, given CAPAB's history of racial exclusivity and its serving a primarily privileged audience, TAG — particularly community groups associated with TAG — was concerned that CAPAB does not gain increasing legitimacy through an association with TAG without being prepared to make fundamental changes to its structure and aesthetic practices which would reflect a greater sensitivity and commitment to the aesthetic needs and aspirations of those communities which had been excluded from CAPAB in the past by apartheid and its legacy.

At a broad, representative TAG-meeting on 10 February 1991 to discuss TAG's relationship with CAPAB and which was attended by numerous CAPAB employees who participated actively in the meeting, including Mr. George Loopuyt, Director of CAPAB, it was overwhelmingly agreed that the minimum requirement for any relationship with CAPAB was a public statement by CAPAB in which it acknowledged its past limitations in serving a primarily élitist audience, committed itself to serving the performing arts' needs of all the communities in the Cape, making structural changes where necessary to give effect to this and finally list practical steps that it would take within a specific time framework to realise these changes.

Once such a public statement was forthcoming, TAG would be prepared to nominate persons for CAPAB's Board (no-one with credibility within the larger community would want to be on the Board without being convinced that CAPAB was really committed to change), to co-host events with CAPAB, to facilitate exchanges between CAPAB and community groups and to assist CAPAB to change to a performing arts institution more appropriate to the changing political realities.

To be as constructive as possible the meeting elected a committee consisting of Mavis Taylor, Ronnie Govender,

Charlton George, Dumile Makgodla, Mike van Graan and Thys Odendaal to draft a statement which would include all of the above concerns, submit it to CAPAB's management and then arrange a meeting with them to discuss the draft and make changes so that consensus could be reached where CAPAB would feel happy with the statement and TAG would feel that it satisfactorily covered the areas that concerned its constituency.

The draft statement was drawn up by the elected committee in consultation with past and present CAPAB employees and academics to ensure that it was factually correct and reasonable in its content and tone.

It was submitted to CAPAB on 20 February 1991 and a meeting was requested at CAPAB's earliest convenience for TAG representatives to meet with CAPAB's management team to discuss the statement. However, for nearly two months TAG did not receive an acknowledgment of receipt of the draft statement, let alone a response to it.

The draft statement reads as follows:

CAPAB acknowledges that laws such as the Group Areas Act and the Separate Amenities Act which governed its initial inception excluded the majority of people from its activities on the basis of racial classification.

Furthermore, CAPAB acknowledges that while it has been open to all since the mid-seventies, the legacy of its racially exclusive history, the geographical location of CAPAB and its relative inaccessibility to those without transport and the kinds of aesthetic work which it does and which does not fall within the life experience of the majority, has meant that CAPAB serves and is seen to serve an élite, privileged audience.

While we believe that it is important for the state to subsidise the arts, we accept that CAPAB's history, coupled with the receipt of a substantial state grant, has led to the performing arts councils being regarded as representatives of and apologists for "state culture."

Some of these factors have been beyond CAPAB's control, yet we acknowledge that until now we have not fought hard enough to redress this situation. While we recognise that the future of the performing arts councils will be one subject in the overall process of negotiations, we believe that we must now take pro-active steps to rectify the legacies of the past.

Accordingly, CAPAB commits itself to serve the performing arts' needs of all the people of the Cape, irrespective of race, gender or creed, in accordance with our mission statement. We recognise though that past legacies will require us to make extra efforts to serve those communities which have been denied or had little access to skills, resources, performances and expertise.

Furthermore, we commit CAPAB to structural, policy and constitutional changes to reflect and facilitate this mission where necessary.

While we reserve the right to make decisions as an independently constituted institution, we commit CAPAB to regular consultations with representatives of community cultural structures.

Finally, we commit ourselves to actively nurturing the aesthetic development of all and to change our aesthetic practice where necessary, to encourage and give expression to the aesthetic needs and practices of all. In this regard we commit ourselves to discussion, debate and practical work regarding aesthetics, standards and values and assumptions about the performing arts, so that we are informed and understand the aspirations and insights of all.

In practical terms this will mean:

a) Working towards changing the Board so that at least half of the members will be nominated by community or more representative cultural structures and changing significant positions on the Executive Committee so that the broader community may have faith in the Board that their aspirations are taken seriously. This we will try to achieve by the end of 1991.

b) Setting up a consultative group with representatives from community based cultural structures to meet with CAPAB management at least monthly to give guidance, advice and whatever assistance may be necessary in transforming CAPAB. This we will do within two months.

c) Making technical, material and human resources available for the development of theatre in deprived communities. This may include equipping venues, training people to run them, sponsoring shows to tour such venues, providing skilled people to run workshops, making CAPAB's facilities available for rehearsals, performances, exhibitions, recordings, etc.

d) Improving internal channels of communication and exploring the internal democratisation of CAPAB, e.g. through the distribution of minutes of Board, management and consultative meetings to all employees, greater consultation and consensus decision-making at management level, more direct access to and representation on management structures by performers, technicians and other categories of staff.

> While we accept that these will not happen over night, we
> commit ourselves to the speedy implementation of these.

To this draft statement the director of CAPAB, Mr. George
Loopuyt, replies in a letter, dated 16 April 1991, as follows:

> Thank you for your letter dated 20 Feb. 1991 and the attached
> draft statement which I have read with interest and discussed
> fully with my Management team at CAPAB.
>
> I must make it clear at the outset that CAPAB is not
> prepared to make a public apology or statement with regard
> to the past government apartheid policy. CAPAB never cre-
> ated, championed, promoted or supported these policies, but
> was subjected to them like everyone else. Indeed, a great
> many of our productions viciously attacked or exposed these
> policies. We find it difficult to accept that we should become
> apologists for something for which we were not responsible.
>
> CAPAB has always been open to all races and has always
> employed people of all races. Although the Nico (Malan
> Theatre) began its history as a whites only theatre, CAPAB
> did all in its power to have it declared open and succeeded
> in achieving this just a few years later. In fact the Nico should
> be seen as a monument to the very first practical steps to
> dismantling apartheid!
>
> If there is any major reason that CAPAB did not employ
> great numbers of black or so-called coloured artists in the
> past, it is that they have boycotted CAPAB and the Nico, not
> the opposite. To a lesser degree this is still the case.
>
> CAPAB has never applied for a permit in order to perform
> before mixed audiences or to have a mixed cast in stage and
> furthermore it has been CAPAB's policy to perform only in
> venues that allow all races since the whole system of permits
> was introduced, albeit without a permit in CAPAB's case.
>
> There are no structural or constitutional changes neces-
> sary in order to permit CAPAB to carry out its job. All that
> is needed is a willingness on the part of the public to acknowl-
> edge that CAPAB stands for the rights of all and to come
> forward and co-operate.
>
> I have already made known to you that the Administrator
> has set himself the goal of appointing a Board which is more
> fully representative of the wider community and will con-
> sider all nominations. Your suggestions for appointments to
> be considered by the Administrator should be forwarded to
> me for onward transmission. I give my assurance that these
> suggestions will be passed on: of course the final decision is
> still always the prerogative of the Administrator.
>
> CAPAB is committed to serve the needs of all people of the
> Cape Province and I am more than willing to talk about the
> best way to do this, bearing in mind resources and personnel.

Regarding changes to aesthetics, this will happen naturally as the scope of CAPAB's activities is widened by the participation of all who are willing and able to further the performing arts.

I speak for all of us at CAPAB when I say that we will continue to do anything to make CAPAB a worthy arts council presenting work that is enjoyed and loved by all who wish to participate, and am more than prepared to speak to you or TAG and to listen to constructive suggestions for achieving this. I am not prepared to listen to destructive ideas that seem intent on breaking down what has taken a multitude of dedicated and talented people many years to build.

The performing arts must surely transcend racial, social, economic, political, gender and all other possible differences and be a vehicle for building confidence and fellowship in the new South Africa. As I have often stated before, actions speak louder than words and I appeal to you to join us in carrying out the joint projects which we have already launched most successfully and in starting others which are so drastically needed.

The last part of this letter sounds very laudable, but it will remain wishful thinking which is not worth the paper it is written on, as long as the Director of CAPAB is "not prepared to listen to destructive ideas" without at least suggesting where in the draft statement these "destructive ideas" might be hidden. Needless to say, the debate, discussion and consultation which were envisaged in the draft statement have not taken place yet. It is difficult to see how to engage in constructive discussions with a man who says on the one hand that "there are no structural or constitutional changes necessary" and on the other that "the final decision" on who is appointed to the Board "of course . . . is still always the prerogative of the Administrator." This means that the people or group who elect or nominate a person to sit on the Board have no say and it also means that the Director of CAPAB has not got the faintest idea of what democracy is all about.

On top of it this man has the cheek to turn facts upside down. It is quite true that black or so-called coloured artists and their communities have boycotted CAPAB and the Nico Malan Theatre, but they have done so, because when the Nico was inaugurated in 1971, they were neither allowed on stage nor to be present in the audience. This also applied to the Hofmeyr Theatre which CAPAB had used for many years before it could move into the Nico. And then it still took a couple of years before the Nico was finally opened. At the same time, however, in the early and mid-seventies there existed a theatre in Cape Town called The Space and there all hues of skin colour were to be seen on stage and in the audience. Of course, there have always been black and so-called coloured employees in CAPAB, but they were not seen, as they were the cleaners and carpenters in the workshop. A sentence like "CAPAB has always been open to all races and has always employed people of all races" is thus grossly misleading, to say the least.

When the draft statement refers to CAPAB's "aesthetic practice" and says "that CAPAB serves and is seen to serve an élite, privileged audience" it means that the less accessible art forms are favoured to the detriment of the more accessible ones. In 1989/90 all four Performing Arts Councils, of which each one is responsible for opera, drama, ballet and music, together received a state subsidy of R 77.8 million. Between 1987/88 and 1989/90 the attendance figures for drama in all four Councils rose from 414,784 to 459,130, thus by 10.7%. But in the same period the attendance figures for opera in all four Councils rose from 498,333 to 671,768, thus by 34.8%! State subsidy, however, is granted according to a rather stupid "bums-on-seats" formula and this in turn means that more and more money is channelled into the opera sections of each Council. But opera is the artform which least of all falls "within the life experience of the majority." An increase in state subsidy thus means a direct benefit to the mostly white opera-goers. This is the sort of imbalance which has to be redressed.

The story does not end here. On 25 July 1992 the Afrikaans newspaper *Die Burger* reports on a statement issued by the Performing Arts Council of Transvaal (PACT) in answer to suggestions to PACT made by Wally Serote, secretary-general of the ANC's Department of Arts and Culture (DAC). The report says:

> Mr. Wally Serote . . . has accused the Arts Council of interrupting the discussions about the future of the performing arts in the country.
>
> Decision making, administrative, artistic and fund-raising structures in the arts councils have to be restructured so that they mirror the composition of the communities which uphold these institutions, the ANC said in a statement yesterday.
>
> The ANC has suggested a joint working group as facilitator in this process. This working group could consist of PACT and members of the different democratic cultural structures which up to now have been sidelined by the apartheid system. They must reach an agreement about the framework for

the restructuring of PACT. The role of the ANC would be to act as facilitator in this process.

Sapa reports that the ANC has said it did not say that Eurocentric art deserved no place in PACT, but that this could not happen at the expense of Afrocentric art. In reaction to this PACT has issued a statement . . . : "The suggestions of the ANC boil down to a total take-over of PACT" (my translation, A.B.).

In the same issue of *Die Burger* the editor comments in an editorial:

In the final instance the fight actually seems to be a battle for nothing but power, for the sake of which civilised standards may be dragged "to hell" together with the masses.

PACT is correct. Cultural imperialism is always an enemy of freedom, it doesn't matter how seemingly sincerely it is represented (my translation, A.B.).

It is fairly incomprehensible how PACT can arrive at the conclusion that what the ANC suggests "boils down to a total take-over," because in the same report it is stated explicitly and more than once that the ANC sees itself as facilitator. Apart from that mention is made of a "joint working group," which is the most efficient democratic mechanism to prevent a "total take-over." So when the editor of *Die Burger* speaks of a power battle he does so on the grounds of ideologically biased, anti-ANC sentiments.

If there is a power battle going on it is a somewhat different one, namely the battle of the present Councils and their Directors to remain in power, as is shown in two reports which appeared in the alternative Afrikaans weekly newspaper *Vrye Weekblad*. Under the heading "PACT — where the arts unite people?" the following is said:

The opening night of PACT's production of *Beyond Therapy* was greeted by a PAWE picket in front of the theatre. Charl Blignaut was there and spoke to PACT director Dennis Reinecke, who has consistently refused to comment.

The progressive theatre organisation PAWE (Performing Arts Workers Equity) has been making things very uncomfortable for Dennis Reinecke by making their presence felt at opening nights.

Spurned by the recent run-in between ANC Department of Arts and Culture (DAC) head Wally Serote (aided and abetted by members of democratic cultural organisations) and the intransigent PACT management, several PAWE members gathered outside the Alex Theatre at Tuesday night's opening of *Beyond Therapy*. The aim: to state their case. Placards displayed some of their views: "Pact is a disgrace," "Reinecke must resign," "Pawe demands safety on our stages," "Long live Gaynor Young," "The people will perform."

PAWE give their reasons for the protest in a leaflet entitled *Pact Must Change*. The reasons are:

– PACT's refusal to negotiate with democratic cultural organisations.
Dennis Reinecke says that he last met with PAWE a year ago and was still waiting for them to get back to him. According to him he had PACT's legal advisors write to PAWE in this regard. He has met with Serote and the DAC at least three times this year and claims that "frequent negotiations have taken place between PACT and democratic cultural organisations."

– PACT's arrest of 150 peaceful demonstrators in the State Theatre on August 7.
Reinecke responds that PACT cannot be accused of arresting anyone because they have no jurisdiction in that area. He adds that certain laws were broken with regard to peaceful protest — only ten people can gather in one place to protest; a larger crowd constitutes an illegal gathering. Neither he nor the police were informed of the protest, so it became a security issue.

– PACT's squandering of taxpayers' money on defending their position — notably the court cases involving 317 unfairly dismissed workers and actress Gaynor Young.
Reinecke says that the dismissals were not unfair as the strike was illegal, regardless of the court ruling. He says that the court had in fact exonerated PACT in the Young case. Not only managements, but also artists had certain responsibilities to uphold.
– Further reasons include PACT's "squandering money by mounting the same ballets year after year with entirely new decor and costumes," as well as their exemption from work permit procedures for international artists.
Reinecke dismisses the charges, claiming that PACT's approach to the repertoire is similar to that of other international companies — i.e. that sets and costumes are subject to wear and tear and must be replaced. He says PACT is not exempt from obtaining permits for international artists.

PAWE remains adamant that Reinecke resigns. Reinecke refuses to comment on this, but couldn't restrain himself from saying that the demand was not a particularly democratic one and that it was unjustified.

PAWE spokesman Dan Robbertse is pleased with the protest's friendly nature and the absence of intimidation. He says that the intention was not about "not attending PACT productions, but rather highlighting certain problems." He adds that the protests will continue until PACT addresses the problems.

PAWE will shortly be affiliating with the International Federation of Actors (FIA), a worldwide umbrella body, who will help them to put on the pressure (*Vrye Weeklblad,* 11–17 September 1992: 35).

To this the PAWE executive replies:

> In his article entitled "PACT — where the arts unite people?" Charl Blignaut reports on PAWE's picket of the opening night of PACT's production of *Beyond Therapy* and the response of PACT director Dennis Reinecke to the leaflet that PAWE distributed at the picket. Our quibble is not with Charl Blignaut — we appreciate his well considered coverage of the event. PAWE wishes to point out a couple of the inaccuracies in Reinecke's statement.
>
> Reinecke denies the fact that he blocks negotiations between PACT and democratic cultural organisations. Just one example will make our point. To paraphrase a letter from PACTs lawyer dated 12/09/1991: *PACT cannot respond to PAWE's request for recognition agreement negotiations because PAWE is a political organisation and hence not a bona fide union.* This is pure obfuscation. If unions and politics are mutually exclusive then COSATU and NACTU would not be unions. PACT's letter is simply a red herring — another obstacle in the path of PAWE's attempts to negotiate with PACT.
>
> – Reinecke claims that PACT was not instrumental in the arrest of 150 peaceful demonstrators in the State Theatre on August 7. The delegation that staged a sit-in that day made it clear that they would leave the State Theatre as soon as Reinecke accepted their memorandum. Instead, he chose to get a court interdict to evict the delegation which led directly to their arrest and prosecution.
>
> – PAWE — among others — accuses PACT of wasting the taxpayer's money on unnecessary industrial relations battles. Reinecke denies this. PACT's firing of the 299 State Theatre workers last year has been declared an unfair labour practice by both the Industrial Court and the Labour Appeal Court. The Appeal Court recently upheld the earlier ruling that the

> fired workers should be reinstated with full back pay. Both
> courts reprimanded PACT and its lawyer for its outmoded
> industrial relations practices. The costs to PACT in this
> senseless and unwinnable legal battle they have undertaken,
> before consideration of legal fees, are around R 2.5 million.
> Taxpayer's money. Reinecke indicates in the Blignaut article
> that "the dismissals were not unfair . . . regardless of the
> court ruling." This now notorious intransigence and disre-
> gard for the findings of two of South Africa's courts indi-
> cates a flagrant lack of respect for the law (*Vrye Weekblad*,
> 18–24 September 1992: 35).

In the meantime it was reported that CAPAB would be willing
to resume negotiations with the Federation of South African Cultural
Organisations (FOSACO). What the outcome will be, remains to be
seen. But one thing is certain: the political and social changes in the
country will also affect the Performing Arts Councils and their structures.

In the ongoing debate, however, both sides again and again
assume that the state will continue to subsidise the performing arts.
But the state is close to bankruptcy. There is a negative economic
growth rate of –2.6%, an unemployment figure of 45%, a deficit of 6%
on the gross domestic product is looming on the horizon and the
inflation rate is officially said to be 15%, but probably it is much higher.
Money is desperately needed for housing, education and medical care.
In these circumstances it seems to be futile to demand the total (and
expendable?) luxury of ongoing or even increased state subsidies for
the performing arts. Quite rightly it is demanded that the performing
arts be made more accessible to broader sections of all communities,
but it would be a fallacy to assume that with the democratisation of
the Performing Arts Councils the state theatres would attract crowds
as large as those attending soccer or rugby matches. In comparison the
performing arts audiences will always be somewhat smaller, somewhat more "élitist." Should this not be taken into account when one
talks about the future funding of the Performing Arts Councils, e.g. by
selling those artistic products for which there is the least demand for
the highest prices? But at the same time mechanisms should be developed which prevent excluding those who can't afford high ticket prices.

Be that as it may, at long last it seems to have been realised
that unless debates and discussions take place amongst all concerned
parties there will be no future for the Performing Arts Councils and
the state theatres.

According to recent newspaper reports the Natal Performing Arts Council is in the process of revising its constitution so that its members represent a broader community than before. And rumours have it that PACT, after all, is planning something similar.

"IT'S TIME TO HAVE A
SOUTH AFRICAN CULTURE."
AN INTERVIEW WITH RAMOLAO MAKHENE[1]

The founding of the Performing Arts Workers Equity (PAWE)

Question: Perhaps you could begin by telling us what the acronym PAWE means and when the organisation was founded?

Makhene: The past twenty-five or twenty-six years there's been SAFTU — the South African Film and Theatre Union. It catered for the white folks, they tried to woo us in. I was still working at Wits, and I kept on saying to them: "Guys, there's no way we can come into you, if you don't come out in the open." They used to have some words in italics that you also involve blacks, and we just said, "No!" I was still with Robert McLaren at Wits and they said as they'd used the name of Workshop '71, they'd send us some percentage. They sent us R21 or R27; we sent it back. They didn't have the right to use our name in the first place without consulting with us.

In 1976, a group of mainly black artists, right through the spectrum — musicians, actors, visual artists, the lot — met at Donaldson Orlando Cultural Club. Our idea was to put together a school of the arts, then also have a union. What came out of that was FUBA (the Federated Union of Black Arts). Now what worked better was the school which we have, the FUBA Academy next to the Market Theatre; the union side fell off. Then there were a number of other attempts. I remember, one meeting was held in Mofolo. It almost looked like things were going to happen, but one of the people — I won't mention names — who had put those people right up front to do certain things for us suddenly got some sponsorship from some Italians and they just

[1]Anne Fuchs and Geoff Davis interviewed Ramolao Makhene at Malcolm Purkey's home in Bertrams, Johannesburg on 8th September 1992.

threw all our work out of the window, put it in abeyance and nothing happened.

And then came CASA (the Conference for Another South Africa) in Amsterdam. At that time there was the UDF Cultural Desk. How that started, they pulled in people, from the top rather, it was at that point that somebody said, culture needed attention and they called people from organisations, and also as individuals, to sit on the desk. So they kept on saying that people must get their act together. There was a realisation that we cannot have a union of all the arts combined like that, just at a go; that it was important that we divided ourselves into our disciplines. The first president was Marolo.

The visual arts had their own problems. They said a lot of artists were working as individuals like the visual artists, the musicians are more problematic. The most troublesome area is PAWE, it's going to be the actors' area. One of the things that came out of CASA was the resolution, that we have to form ourselves as disciplines. We can then later have a federation of these organisations. I think just before CASA we had met as actors and we had formed something called Theatre Alliance. Looking back, we created a paper union. I don't know if you know what I mean by that? With all our honest intentions of getting things together, that's what it was. Then the people up front — there was me, there was Siphiwe Khumalo, John Kani, Gcina Mhlophe — we went to CASA.

When we came back, I personally started going round asking questions, because I was working a lot with the COSATU unions, running workshops with them, trying to ask them to get a union together. And then I took this initiative to invite people — largely the Malcolm Purkeys — and I also invited people from the Living Wage Campaign. They had a play that they took to CASA, and which I had helped direct. I invited those guys as well to come into this meeting.

Before the meeting started, I saw people conversing and I realised that there were some problems. When the meeting started, people said, this is not Theatre Alliance, because the people we see here aren't Theatre Alliance. I tried to explain, I'm trying to open this up. I was really *"fokked"*, if I can use that word. People like Laurens Cilliers and Malcolm Purkey had to be asked to leave. It was quite a problematic time. What was happening there was that — quite rightly — the black caucus said: "Guys, we have a problem. Before we can say Theatre Alliance is this type of union, we need to sort out our backyards first, because we come from different political ideologies, the Matsemela Manakas, Maishe Maponyas, Ramolao Makhenes . . . ." It was important that we get this right. The criticism coming was that we were BCM, we were practising racism in reverse, which wasn't true. Altogether the problem was, one must openly say, that lots of us, my white friends, were so afraid or anti-BC. You mention the name of Maishe Maponya, that's BC [Black Consciousness], that's AZAPO [Azanian People's Organisation]; you mention Matsemela Manaka, no, those names were now involved in the alliance. Then came the UDF [United Democratic Front] and COSAW [Congress of South African Writers]. Together they called for a meeting of all the actors at the — what do you call that place? — the Market Theatre! The meeting was called there to say: "Guys, we're asking you to get your act together." Problems were put across: that why we wanted to come together to have another union was because SAFTU is not representing us, it's history; even if we say we join it, we change it from within, it cannot work, because it is an apartheid structure. It was agreed that something had to be done, we must have a new union. A committee of 17 people was chosen.

I was amongst those, Carol Steinberg was, Malcolm was, Siphiwe Khumalo and Debbie Watson, and a host of other guys who used to work for LEP. We divided into commissions, I was amongst the group that was working on the constitution. We looked at other constitutions, SAFTU, COSAW and others. One of the biggest realisations that came to us was that we have all been products of apartheid culture, we've been this apartheid culture all this time, it was now time that we should have a South African culture. And therefore, if we were to form whatever it would be called, one of its principles should be non-alignment and that has been the thing that helped to put PAWE where it is, helped PAWE to gather momentum, to get people into it, and get people to respect it.

Actually we were either the first or among the first organisations that said, culture should be non-aligned. Other organisations formed before like the Congress of South African Writers (COSAW) and AWA [the African Writers' Association] were ANC-aligned or PAC-aligned, but now people are beginning to realise that it is important that culture should be non-aligned. After this another meeting was held at the FUBA Centre, where they were calling in people to come and tell us what an association is, what an alliance means, what a union means. Out of that workshop the people said we need to have a union. Then the committee was set up, but the interim committee kept going ahead with the constitution, we were given about 6 or 8 months to get this constitution.

A meeting was called again in the Market, I was in Natal in 1990 working with the SARMCOL workers' latest play, *Comment* there. I was called in. It was May 20th: when we were going to set up the union officially. Lots of names came forward: "Congress of . . ." And I said, once you say "congress," it cannot work, people say that's ANC. The name that actually worked was Performing Arts Workers Equity, and everybody was very happy about it. A committee was chosen and I was in the singularly unfortunate position of being chosen the first chairperson. And I've been in the hot seat since. I was re-elected and it's the third term I'm serving.

Question: How many times can you be re-elected?

Makhene: I don't know. The constitution does not actually say how many seasons one can stay on. One of the major issues now was that we should form one union. The management association was also falling apart, because PACT had withdrawn out of it and had started writing out their own contracts. And then there were SAFTU and PAWE and there were people who were members of both. We were being labelled the radical union, the political union, rather than an equity.

Amalgamation with SAFTU

We had battles. I remember, we had our first AGM, it almost became a SAFTU meeting, rather than a PAWE AGM, because they came in en bloc, and by that time we had a committee working on amalgamation. We were swallowing them and they were seeing it as amalgamation. There were a number of things that we had said were non-negotiables, like the name. They had said once, if we amalgamate, they still want to show that it's two unions coming together, we can say "PAWE incorporating SAFTU." We said, we cannot change the name PAWE, it has become such an important thing for our membership, when you say PAWE it's a kind of empowerment for the people in the existing union. You talk about SAFTU, you talk about something else. So we agreed that the name would not be changed. Then we ultimately came together, and they all came in. We did not want to take SAFTU into us with its problems, they had debts which were outstanding, and we said, we are not going to take these over, and we started to negotiate for money. Phillip Stein came in and helped us to clear that up. And that's how we came together.

It was not an easy road. Because of apathy people were not taking part. We found that a few people were running the union, some of whom had gotten used to taking decisions on their own. We found that very problematic, people would just ring and say, this one doesn't have the power, that one doesn't have the power. Once Megan Wilson made a horrible statement about women's rights that infuriated people, saying this is PAWE's stand, and it wasn't so; we'd never discussed that, she was never given that mandate, and that was a huge problem, because we mandate people. You've got to do, that's how we're working, because we consult quite a lot. That is the type of line we are taking: everything must be by consultation, they had lost that way of working.

Question: Does SAFTU still exist, or has it been completely dismantled?

Makhene: Completely.

Question: And have all the members of SAFTU joined PAWE or have some of them stayed out?

Makhene: Some have stayed out, some have joined. Some joined immediately, some joined while SAFTU was still operating. After we had started to negotiate for amalgamation and they went on to hold other meetings, and we heard from some of those meetings, they said we had to go on for another year or two. And we thought, these people must be crazy. Then we immediately informed all the unions in the country and also British Equity and FIA, and were recognised and have become the latest child of FIA. At the end of this month I am going to the 15th FIA conference in Montreux.

Question: What roughly is the strength of your membership?

Makhene: We're just getting on to a thousand. The industry is based mainly in Johannesburg, Durban and Cape Town. SAFTU was national, but we do not want to assume that we are national. In Soweto when a thing starts people call it South African this and that, but it's just a Soweto thing. Last week I was talking to Kessie Govender, who wants to get things going; there are people at NAPAC, who want things to happen. There was a Theatre Alliance thing happening there. Ari Sitas was doing that, but it looks like he had his own problems as well. The Western Cape has its own problems; they personalise things quite a lot. I thought we'd got a lot of groupings in Johannesburg, but there they are really at each others' teeth. For example, if Vanessa [Cooke] goes and talks to the black folks there, they say they don't trust her, they're being sold down the river. This I was told to the face, so I have to go and speak to those folks. So you can see the complexity. Even during the days of the UDF, there were all those complexities. Last year I was working at the Baxter Theatre and we started again getting meetings together, Dale Cutts was in the cast and was also our syndic, and together we went to do the play there. I had to go to talk to the people at the Nico Malan Theatre, there were about sixty or seventy of them. Before this meeting Bo Petersen got together a meeting of a few people, then about ten people came and Malcolm was there as well, she forgot about the meeting and went to the beach!

Relations with the Performing Arts Council of the Transvaal (PACT)

Question: Could you perhaps tell us something about some of the specific issues PAWE has been dealing with, the issues you set the organisation up to address?

Makhene: Well, Equity is mainly to protect the actor at work. We are non-aligned, but we are not apolitical, and lots of issues that are happening around our industry have got to do with politics. Politics is bound in them. This is one of the things that was different between us and SAFTU, because SAFTU was not engaging in those issues; they were engaging PACT, but I think they were engaging PACT with kid-gloves, because lots of their membership was mainly getting work from PACT, and they were afraid of losing jobs and house subsidies and the like.

Question: Perhaps you could tell us something about the problem of PACT?

Makhene: For us, PACT is a state-subsidized institution which is using our taxes. Like all the other places, these institutions were put up to foster apartheid culture. The performances that go on there and all the advantages are mainly for just a section of the South African community. That is one of our biggest problems, that so much money should go in there, while there's not even one theatre in Soweto or any other township. All we've been getting is these township halls, that cannot be used because they've got no lighting or anything of the sort, but there's so much money, our money. Also, we as tax-payers are not able to get the fruits out of PACT.

It's only very recently that they are trying to do things that are political or with a South African flavour; they are for mainly Eurocentric theatre. Some people used to call me and say that Eurocentric theatre has got no place in this country, and I said, that is not true, we just have to promote South African theatre. Whilst we have to go out and about and see what other people do, it is important that our theatre must also get on its feet. There are people who are still propounding apartheid culture and fear another type of culture that comes in, thinking that they are fine, people are living protected lives. A person comes out of school, a job is definitely there, a house is there, everything is there, people have never lived lives of questioning issues, questioning values, questioning principles. PACT is part of that whole structure of life.

We feel that that structure is there, we cannot destroy it, we cannot go through what Beirut has gone through in order to start again. What should happen is that the way the place is run should be changed, and through negotiation. We are trying to start talking, first to get a recognition agreement with PACT. Just before we amalgamated with SAFTU, the two committees went to see Reinecke and Bezuidenhout, and we asked that their lawyers should not be there, because we wanted to have unprejudiced talks. He just sat there and refused to leave. We were arguing with him, what type of a person is this one, who is supposed to be the person who advises them? He is so stubborn, he's stupid. We walked out of that meeting, we sent them letters to say we want to have a recognition agreement. They took a newsletter of SAFTU which had a letter that I'd written that quoted from the AGM Report, and some words were "PAWE is a political organisation." He just took that line and said, "we cannot talk with you, because Equity is a political organisation." He just quoted the thing out of context.

And they were the people again who write to us wanting to get rights from overseas for a certain play and we said, "we don't censor plays, don't think this, but you have to go through RK/CC Consultative Committee for work permits"; it was done by the Home Affairs Dept. I can't remember who is in it, but we are outside. We were going to be in it as observers, but we realised that we have to be part and parcel of this, because so many things are going on. At the moment people are just rushing into our country, they are coming and taking our jobs. That was one of the battles we are waging with PACT.

And then at one stage they fired 317 workers. There are a number of other unions that are inside PACT. There's SACCAWU (the South African Commercial Catering Allied Workers Union), there's PPWAWU (Paper, Printing, Wood and Allied Workers Union). Most of the PPWAWU people are without work there, people who have worked fifteen or twenty years at PACT. They were all fired. I can't remember how the strike started. We had members there.

Now before this, when we were launched, we sent letters to all the unions in the country and said, we have just been launched, please recognise that here is another sister union, we are all in this, we are going to be working like all other unions protecting the rights of workers. The letters started at the top to filter down, it took long, but at that particular union there, they asked the organizer to work hand in hand with our people to get things going. Because we are saying we are non-aligned, and they do not understand how on earth at this time in terms of politics you can say as an Equity you are non-aligned, the organizer did not start working with our people.

Question: Is there any issue beside PACT? Have you had any other disputes where you have had to intervene?

Makhene: We've had a number of them. The very first one was with a group called Street Sisters, that was going overseas. Just before they wanted to go, a number of the musicians were owed money and before they left they asked James Mthoba and me to go in and speak to the actors, it is important that they have contracts. We spoke to them the night before they left. None of them had a contract, they all ended up in the rubbish bin. Some of the musicians stayed behind, about eight or twelve of them and the total amount of money that was owed was about R 12000. We went into this, we spoke and every cent of theirs we got back. That was our very first case, the first we won. All our actors have had their money back. The big one that we got involved in was *Rabelais*. And then there was the other one: Colin Law and *The Rocky Horror Show* . . .

Les Misérables

Question: Tell us about the problem of *Les Misérables*.

Makhene: We heard that there were going to be auditions. We quickly checked out what is happening and we found out that it's *Les Misérables* happening. The auditions were held, the guys came in, auditioned, and out of the country they went. Then, one started finding out what is actually happening. They told us, *Les Misérables* was being brought here. At first they were going to bring in a cast from out there, that's the impression that we got from the beginning. Then we started fighting. We said no, we said if this should happen it should be done in the proper fashion. A workshop was held by PAWE members at which we got a mandate from the people what we must do. We said no. A union can only be a union when people are working, and therefore one should not stop work coming into the country, but if the work comes into the country, it must benefit our own members. Therefore find ways to let it happen well for our people.

We said fine, first we would love to have the original director come in — with an understudy of our own. We've got a number of people we feel can handle such big musicals. We'd love to have a totally South African cast. Give many blacks parts, even 60%, and also give it a South African flavour in terms of the story-line — it was mainly around the French Revolution — and also have people on the technical staff, people that are going to be trained. We were discussing with Pieter Toerien, and it was ding dong, ding dong all the time.

Then, suddenly, Mackintosh withdrew. He wrote to us a very horrible letter: they've sent people here, there's no one in South Africa, not one actor who can handle his type of work. There was a second very arrogant letter he wrote to us. And then in the meantime Pieter Toerien and the press went to town, saying that PAWE was responsible for the cancellation of *Les Misérables*. Even some of our members were saying we were the cause of this. While he was saying this, the people were shouting at us, saying we have stopped the work. In the meantime, Mackintosh was saying, they are not fit for his work. OK, then we had another meeting where every letter of correspondence was shown and read to our membership, and it was only then that the people understood that PAWE had done all it can to protect its members. Then the media first interviewed Pieter Toerien and they interviewed me and Malcolm. The trouble of it was that Pieter Toerien was just fumbling about what we had put across, while we had put our facts together, we were also on 702 radio.

At that time one of the reasons that we think Cameron Mackintosh withdrew on us was that that was the time when the *Graceland* guy, Paul Simon, was coming to the country. AZAPO was giving him problems, and it was at that time that he withdrew. I think he was afraid of the South African situation as well, not to get himself involved; there were the cultural boycott issues that were still hanging in the air, so he just withdrew. But in withdrawing, he wrote this arrogant letter to us. We were getting a lot of flak, the media were really going to town on us; we sent them the facts of what has actually happened that they just manipulated.

The Rocky Horror Show

At one of our AGMs there was a guy called Colin Law, who is also a producer. In the past, before he started this show, he was owing so many actors, and in the AGM we spoke about him. And the people said an *escroc* fund must be started, that he must put in two weeks' salaries of people in that *escroc* fund. This trust was started, people auditioned, they also asked me to come and audition for them, but because of lack of communication and time I never got round to it.

It started in Cape Town. We sent membership forms down, we sent cards, we even sent the money for people to go and get things going. And Colin Law kept on saying, "I'm waiting, where is this PAWE?" He spent seven weeks in Cape Town, and nothing happened! We were made the laughing stock by the people in Cape Town. Somebody actually said: "We don't agree, we don't really have a need for a union here in the Cape." Oh, the people of Cape Town, you just feel like taking a *sjambok* and chasing them into the sea sometimes. Then we came up into Jo'burg. I had to go and speak to the actors, he allowed me to speak to the actors, they all joined, it was beautiful. Ultimately he did put money into the *escroc* fund. He's making money like dust with the *Rocky Horror Show.*

PAWE begins to picket PACT

Question: You mentioned that you were going to picket the Alexandra Theatre and that that would be part of the campaign against PACT. Can you tell us how you moved onto this very practical way of bringing yourselves to their attention?

Makhene: Actually, while we were starting talking with PACT as a union, and they were pushing us out and telling us they don't recognise us, the ANC through its Arts and Culture Dept. (DAC) were talking to them. And they were looking down on us and saying, "who are you to tell us this, when we are talking to the ANC?" Then agreements were made between the two, that they had got to come forth with this and that, and nothing was happening. In the meantime, we also had another workshop around how do we tackle PACT? We don't just want to work out of the committee, we call the members together.

Out of that first meeting we had two committees, one of which was "Slash and Burn," the other was "Plant and Water." The "Slash and Burn" Committee was going into PACT and investigating, how do they use their money, how are they funded, how do people get paid, are there any scandals going around? Then the "Plant and Water" one was to draw up a programme and go up to them and say, "give us the Windybrow Theatre for a particular time. Let us run the Windybrow. Let us show you how we can bring people to that place." These things were moving very slowly.

One of the things that we have a problem with at PAWE is manpower; we are over-extended. And some things we start with just fizzle out. Some of our members that were within PACT were a little bit afraid, they openly withdrew from the "Slash and Burn" and said, we don't think we can manage this; it's too hot a cake for them. Then Janice Honeyman and other people got very busy. So it's still hanging in the air. While they were talking like this, they had already fired these 317 people, they appealed in court, and won the case, and PACT went to appeal. But last week they lost the case, they've got to repay people . . .

Then came in the ANC campaign around the whole country, this mass action issue. So all the organisations joined in, FAWU, PAWE, COSAW, people as individuals, all the other committee groups were going to go there to present this memorandum. When we were still around there, the delegation walked up, and Reinecke refused to come out. We were asking for his resignation, he sent his tenth second, and the guy said, until he comes we are not moving here. They were also arrested. But we were arrested first. People were still *toyi-toying*, waiting for the bus to come, and a concert was going to be held on that square in Pretoria in front of the PACT building. We were all piled into trucks. Some of the guys were coming out of the bus straight into the trucks, and we were locked up. We spent the whole day. I had to miss a performance of *Death and the Maiden*. At three, I started telling these guys I had a job to do. At six o'clock, they started dividing us, putting men one side, women the other side, and handling the juveniles. At quarter past eight, there was a call then, this top top policeman comes: "Do you know Alan Joseph?" "Yes." "He wants you now in Jo'burg." He tells these people, "this guy must go now." This show is supposed to start at quarter past eight. They're releasing me, then I pick up the phone and I say, maybe I can be there at nine o'clock. I get Carol's car, which doesn't go over 100. When I arrived here, they had already dispersed the people. I spoke with some of the audience. So out of that we felt, ANC are doing it in a particular way; it was this mass campaign. We agreed with them that every other group must have its own initiative. If they want to do it together with the ANC, they can. One of the big problems we found was that everytime we do anything with the ANC, we are accused of not being non-aligned. So we'd rather do things on our own, without ANC with us.

We decided that we are going to have our own campaign, and the beginnings of it is that we should picket each and every opening and make the people aware of what is happening. We did picket them at one stage. They brought in the Baden-Baden Symphony Orchestra from Germany. Whilst they had fired 317 workers, they spent all these monies to bring in these people to the City Hall. We went and asked for permission and we had people walking across from going to watch the show and join us around the picket. That was our first major picket against them at the City Hall. We even spoke to some of the people, we had such a hell of a row with them, because they had been told lies about coming, they were not told the facts about this place. And that is the reason why we are picketing tonight.

Workshop '71

Question: Perhaps we could now come to your own career in the theatre. What have been for you the most important things you have done in the theatre over the years? How did you start?

Makhene: I started working when I finished matric, in '68 and '69 at the Anglo-American Research Laboratory. From there to another small place called General Superintendant in town. Then I was working with this terrible Jewish person called Mr Sher, who used to say, every time he sees a black, "he's rotten." He was a terrible person. And then I went to work at Wits. There's a friend of mine, James Maliba — he's late now — he helped me apply and I got the job. I was supposed to go into one of the laboratories, but the personnel manager, a white person called Mr Hindle — they called him "two minutes," because every time he came into the office, he said "I haven't got much time, I've only got two minutes" — he said, your cv is fine, I haven't got a place in any of the laboratories, but for the meantime, please go to the library, and once there's some place, please apply and we'll take you up. And I got into the library, and I never got out of the library!

I worked 11 years at Wits, but the second day I started working with a guy called Jabu, who was a pro of Workshop '71. They invited me to go and see a performance of a play called *Crossroads*, which was an experimental play based on ideas from *Everyman*. It was directed by Robert McLaren. I was sitting in the audience enjoying myself and it just happened that Robert was in there and my reactions to what I was seeing were what he was expecting of the audience. My reactions attracted his attention and he asked Jabu who I was and Robert said, "can you invite him to come to workshops?" And that's how I started.

Question: The next highlight . . .

Makhene: People always ask me which play is my best play. And I always say, I thought the last play I did was the best until I do the next one.

Question: What do you think is your most important contribution?

Makhene: Let me blow my trumpet! I think one of the things that was a good foundation for me in the theatre was starting with Workshop '71 and being made to fall in love with the work. Things opened up quite a lot, this educated me being involved with theatre and doing experimental work and taking theatre to the people. When we were in Workshop '71, at one stage we had about three, four or five plays actually at a festival of Workshop '71 plays. There was *ZZIPP*, there was *uNosilimela*, there was *Crossroads*, there was *Happy Ending*. *Survival* had not been done yet, but James Mthoba had already done his one-man show, *The Reed*. At that time Gibson Kente, the Sam Mhangwanes, the other guys in the townships were running plays, and the fees that were being charged were R 1.50 and that was quite a lot still for people to pay. I remember when we went to Port Elizabeth, they were charging R 2.50 because of the transport to get there. And here we are, we're coming there to charge 50c. So people said, "I'm sure this must be rubbish of a play, 50c. Anyway, let's go and see." It had two forms: either people were saying, "we won't go there and see a thing that is worth 50c." And others were saying, "let's go and see why." And the reason why we were charging 50c was because we were trying to take theatre to the people.

Taking theatre to the people

And then James came with this idea, and handpicked people up with Workshop '71 — me, himself, Themba Ntinga, who went over with *Survival* to America, my former wife Mpho Makhene, who's stopped acting — six of us. We did two things. One was a series of workshops: what happens to a man when he comes home from work up to when he wakes up in the morning? We called this *Footsteps*. That was the first half.

The second half was a play by Douglas Turner-Ward, *A Happy Ending*, which was a very fine comedy. These two ladies worked for this very rich white couple, and they were about to get divorced. So this young boy comes home and confronts them crying at the table: "why the hell are you crying for?" And they say," Mr So and So is getting divorced. Are you crying for this madam? Let them get divorced." The woman says, "look they've given you these clothes." We take the clothes to the tailor's and have them changed and the boy becomes the best-dressed boy in America, and then he sits down and starts to cry. And then the father comes in, and he knows what it means for them to get divorced, and he starts to cry. And as they are all crying, the phone rings. One of them goes and picks it up, and he tells them, "no, it's alright, they're not getting divorced anymore. They've come together again." It becomes very hilarious. And with that we are able to take it all around, wherever we wanted it played. We were in Pretoria in a church, it was a mixed audience, and we took these two children and put them in front of us and this couple kept on pointing fingers at them, they were having so much fun, they were collapsing. But the nicest one was when one of the brothers of one of the women who was acting with us was having a wedding anniversary, and he asked her just to bring something. And she said: "OK, I've got a present for you." He didn't know what it was. So they went through all the niceties. "Now for this part of the programme, let's go outside, because there's no room here." They all went outside, we cleared the stage and we put them there, and the table was our only prop, and they went to town. It was so full, there was this guy, he went up into the tree and sat there, and as they were laughing, he forgot he was in the tree, wow! He came down! It was such fun with that play, taking theatre to the people.

Then we took it to a place in Evaton. We couldn't get started until quite late, and we had to use paraffin lamps, lanterns to hang up under a grapevine, and we started acting. When we finished, they said "encore." Most people had never seen theatre before; they wanted it again. We had to do the play again. Well the guys just kept cutting and cutting! It has never happened in my life to be asked to do a play again! And for me, that area was a really good thing, to be able to take theatre to the people and see how people react to it. It was the most wonderful thing to happen.

The Sun will Rise for the Workers

In 1982/83 I was still working at Wits, I was still acting part-time, still working at the library. I hadn't moved to the Centre for Political Studies. This was the days during FOSATU, before it became COSATU. There was a foundry near Boksburg, there were such horrible working conditions there, people during working hours were not allowed to move off the working premises, the only person allowed to was the *induna*, the boss-boy. So this particular day, one of the workers was looking for a screw, he didn't know which one to use, and the only person who knew was the *induna* and the *induna* was not on the working premises, gone to the shop or something like that. They couldn't go on working; so he decided to go and look for this person, after he consulted with everybody. And when he went to go and look for him, the boss boy saw him. He said, "you're fired." The people said nothing, they sat down and created a sit-in. They called in the police, piled the guys into a truck, when they got to the police-station, they reversed in. As they came out, they beat up everybody individually, they went to court, they were given a five-years suspended sentence. Then the union went in and sued the Minister of Police. The case went into court for about three days. The third day the police realised they are going to lose the case, they settled out of court. I think they got something like R42-45,000. There were 42 workers involved; the most hurt person got something like R250. The important precedent here was that the money for the fines came out of the policemens' salaries that had done the beating. For some time that helped the police not to jump into a situation.

Then, Halton Cheadle, who is a labour lawyer, came and asked Junction Avenue, can't you do a play about this? So Ari Sitas and Siphiwe Khumalo started working, and they called me in later. We started working with this whole group, the three of us went in. I left it to Ari and Siphiwe; then I was called back again. We ended up with about six of the guys out of 42, the others got jobs and the other problems of not being able to stay in the hostel and things like that. Being without money, they went to other places.

Then we got this play together and called it *Ilanga Lizophumela Abasebenzi (The Sun will rise for the workers)*. We put up the play at Wits, and students with a video camera trying their luck put it on tape. Halton Cheadle wanted to look for funds with this tape overseas and he came back with something like R50,000 which was put into the education fund. Then this cassette was sent around the workers in the country. This was the beginning of the Workers' Theatre, which is running very high at the moment. All the workers are realising we can actually do this. Lots of the workers, the shop stewards on the ground floor were either illiterate or semi-literate and to teach them to read the *Government Gazette* was very difficult! Rôle-playing was the best thing and writing scripts, and that was my work mainly, going round all the unions doing the play, carrying with me videos to show them. That for me was one of the best things to see a person who had no confidence, could not say things, who was always cowering, but suddenly seeing a person blooming.

The SARMCOL workers and *Comment*

Then I was called on a number of times back to Natal. I had worked with the SARMCOL workers. The guys also had the same kind of background: they were fired. The whole township was working in Howick, this huge SARMCOL rubber company. So instead of just sitting down, they opened a cultural cooperative, agricultural coopera-tive, T-shirt making cooperative and a health cooperative. And they did their first play *The Long March*. Then I was asked at one stage, because Ari was working with them and he has no Zulu. With Malcolm during the days of Junction Avenue, he kept on saying "guys, are you going to learn?. Yes, next week I'm going to have lessons." 10 years have passed. I went down and helped with that and then they called me again, they had done another play — *Bambatha* — they were going overseas. It was 99% in Zulu! It was quite challenging work. While I was working with these people — some were very literate, some were semi-literate — I had to make them talk the English that they under-stood and also at the same time not interfere with the quality of the play, the message of the play. And there were certain things that we had to leave out, that we were not going to change into English, because they were just going to throw the play into another direction. It was a very difficult job, but a very challenging one.

Then they called me back again. I stayed there for three and a half months. When I went back, they said they wanted to do a play that they can perform anywhere else, like at the Market Theatre. It should not be seen as another worker play. And before going down, I asked, "please let the guys research what they want to do, let them look around." At that time Mandela had just come out. So when I got there, I said, "what have you researched? What have you done?" A guy shows with three sentences, it was absolutely nothing.

We had to start from scratch. I asked the guys, what do they want to do? Tell me all the areas they want to look at. They wanted to look at what has happened since Mandela came out, the exiles coming back, what happened to the exile families, what happens to these people? And we chose this exile family, the father coming back, he had left his wife behind, got married there, he's coming back home, but when he comes back home, he finds his wife has got a child with a policeman, who has almost killed the other son, they almost kill each other. And at the end, they had all these different people, they had Mbeki, they had Vlok, they had a scene between Vlok and Buthelezi, they had a helicopter over Howick, because that was a very problematic area for them, they got it right ultimately.

Question: What was the play called?

Makhene: The play was called *Comment*.

Question: Has it been performed anywhere else?

Makhene: They went overseas with it. I met Nise Malange two weeks ago; she said they're putting on another play about hostel violence. And they're going to call me down.

The Alexandra Arts Centre

Question: Would you like to tell us something about your work with the Alexandra Arts Centre?

Makhene: When FUBA was still running, because of the lack of training for black people here at home, the community centres came up, and most go around on Sundays and in the evenings and run workshops. I used to run some workshops for FUBA and when Alexandra Arts Centre was started — we still were using the clinic — Mbongi Dhlomo, who was the coordinator then, called me in. What she did, she went out; somebody else was the coordinator and fund-raiser and now it was a hell of a problem, because what they did was get this white woman, who was raising funds for them. She was never seeing herself as part of Alexandra Arts, and money was not coming in. Then the committee themselves called Mbongi back in. She looked for people she knew had been in this area, she got hold of Mgali for the music, she asked me to coordinate after we found a space in Marlborough, a building with just one floor above, a ground floor and a first floor.

Things were going well for almost two years. Alexandra is a place — the nicest thing about what was happening there, they were allowing us the people that were coordinating the disciplines to carry on with what we were doing. "Go out and do your *Sophiatown*, so that you can come back with the experiences and teach." And also what we were doing was always, call people from outside to come in and give their expertise as well. We first started this part-time, in the afternoon, we also started having people coming full-time. These had also a number of problems. When people are unemployed these days, a certain culture has come out. People see you on television, and say: "Hey, Ramolao, come here man; give me a job. I also want to appear on television, man. I can play a drunk person, you know how I drink, man. I can do that with ease. I can always drive a bike." People just think that it's all that easy, and you say, "go in then," and if a person is unemployed, they come in, they become full-time students.

With that we also started inheriting other problems. People seeing that place as their home, and they are not seeing themselves after a year or two going out. What we were also doing every six months or every year is a thing that we had started trying to promote Alexandra Arts Centre. You just say, art's on the move, get a truck, get a band, put up things, and come with students; just a place in Alex, we stop, people follow the truck, and we stop, and students put on a performance, a dance. Then to the next place. We give out forms, and people actually start to come in. I started taking the Alex combi and just going out to the schools, talking to the people in the schools and people are really into acting, you know. Then the students started to come in.

Then there were other types of political problems coming in, that people had. Whilst they called people from outside to come in and run the centre, and the centre was becoming a model of all these arts centres, they were thinking that the thing was being taken out of their hands, was getting out of their control. Certain things were being manipulated, the students were mainly manipulated. This came out.

People confessed later and told us. We had to leave the place unceremoniously. Our lives were threatened. Now three or four years later, people are coming back and saying, "Guys, a mess has happened." Meetings were held, there was a trial, a tribunal you can call it; another meeting was held, where people from the cultural desk — known, respected people in the cultural world — came there to try and resolve the whole issue.

Alexandra is a very sophisticated place, because it's so small, it's got so many people, there's thuggery, they have their own communal life and it also attracts so much international attention. Alex will always be on peoples' minds. Some people have come to believe that when culture is coming it is their right to be given handouts. And what used to happen was, you'd see the students coming in, they'd buy fat cakes for lunch, and buy a packet of cigarettes, R2, R3. We said, "let the centre buy food, let's cook because we've got kitchens," we were starting a kitchen as well and a cooking class. "Let's cook here, and let's sell you the food." They said, "Rubbish. We're not going to. We're going to eat for free." That started the whole thing. "We have this money here that belongs to us, and we must be paid for" — and we're trying to put this into them: "Be on your own." We'll never stop getting attention from outside and it's such a terrible thing to hear that.

Then other things came. I went away with *Sophiatown*, and we ended up coming to Nice. I had called in Bobby Rodwell, and then Soli Philander, James Mthoba, and Andrew Buckland. I sat down with them and explained to them: "Guys, I'm going off for three and a half months. Can you come in and work with these guys?" There was a group teaching English, so they came in and ran the drama classes. The students couldn't express themselves in English. Half the time I was teaching English with my own bad English, and we started bringing in this other woman who was teaching them, and they were getting better and better.

When we came back with *Sophiatown*, one of these students — the leader — came to me, they phoned me in my house in Soweto to say, Ramolao, "we were given names, when we wanted help with our play, we were given your name and Peter Sephuma's name and we decided we must call on you to come and help us." I went there and looked at their play. I started helping them, and when we went full-time to the centre, we made them full-time students. It was these students that ended up saying, that I and Mgali and Mbongi, that all of us who had been going overseas for different reasons were using the centre's money in going overseas for our own thing. Every time one was overseas, one was talking about Alexandra Arts Centre all the time and things were happening to the centre. Then you came back and are told this. It was one of those terrible things.

Administrative problems

After that I started working on a project which was the brainchild of the South African Catholic Bishops' Conference, and getting money from the Germans too. One of their projects was to adopt community centres in the townships, and they called me in to come and coordinate the drama department. At the same time I and Mi Hlatshwayo were trying to start a full-time thing within COSATU of workers' theatre to train other workers. At that time COSATU was not yet seeing culture as a priority. Today they've got a culture department together. So, they'd already got the money, and they didn't know where to put the funds in, so I started working with this, combining the two there. One of the biggest things we had was having people who were administrators that had no inkling about culture, that just climbed on the bandwagon.

In coming to a place, when a person had been running a thing, and had put up suggestions, this person starts thinking that now you are taking over their work. That is one problem that I met there. For example, I was taking the kids out, organising them, making their department subsidised. I asked the kids to pay half the fare, asked the Market sometimes, they had a fund where they just provide the bus, we just come in and they just pay. I would get the kids around to come in. They said to me, I'm wasting money. The kids must see one or two plays a year. I said but that's madness, no ways can you encourage anything in kids when you're doing that.

A group of kids in Kagiso heard about what was happening and they complained and said: "We are disadvantaged, why don't we get this thing?" This person bought them a soccer ball and said, "keep yourselves busy." What type of thinking is that? This same person wrote an unsigned letter with a group of other people to get me fired — and sat around the table with me. And this very same person is sitting in a very high position in some of the organisations that we are talking about. Is this where we are going? We don't have cultural administrators that have a cultural inkling, that can help us out. If we can start training in that area, then we're quite a way.

The Grahamstown Festival

Question: Recently you have been much involved in the Grahamstown Festival, too?

Makhene: Yes. The Grahamstown Festival is a project of the 1820 Settlers Memorial Foundation — a memorial of the English colonialists who came into Grahamstown and settled there. They started a number of years ago as a celebration of the English language, but throughout the years, as it grew up, it ended up including other things, and now at the moment it's a fully fledged festival, which includes on the main programme theatre, music — contemporary and classical — it has visual arts, it has dance, and on the fringe there is everything. 90% of things on the fringe are drama, but there's cabaret, and music is starting to come in, and the flea markets are happening there. It's happening at Grahamstown, which is a very small town. The town comes alive in those ten days, and the rest of the country comes down there. The people don't stay, they go on holiday, and hire out their houses.

So the first time I performed there was when I was doing *Master Harold and the Boys* by Athol Fugard in 1983, and we were part of the main programme. There is a festival committee that is independent, at one stage it was funded by Five Roses, but Standard Bank has been funding it for the past five years. It's growing, and Standard Bank is still putting lots of money into it. But there was that time when everybody was going to Lusaka, the "Lusaka Safaris" — and Mannie Manim told the committee that this committee is all white, and if it is to become a South African Festival, it has to start changing as everything else is changing. They started inviting people. I was invited with Sipho Sepamla, Saira Essa, Mike van Graan, I think Alan Joseph was also invited. I remember at the very first meeting Saira Essa did not spare them and she told the committee, what rubbish they'd been doing, how much they'd been making this an elitist thing. And I suggested, if everybody's going to Lusaka, there's no need to go to Lusaka, there are people here, so we must go around here. I'd started arranging a number of meetings with COSATU and suggested names, and they went around and listened to people and they were hammered left, right and centre. Since a new chairman came in, Prof. Alan Crump, he's also trying to change things, the way people are appointed now to the festival. My work on the festival, I and Mannie are in charge of the drama content, that goes into the main festival. People send in scripts, we read the scripts, I've got about four thick scripts to go through now. They give us the scripts, we read them and if we say it's a good script, we go ahead and they send in budgets.

One of the other battles we had, I and Mannie, was because lots of money was being spent on Pact and Napac, the people that already had lots of money. While they were the people who had an advantage, they were the main part of the festival. Last year we almost managed not to have any of these PACs, but because there was an anniversary of the English language, and there was one doing *Romeo and Juliet*, it went to the festival for that reason.

We have a problem, whilst we are saying, people have got to be empowered, things have got to be on a par, these people the "haves", have so much, and the "have-nots" have so little, that it is so difficult to say that people are on a par. So it's a huge battle, we are trying now to say it should be advertised, people must send in their scripts, because other people don't know about it, those people who know about it already send in their scripts very early and we start reading. Some of these that don't know send their scripts about May when the thing is happening in July, and at that time there is already a programme set up. So it's a huge battle.

I've written an article for the official programme two years ago, trying to say the type of things I think what a festival is, what we should promote if we say we are promoting a South African festival, because it has been so Eurocentric all the time.

The latest thing is that a Joint Committee has been formed, part people of the festival committee and people from PAWE, FAWU, SAMA and ACAC (the Association of Community Arts Centres). The grand idea was to have this joint committee to help find ways of appointing people onto the festival committee, trying to change the ways and means of the committee, how it should be the people's thing, how much it should help empower the people, especially in Grahamstown.

One of the things which was said, the people of Grahamstown said, here comes the week of Christmas, because it was the only week things happened. It was just happening on the Monument, now we've made that venues should be used in the townships and those buildings are being improved, the lighting, the stage, they are in use all over the year. Now the bank has just come in with a development programme and they have a budget different from the festival committee, which for me was one of the things that I said, "hooray!" We've been crying a lot and saying, the bank has got to put in money and educate people or some other people should come in. And the function of this joint working committee is to administer that this thing is done properly.

The Future of South African theatre

Question: What is your feeling about the general direction South African theatre is taking? Do you think it will follow *Sarafina* or *Woyzeck on the Highveld*?

Makhene: I think things are changing, and I think they are going to change for the better. When we were on that long trip, we were in Toronto at the Harbourfront Festival, and there was a seminar going on where people were saying they didn't know what direction to take, because it looked like they'd done everything else. They were looking for new ways out. We were almost at that stage where people were saying, enough of sloganeering theatre, enough of township theatre, as they call it, enough of that. But how can you say, enough of that, when the country is still in this state? What is needed is, *how* should we say these things and *how* should we change them? That's for me — the line of *Death and the Maiden* is another one — when we did *Tooth and Nail*, that was another change. When we did that, we really got the most praise from people like Barry Ronge saying, here is a new way for South African theatre. I haven't seen *Woyzeck*, but the people who are in *Woyzeck* were the people we were working with in *Tooth and Nail* — and I heard that it's another very beautiful direction.

One thinks of some of the people like the poet Mzwakhe Mbuli, where they say things like that, they still do some of those old poems, but the new things he's coming up with! Apparently he's still fighting with which company must promote his records here, he's recorded something overseas, so they're still going through these problems. I hear that people are saying it had taken another direction, it's now telling people how to go through this transitional period. Obviously the fact that people in *Bambatha*, these SARMCOL guys, they're doing a play about the hostels. For the students for example, they can say enough is enough, but in one way or the other they're going to end up talking about politics.

For me, I think, one of the other directions that theatre must take, if theatre takes a change, is that you have to start teaching reconciliation, you have to start teaching people how to vote, start teaching people knowing what is democracy, people knowing what politics offer, tolerance. There's so many other things that theatre has to offer, the only way that can happen is if the people with the money start also changing their minds, like Nedbank has already started doing. Culture, I always say, culture is missing out on the wealth of this country, and if those people with the money can start realising that we have a rôle to do, we have to educate.

They too were concerned, the people that are in education, they were saying how many people are illiterate, the statistics vary from 6 million to 12 million people out of a population of about 40 million, and that is a lot. Those people are fathers and mothers and workers. That is why we are fighting SABC, we are saying to them, "change over, do things this way, start putting money into South African productions, because when people sit at night watching that, it makes such a lot if we give them educational matter." That is a line I think theatre will take.

Sarafina and things like that are entertainment, the type of things that people laugh seeing, musicals appeal to them quite a lot. If you have people like Mbongeni Ngema doing these things, what they should do is come up with the idea, just concentrate on the music, ask someone else to come and choreograph for him, ask somebody else to come and direct the play, ask somebody else to write the script for him. Start combining, and I'm sure you can come up with something very new for the theatre. We are starting working together with people cross-colour, cross-cultures, you know the experiences one went through when working on *Tooth and Nail*. I'm working with Neil McCarthy right now. After I did *Rainshark* some people saw it and said, you must write the film-script for *Rainshark*. Then came this idea, we should write a thing, they just asked me and said, "what do you think is a thing you want to put up?" I said, "one thing I want to write is about one character in black family life, one important person, the uncle. A lot of decisions in family matters have to go through the uncle, the maternal uncle." So we should need a thing that revolves around an uncle, and use that directly to act to the youth, talking about politics, tolerance and things like that, and his past history.

Recent Work

Question: Let's draw to a close and ask you to say something about your own most recent work.

Makhene: I have just finished doing *Death and the Maiden*, a play written by Ariel Dorfman, directed by Barney Simon at the Market. As I said, people always ask me which was your best play, and I always say, the last one. But this one was totally different. It's a play written from outside, but every other sentence of it says everything about this country this very minute. The thing that happened yesterday at Bisho, the fact that at this very time the government has said there was a moratorium on the death penalty and suddenly they say, they are going to bring it back, because there are certain cases that have happened that definitely warrant the death penalty. At the same time they are saying they want a general amnesty for the cabinet ministers, because things were coming out. And this play is talking about forgiveness, forgetting, about giving amnesty. It was also a very different kind. I've never played a lawyer in my life, it was an extremely serious play. Somebody was saying, "I've always seen Ramolao in a fun play, fun characters. It's the first time I've seen him in such a serious part." It was a very, very difficult rôle.

Besides that, there have been some television adverts that I've been doing, there's one that has been running since I did it in 1986. Everybody who sees me in the streets calls me "Triple X mint!" It's the longest running advert actually. There are other adverts. I suppose if I had been in America or England I would have been rich. I started doing adverts at the invention of South African television. I think I did about six or eight of them. Most of them have run for quite a long time.

Besides that, there are little movie parts that one gets, feature movies, that keep coming in. There are in-house movies, radio spots. One of the nicest things I started doing yesterday. I was doing four jingles for Old Mutual. Mutual is starting to introduce itself on the Black market. I did four radio spots yesterday. So my voice is getting marketed.

The Market Theatre Laboratory

I've also started working with the students at the Market Laboratory. They, like the workers, said they're tired of doing politics and politics. I said, "fine, let's look at what you want to do". They said they wanted to look at the experience of how they ended up at the Market Theatre. Some of them had been in these crooked places that call themselves agencies, that make you instant models, instant actors. They tell you they can turn you into a model — that's got *no* chance at all. And their money went down the drain; then they met somebody there, they end up at the Market, they sleep at the Lab. I said to them, "how about also that we do other things, because what is happening at the schools now, the culture of education is flat. This is the second generation that has lost out in terms of education. Can't we do something that we may take around schools or people's houses next year, that talks about what affects you? Some of you have just come out of school, some of you are still at school, a thing that talks about cultural education now. What can we do? What can be done? How do you help people to get back to school?"

Those are more or less the things that I'm doing, except running my family, and eating quite a lot and drinking lots of beer, especially when I'm not performing . . .

Appendix I

PUBLICATIONS APPEAL BOARD DECISION ON PUBLIC ENTERTAINMENT: *FAMOUS DEAD MAN*

We reprint below the official record of the deliberations of the Publications Appeal Board under the chairmanship of J.C.W. van Rooyen on Robert Colman and Matthew Krouse's play *Famous Dead Man*.

PUBLICATIONS APPEAL BOARD
REPUBLIC OF SOUTH AFRICA

PUBLIC ENTERTAINMENT: *"FAMOUS DEAD MAN"*

AP 181/86

PRESS EMBARGO

14 November 1986 12H00

PUBLICATIONS APPEAL BOARD
REPUBLIC OF SOUTH AFRICA
Date of Examination: 1986–10–21
Case No: AP 181/86
Date of Hearing: 1986–10–29

ROBERT COLMAN and MATTHEW KROUSE Appellants

v

THE COMMITTEE OF PUBLICATIONS Respondent

In regard to the Public Entertainment: *"FAMOUS DEAD MAN"*

Appeal Board: Prof. JCW van Rooyen (Chairman)
              Mr JJH Malherbe (Deputy Chairman)
              Prof. AP Grové
              Mr CD Fuchs
              Rev. PR van der Merwe
              Mrs L Gilfillan

For the Appellant: E Cameron, instructed by Bell, Dewar and Hall, Johannesburg

For the Respondent: LJL Visser SC, instructed by the Office of the State Attorney, Pretoria (represented by S Rudolph)

OPSOMMING

1   Kabaret waarin vroeëre leier se filosofie en beleid gesatiriseer word. Appèl teen verbod van die hand gewys.
2   Oordadige seksuele kruheid in aksie en dialoog lei tot bevinding dat die geheel ongewens is.
3   Aard en toon van stellings waarin na die Godheid verwys word, aanstootlik vir die godsdienstige oortuigings of gevoelens van die Christelike bevolkingsdeel.
4   Bevolkingsdeel word nie veragtelik of belaglik gemaak nie. Gronde 2 en 3 egter afdoende vir verbod.
5   Plekbeperking nie paslik nie.

JUDGMENT

JCW van Rooyen: A Publications Committee found the public entertainment *Famous Dead Man* undesirable in terms of section 47 (2) (a), (b) and (c) of the Publications Act 42 of 1974 as amended. The writers and performers of the entertainment appealed to the Publications Appeal Board against this decision.

I CONTENT AND ARGUMENT

The entertainment, which lasts just under an hour, satirises in a cabaret the life, attitudes, philosophy and historical legacy of Dr HF Verwoerd, Prime Minister of South Africa from 1958 until his death in 1966. The chief features of Dr Verwoerd's life, which are canvassed, are: his non-South African, non-Afrikaner origins; his intellectual brilliance; his career at Stellenbosch as a gifted student and debating leader; his marriage, tours and editorial role; his rising political dominance; the (alleged) intransigence of his political thinking; his intellectual contribution to political thought in South Africa; his proposed geopolitical blueprint for this country; the attempt to assassinate him in 1961 and his death by the hand of Dimitrio Tsafendas in 1966 in Parliament.

As indicated earlier, these different aspects of Dr Verwoerd's life are satirised by means of a cabaret. This comprises a series of sketches, songs and dialogues to lampoon, at times mercilessly, the thoughts and public life of Dr Verwoerd. Elements which are used in this cabaret include a simulated fellatio scene between "Dr Verwoerd's parents" in Holland, movements obviously indicating sex between "Dr Verwoerd's parents", a scene in which degree scrolls are held as penises and masturbatory actions are made with them and the following song which is sung at the beginning of the play and also at the end:

	"If you don't want to fuck then baby fuck off
Chorus	If you don't want to fuck then baby fuck off
	Nobody wins
	You play with my knee
	You know you're nothing but a prick-tease
Chorus	
	If you don't want a piece of the action
	then baby take a walk
Repeat	
	I ain't got time
	For yesterday's news
	So don't shoot me up with your bullshit blues
Chorus × 2	
	I love history
	It fucks up my mind
	It's going to give you real good time
Chorus."	

There is also a scene in which "Dr Verwoerd" arrives in heaven and orders God out of his chair: "God, aikôna God, you're in my chair — get out of it!" In the dialogue mention is also made of "Dr Verwoerd" studying to become God. "Mrs Verwoerd" is heard to say "I always wanted to fuck a future Prime Minister . . . Oh if I could fuck a Prime Minister every day, I'll probably live for ever!" There is also a scene in which a pair of woman's panties, made from or substantially from the South African flag or the Vierkleur are held up to the audience. There is a slit cut into the panties and one of the actors pokes his fingers or finger through the slit, clearly implying sexual activity. On the other hand, most of the other songs in no way contravene the Publications Act, for example, the Hosanna song, "I only Want to Start a Flame in your Heart", "Let's Go Get Stoned", "When the Night" and "Winds of Change". "Speeches" are often made in the typical style of a well-known earlier politician, obviously not Dr Verwoerd.

Mr Cameron, who eloquently put the case for the appellants, had obviously done research concerned with satire and cabaret as well as the broad outlines of Dr Verwoerd's philosophy. He argued that the present entertainment has received high praise: from experts who are acquainted with the nature of the art form which it expounds and who also have an extensive knowledge of drama, public entertainment in South Africa and the audiences which these forms serve. He also argued that the work has been carefully integrated into a form which diverts, shocks, provokes, entertains and amuses. He quoted from Hennie Aucamp's book on Cabaret where he says: "Kabaret teer op die spanning tussen burgerlikheid en vrysinnigheid." From the opening song, he argued, the audience is challenged to react; but the lyrics already seek, according to this argument, to convey something of Dr Verwoerd's well-known reputation for uncompromising adherence to his own views in the face of sustained dissent. This view already, according to Mr Cameron's argument, is brought to the fore by the opening song referred to earlier. It also, according to Mr Cameron, presents something of the present government's attitude towards the outside world: "We will move on our own terms, or not at all." He also argued that the work exposes human vain-glory, and ways in which men make idols of their own ambitions ("Jesus, you're in my way, get out of it"). The work raises questions, according to this argument, about delusions and about the wholeness of any one person's visions. It was argued that the work shows private ambition for public power transcending selfless service to the public. The scenes between "Dr Verwoerd" and his wife seek, by distortion and ridicule, to demonstrate the single-mindedness of the chief protagonists. The fatuous representation of the couple's wedding night is supposed to shock, but also disillusion, those people who have, according to the argument, defiled Dr Verwoerd and elevated him above the level of an ordinary man. But, most importantly, according to the argument, the entertainment tackles the current situation in South Africa. Dr Verwoerd is not selected, it is maintained, for incidental reasons: he left a considerable legacy to the rhetoric of today's politicians and South African public life in general. According to this argument, we live in the world of the AWB, the CP and the HNP which represent dominant political forces within the white community. *Famous Dead Man* is a reaction against, and a commentary upon such exclusivist thinking amongst Whites; although it is conceded that Dr Verwoerd cannot be called a white supremacist, for he developed the "homeland policy" and pursued it, intellectually, to its logical conclusion, he was nevertheless a wholly uncompromising white exclusivist. The present government has expressly abandoned the notions of white exclusivism — but Dr Verwoerd's thinking lives on strongly in public rhetoric and the campaign platforms of the organisations referred to. The entertainment seeks to address itself to the present by raising a spectre from the past. It does so violently, at times, heavy-handedly, always irreverently. Its background, context and intrinsic artistic cohesion, it was argued, sustain its individual components, even where these might be deemed to be annoying, vexing or in questionable taste. This constitutes, according to the argument, a substantial mitigating factor in regard to any potentially questionable material.

On the other hand Mr Visser argued that certain aspects of a political nature do bring certain sections of the South African population into ridicule or contempt. He, however, based his argument mainly on the sexual aspects and the religious aspects which, in his view, were indecently and offensively presented in this play. It is unnecessary to repeat his arguments here, as they generally correspond with the Board's conclusions.

II MERITS

Insofar as the merits of this cabaret are concerned, the two witnesses called by appellants (the well-known actors Pieter-Dirk Uys and Des Lindberg) both said that they were pleasantly surprised by the play. Mr Uys, in fact, indicated that when he started, like the present actors, he was much less successful. He also thought that the humour and shock technique used by the actors created an interesting theatrical device. Mr Lindberg indicated that he regarded the play as an example of the theatre of the grotesque and added that although he initially did not expect much from the performance, he afterwards thought that he had seen a very good "putting together" on the stage of such a play in its own terms. Although it is not the task of this Board to pronounce solely on the merits of the play we find it impossible to express an opinion on the questions concerning section 47 (2) without taking note of contextual justification of the parts and this, inevitably, is connected to merit. It is obvious that the lack of merit in itself is not sufficient ground on which to base a finding of undesirability, but on the other hand, the more morally risqué material becomes, the more it needs contextual justification. This Board is unanimous in its view that although this cabaret has some interesting aspects to it, the depth attributed to it by Mr Cameron, in his well prepared address, was lacking. Although the initial song obviously indicates an attitude of harsh inflexibility, one gained the impression that it was mainly there for entertainment and that the scant references which it has to history and "yesterday's news" do little to integrate it in the whole. One can also not help but wonder, for example, why the scene between Dr Verwoerd's parents had to portray such sexual crudity.

III THE COMMITTEE'S REASONS

Section 47 (2) of the Publications Act provides that a play or any part of it is deemed to be undesirable if (a) it is indecent or obscene or offensive or harmful to public morals or (b) if it is blasphemous or offensive to the religious convictions or feelings of a section of the population of the Republic or (c) if it brings into ridicule or contempt a section of the population of the Republic of South Africa.

The Committee gave the following reasons for its decision:

> "The question to be asked regarding this cabaret is whether it brings any section of the inhabitants of the Republic into ridicule or contempt within the meaning of s 47 (2) (c) of the Act.
>
> It is acknowledged that the Act does not protect the individual personality or for that matter political figures against criticism. But in this instance Dr Verwoerd is chosen as a symbol or representative of a large section of the Republic in an attempt to insult and degrade them.
>
>> 'It must be observed that the word insult does not in this context bear its ordinary meaning, but is used with the narrow meaning of degrading, humiliating or ignominy.' — See *Publikasiebeheer in SA*: JCW van Rooyen p 116.
>
> The scenes of gratuitous sex would exceed the tolerance of the average balanced person and the blasphemous material would be offensive to people's religious convictions within the meaning of s 47 (2) (b) of the Act.
>
> The Committee decided that this public entertainment would be offensive to the average reasonable person who is neither a prude nor a libertine as stated in Appeal Board case Rumpff HR in *SAUK v O'Malley* 1977 (3) SA 394 (A) — within the meaning of s 47 (2) (a), (b) and (c) of the Act."

IV SECTION 47 (2) (A)

Section 47 (2) (a) of the Act provides that if a public entertainment or any part of it (as understood in context, of course) is indecent or obscene or offensive or harmful to public morals, it is deemed to be undesirable.

Indecency must be judged according to prevailing community standards and after due consideration of all relevant factors such as likely audiences, content and manner of performance, the ultimate question is whether the well-balanced modern viewer would be outraged or whether a substantial number of well-balanced likely viewers would be outraged.

The word "offensive" in section 47 (2) (a) requires, in the light of Rumpff CJ's interpretation of the word "offensive" in *Publications Control Board v Gallo (Africa) Ltd* 1975 (3) SA 665 (A), that the material should be more than irritating or annoying and indeed mortifying, painful or disgusting. In *Publications Control Board v Republican Publications* 1972 (1) SA 288 (A) the majority of the Court applied the test of a substantial number of likely readers (viewers, in this case). Rumpff JA (as he then was), however, applied the test of the well-balanced modern reader who has a healthy mind as to sex and similar matters. This Board has given preference to Rumpff JA's approach but has, at times, also applied the other test. We have, however, taken note of Prof. E Kahn's opinion in "When the Lion Feeds — and the Censor Pounces" 1966 SALJ 278 at 322 that the "notion of a substantial number of likely readers is fraught with uncertainty."

Although the Publications Act 42 of 1974, in contrast to section 6 of the now repealed Publications and Entertainments Act 1963, makes no mention of likely readers/viewers, the Supreme Court in *Human & Rousseau Uitgewers (Edms) Bpk v Snyman NO* 1978 (3) SA 836 (T) held that the likely reader (viewer) remained a consideration ("oorweging") under the 1974 Act. The use of the word "oorweging" indicates that the Court did not regard it as a central criterion. Much stress was laid by the Court on the fact that the adjudicators under the Publications Act 1974 were appointed by reason of their "educational qualifications and experience" and that that was the reason why the Act had not, as its predecessor in section 6, spelt out the meaning of terms such as "indecent or obscene" etc.

The Board attended the performance of *Famous Dead Man* in a small venue with a capacity of 80–100, and this venue, "The Black Sun", is in the nature of a night club and is situated in a cosmopolitan area. This is, however, not conclusive evidence as to the likely audiences of this cabaret. In fact, it was performed at the "Howard Theatre" on the campus of the University of Natal which indicates that it would also fit a more traditional theatre than a night club. In any case, the public entertainment itself is the best evidence of its likely audiences. Mr Pieter-Dirk Uys in his evidence before the Board also indicated that the play could go to larger theatres. Mr Des Lindberg, however, had certain reservations about this, stating in his evidence that the size of audiences depended very much on the quality of the material and the reaction of the public to it and that it was difficult to pronounce on the question of likely audiences. Although capacity resulting from quality cannot be ignored, it is the nature of the audience and not necessarily its size, which is of relevance. This Board has, therefore, come to the conclusion that the present cabaret is directed at much wider likely audiences than sophisticated, "liberated" or avant garde audiences. The entertainment contains some striking tunes which are likely to draw wider audiences and the subject matter, in any case on the face of it, does not contain material of an esoteric nature. It is straightforward cabaret satirizing in no indefinite terms the philosophies of a now deceased prime minister of the Republic of South Africa. Although the likely (adult) audiences would obviously not be the same as that of Pieter Toerien's comedies *Who Goes Bare?* (40/83) and *Funny Peculiar* (158/86) which were both adjudicated upon by this Board, it would obviously draw much wider likely audiences than Berkoff's experimental play *Decadence* (142/84) or Arrabal's *The Car Cemetery* (56/80).

The present entertainment contains a number of sexual crudities by way of dialogue or action: the opening and closing song with "If you don't want to fuck then baby fuck off", sung twice as an opening, and repeated as a chorus four times; a simulated fellatio; movements obviously associated with sex movements; masturbatory movements on degree scrolls held in the position of penises; when "Dr Verwoerd" is asked what "Mrs Verwoerd" wore on their wedding night he says "She wore this pantie thing" (at this stage one actor pokes his finger through a slit in a pair of panties); "Mrs Verwoerd" then says "Make me the happiest woman in South Africa, fuck me up my homeland, put your Union Building up my Government Avenue . . . "; later on "Mrs Verwoerd" says "I always wanted to fuck a future Prime Minister . . . Oh, if I could fuck a Prime Minister every day, I'll probably live forever."' Later on there is mention of "they had to share shit", a "wholewheat fart" and "fuck the Commonwealth". The opening song is also sung in conclusion.

From the above it must not be concluded that these instances are all placed together, although most of the instances mentioned occur in the first twenty minutes or so. The play has various other songs: most of them quite entertaining but none of them morally pernicious. There is, furthermore, some reference in the dialogue to Jews, the

Broederbond, the Reddingsdaadbond and Racheltjie de Beer (a girl famous for losing her own life to save her younger brother from freezing). One could say that the "sex" scenes and dialogue referred to above do not take up more than eight to ten minutes. The Board is, however, of the view that they form substantial ingredients of the play. Without them, the play would consist of a number of songs loosely strung together by the "Verwoerd" story, and have a substantially different content. If the songs and scenes are therefore found to be indecent and/or offensive, the play will be undesirable as a whole.

The Board is of the view that except for "they had to share shit", "wholewheat fart" and "fuck the Commonwealth" which can be regarded as vulgar in the light of an age restriction of 2–18, the other "sex" scenes and dialogue are all indecent or offensive to public morals. The opening song is indecent or offensive for its loud and repetitive use of the word "fuck" in its primary and secondary meaning. Counsel's argument that the song indicates the uncompromising attitude of Dr Verwoerd, is overshadowed by this loud and debasing song. Many would find it funny, some would tolerate it, but a substantial number of the members of a likely audience are likely to find it disgusting, and therefore "offensive", to hear this song as part of a public entertainment. In this respect, of course, the reactions of prudes or libertines are not taken into consideration. The same result would be reached when applying the test of the normal, well-balanced viewer. He is likely to find it more than annoying and in fact disgusting in the extreme, in spite of his having taken into consideration that the word "fuck" has gained more common usage in South Africa and that the tune is quite entertaining. He would be outraged by the crude content and the callousness and defiance with which this song is sung. Applying the same tests the same conclusion would be reached in regard to the simulated fellatio, sex movements, poking finger through the panties as well as the masturbatory movements. It is taken into consideration that the theatre of the grotesque means to shock, but the questionable content and callousness and defiance with which these actions are performed in a poorly constructed cabaret and their questionable functionality, would result in disgust and outrage, according to the tests mentioned above. The dialogue in which "Mrs Verwoerd" says that she always "wanted to fuck a future Prime Minister" is shameless in the extreme, not well-integrated into the story-line, and debasing of woman's feelings of privacy in regard to sex. This is offensive. Although the word "fuck" has become of more common usage, its use in public, and on the public stage, remains controversial. This is especially so when used in its primary sense. This dialogue also seems to be without sufficient significance insofar as the story-line is concerned. It is there to shock and although shock is a typical feature of the kind of show, shock has the risk of going too far and becoming offensive.

It is of interest to note that McEwan J in *S v F* 1972 (2) SA 1 (T) found certain movements with a microphone, by which a penis was simulated together with a crude song to amount to public indecency, in spite of the nature of the audience which was a more limited ("Top of the Town") restaurant audience. The present case must, naturally, be decided on its own facts and in the light of prevailing standards. The Board, however, feels that in spite of greater permissiveness in contemporary society, the acts performed, the dialogue specified and the song (repeated) go beyond what is likely to be tolerated, according to the tests mentioned above.

V SECTION 47 (2) (B)

A further problem is created by material which relates to the religious convictions or feelings of the Christian section of the population. It is not necessary to deal with the term "offensiveness" as it is dealt with fully in *Buddy Buddy* (20/86).

Quite early in the play there is an inoffensive, though irritating, reference to things you read in the Bible not necessarily being "so". More problematic is a part of the dialogue where "Dr Verwoerd" says "Jesus, you're in my way, get out of it" and later "God, aikôna, You're in my chair — get out of it." This is followed by a song "Jesus help me find my proper place . . ." Now in themselves these words are quite understandable as part of the presentation which *inter alia* intends to typify Dr Verwoerd as someone striving to usurp God's powers in the political field. This amounts to typical political invective, although many would regard it as in particularly bad taste. But it is the tone in which this invective is expressed that is truly repugnant. The "Jesus" in the "Jesus help me" song is accentuated and repeated several times and within the context of the play with its sexual crudities and innuendos, this is more than irritating and in fact offensive. One realises that it cannot be expected of actors in such a cabaret to sing in the tones of a chanting priest, but nevertheless it was thought that the bounds of tolerance were transgressed. The tone in which the lines are sung are slurred in a manner reminiscent of a drunk. The overly insolent tone of the "God aikôna" and "Jesus step aside" dialogue is also offensive. The juxtaposition of this dialogue with the rest of the play which has sexual crudity as an important ingredient, is particularly aggravating. When "Dr Verwoerd" says "I was studying to become God" this may be irritating to some, but it is not offensive.

This Board is of the view that this cabaret or any part of it cannot be found to be undesirable in terms of section 47 (2) (c) of the Act. As indicated in this Board's judgment in *Head Office* (71/86) and in various previous judgments starting from *Total Freedom* (60/78), individuals, even if they are leaders, are not protected by the Publications Act. If, of course, a leader is assimilated to a section of the population to such an extent that it is the section which is ridiculed or brought into contempt through the leader, the paragraph would apply. This Board is unconvinced that this is the case in the present matter.

The Board considered the imposition of a place restriction to solve the problems, but decided that as this entertainment is a cabaret which can be performed also for wider, popular audiences, a place restriction is not apposite. Such a limitation will, in any case, not solve the problem.

The appeal is dismissed and the decision of the Committee that the public entertainment is undesirable in terms of section 47 (2) (a) and (b) of the Publications Act is confirmed. The finding that it is undesirable in terms of section 47 (2) (c) is set aside.

This decision on paragraphs (a) and (b) was taken by a majority of the members. The decision on paragraph (c) was unanimous.

JCW van Rooyen
CHAIRMAN: PUBLICATIONS APPEAL BOARD

Appendix II

WEEKLY MAIL REPORTS ON *FAMOUS DEAD MAN* AND *SUNRISE CITY.*

VERWOERD SATIRE ACTORS IN HIDING

ACTORS Robert Colman and Matthew Krouse, whose satirical cabaret *Famous Dead Man* was banned this week by the personal intervention of a cabinet minister, have "disappeared", leading to fears for their safety.

The blackly comical revue, which has apartheid-mastermind Hendrik Verwoerd telling God to "get out of my chair", moved his daughter Anna Boshoff (who hasn't seen the show) to warn that she would "speak to the right people" about it.

Since then, there have been several threatening phone calls to the Black Sun in Berea, where the show has already run for eight weeks, and a visit from three plainclothes police to warn the proprietor, George Milaris, that if the show — which was due to be performed again last night — went on, Krouse, Colman and Milaris would be arrested and the audience dispersed.

The police said they were acting on instructions from the Publications Control Committee, which declared *Famous Dead Man* "undesirable" at an urgent meeting convened on Tuesday, at the request of Stoffel Botha, Minister of Home Affairs. Neither members of the committee nor Botha have seen the revue.

Despite this, the committee yesterday released reasons for the banning, saying that although the Publications Act acknowledged it "does not protect . . . political figures against criticism" it found that, in this instance, "Dr Verwoerd (had been) chosen as a symbol of a large section of the Republic in an attempt to insult and degrade them." The committee also found that the "scenes of gratuitous sex . . . would exceed the tolerance of the average balanced person".

However, in his condemnation, Stoffel Botha thought the cabaret far more personal than symbolic. Describing *Famous Dead Man* as "dubious and despicable", he said it discredited a national leader and threatened entertainers with similar intent would find "their efforts time and time again declared undesirable in terms of the Publications Act".

Meanwhile, no-one has seen Krouse or Colman since Tuesday and Milaris says he is very worried about them in the light of the threats he received.

Weekly Mail, 3rd October 1986.

WHERE THERE IS NOISE AND SMOKE . . .

"AS hulle nie eers kultuur kan handel nie, wat kan hulle handel?" Poet Ryk

Hattingh stormed as he left the Oxford Hotel in disgust last Friday night. Others followed. Some stayed to finish their drinks. His was the only expression of outrage. For the rest the mood was polite, disappointed, resigned.

"Hulle" had stopped the End Conscription Campaign's Noise and Smoke Cabaret at the Oxford Hotel. The writing was already on the wall: ANC, UDF, "Zodac" and stars of David had been graffitied on to the hotel the night before the cabaret's opening.

ECC had guaranteed security to a management made nervous by an anonymous and threatening telephone call earlier that day . . . and apologetic frisking (twice) made sure no bombs, guns nor illicit alcohol were taken inside.

And so the show went on. No teargas. No bomb scare. Just cutting cabaret, satirising the South African condition in mime, poetry and song.

There was no interval. And as the audience was drawn into the evening, the reason was announced: the show would be immediately cancelled due to fears for the "clientele's" safety. And that, it seemed, was that.

So there was some quiet milling about and the audience gradually thinned out. Some bad taste jokes, some black humour. Somebody told the stragglers, determined to squeeze something out of the evening; that the police were outside.

Drinks were finished with controlled-haste when tension cracked the waiters' patience. "*Please* go now, we want to close."

At the door a policeman in plain clothes stopped a photographer. "Just let me take your camera." "Why should I give it to you?" "Because I want it." "Show me your card." The official produced the card.

Retreat. He was one, we were 10. But he had the Emergency regulations. An observer stepped forward; "You know the law, you have to say under what section of the regulations . . ."

"It's the Emergency regulations."

Stalemate; He was cautious of the small group. The photographer was insistent. The group was watching. Desperation moved and he grabbed her arm, "look just come outside".

"You just can't find a lawyer in Johannesburg on a Friday night," muttered a concert organiser.

Some uniformed police moved in. Action. The crowd watched as they ran up some stairs. "What are they doing? Why are they running?" "They're arresting one of the actors." "They've detained him." "Why?" "Defaming a cabinet minister." "Is that really against the law?" "No, it's the Emergency." "But why?" Nobody knew and everybody was guessing.

Then the police, and the friends and observers who had been huddled around the actor, Matthew Krouse, moved through the foyer towards the door.

Action. The foyer-standers followed onto the pavement, into the year's coldest night.

Clutching placards from the cabaret, a wide-eyed Krouse, his back against the wall, was ringed by the police. I'm not a politician, he protested. He just went up there and made a few jokes.

The crowd closed in, poking at the police with any piece of law they could recall. They wanted to take him to Parkview police station. But they wouldn't say why. We didn't like this idea. Attack. We wanted to know why.

They just wanted to ask him a few questions. "Ask them here." They wouldn't because of all these people around.

Stalemate. The concerned observers moved back while the police asked their questions of Krouse. There was still no lawyer.

"I don't know. Must I go to the police station?" an exasperated Krouse yelled. "No, Matthew, no." his self-styled protectors shouted back.

Suddenly Krouse picked up his placards and walked towards the crowd. A moment's hesitation, and then Krouse asked for a lift home, quickly. And the police looked at the crowd and the crowd looked at the police.

Hulle kan dit nie handel nie.

• The ECC's Noise and Smoke cabaret will be performed tonight at the Box Theatre at Wits University at 9pm.

Weekly Mail, 3rd, October 1986.

THE TWO WHO DARED SNIGGER AT A NATIONAL INSTITUTION

Those who share the opinion of the Minister of Home Affairs (namely, that a certain Robert Colman, together with a certain Matthew Krouse, did tastelessly and wantonly desecrate the memory of a national leader), will be appalled to hear that the aforementioned duo have chosen their next target: the church. CHARLOTTE BAUER reports.

ROBERT COLMAN and Matthew Krouse are lying low in their

Braamfontein flat, holding their heads as if still cornered by a particularly nasty hangover, trying to work out what the hell happened in the last 10 days.

Two weeks ago they were shimmying about on stage in their Blues Brothers suits trashing the Verwoerdian era of South African history (as she was wrote) to the delighted, drunken approval of their cabaret audience.

Then someone noticed. It didn't take long for the word to reach the large and powerful ears of authority that a *national leader*, (however dead), was being picked on in a most inconsiderate way, considering the leader in question was no longer around to defend himself.

The traditional national consequence for those who think they can have the last laugh followed: the Verwoerd family set about protecting the name of their most famous member; Minister of Home Affairs Stoffel Botha noisily took up his cue and intervened to get the show, *Famous Dead Man*, banned quickly; and gutteral voices used public telephones to threaten the actors' lives.

Unnerved, Colman and Krouse dropped their props, hid their material and left home for a while. By the time they returned this week, it was only to hear they had lost their other job too — selling mock-tile roofs to southern suburbanites on the telephone.

"We've lost our salaries and we've been shut up," Colman said flatly. For now, yes, but the pair intends to appeal the ban as soon as they have taken legal advice.

They are still shaken by the swiftness of the turn of events, especially Krouse, whose near-arrest at the recent End Conscription Campaign concert for . . . well, still no one is quite sure what for . . . came in the same week. "We're going to try to keep out of shit; we're small fry, you know," he says in a voice that rings reality.

Colman and Krouse met a year ago during a forgettable workshop production at the Market Theatre's Rehearsal Room. Two weeks later they started writing comedies together — duologues about leadership, about sex-changes subjectively written, they say, based on their "vast experience of Johannesburg's *demi-monde*" and about suits ("We are very pissed off with suits; we're inundated with suits"). They are currently working on a play about cassocks (and the church), and are still toying with the idea of "doing" all South Africa's prime ministers in a sort of definitive journey through this country's history.

Like Gilbert and George or Laurel and Hardy, Colman and Krouse have discovered a bent for Siamese-twin style, alter-egoish buffoonery at which they are startlingly good.

The sources they draw on are broad: Krouse's work in a military hospital during his national service; Colman's fill-in job as a waiter ("If it's in the north and can guarantee big tips, I'm there in my little bow tie dusting old ladies' laps off"), Krouse's work with the Weekend Theatre group ("We've put on at least 20 plays in the flat downstairs") and historical textbooks.

Much of the research for *Famous Dead Man* came directly from one particular Afrikaans textbook on the role of Hendrik Verwoerd in South African politics. They even opened and ended their show in the same manner as the book — with his assassination.

"We act it and make up the jokes," Colman says, "but we didn't write the history." Colman and Krouse are pleasantly uncomplex in their defence of the show. "We stand by our product," says Krouse, adding that the scrutiny of leadership and self-glorification will never be understood by society's "elders" who have mythologised certain elements of history beyond even the flimsiest truth. "What they don't understand is that, for the youth, there is nothing that is sacred."

Although at first they seem to take refuge in the "I'm just an actor" cosy cushion of defence, what Colman and Krouse mean by this is more subtle.

"No, we're not trying to cop out of the debacle by saying that-of course we're not 'just actors', just as theatre in this country is not 'just theatre' anymore. We recognise the thinning lines between acting and politics here," Colman says, "but we also recognise the clear distinction of our choice of career. We are interested in satirising political situations, but ultimately we get off on the danger of going on stage, which is quite different."

Krouse snatches up the point: "We aren't horny for the baton, we're horny for the stage. Breyten Breytenbach offered a piece of advice in his book *Confessions of an Albino Terrorist*. 'Never go to jail,' he said. Cup of tea, anyone?"

Weekly Mail, 9th, October 1986.

BOARD STALLS ON DECISION

AT the time of going to press, the Appeal Board had still not decided on the final public "desirability" of *Famous Dead Man*.

The delay in ruling would appear to relate to the extremely sticky nature of this particular case, with an interest being shown in its outcome by people in powerful political circles.

The Directorate of Publications' decision to ban the show in the first place, rests on three basic accusations: blasphemy, indecency and racism (towards Afrikaners).

These perceived components led cabinet minister Stoffel Botha to personally get the revue banned by a hastily convened censor committee and provoked Hendrik Verwoerd's daughter, Anna Boshoff, to remark that she would "speak to the right people" about it.

Weekly Mail, November 7th, 1986.

EVEN GOYA HAD TO MAKE A START

As Des Lindberg explained to a disbelieving panel at the appeal against the banning of the *'Famous Dead Man'* cabaret, 'even Goya had to start somewhere'.
CHARLOTTE BAUER reports

"ARE you, if you'll excuse the pun, Mr Uys, prepared to adapt or die for your country?" the senior counsel asked.

' Oh yes," replied Pieter-Dirk Uys, whose vast experience with both satire and censoring committees made him the obvious choice as chief witness in the appeal against the banning of the cabaret show *Famous Dead Man*.

"You are a good patriot, then?" "Yes."

The sort of person Louis Visser, SC, saw in the eye of his mind when he said "good patriot" was probably not the same citizen Uys envisioned when he answered "Yes". Anyway, quite what Uys' feelings about his country had to do with this appeal remained murky (although, if admitting dislike of the way things are run in South Africa equals Marx-worship, this is generally a useful thing to be able to prove).

The cross-examination continued in this bizarre manner for some minutes.

Matthew Krouse and Robert Colman, the newly crowned *enfants terribles* of the theatrical fringe by virtue of the satirical revue they wrote and performed about apartheid's structural engineer, Hendrik Verwoerd, had come to Pretoria to hear the Appeal Board pronounce on whether their show would live or die.

Dressed in the elderly, slightly shiny suits they had worn for a performance the night before and dainty Fifties sunglasses, Krouse and Colman were like "spot-the-mistake" in the quiver of Pierre Cardin shirts and *kultuur*.

Bannings come and go, as do the appeals against them, but this one was special in two ways: firstly, because a cabinet minister had intervened to get *Famous Dead Man* declared "undesirable", and secondly, because the show dealt with a national figure whose still powerful surviving kin had made their displeasure very clear to some very right people.

The politics of this appeal created a tangible tension. And when Hendrik Verwoerd's daughter walked into the room, even Jan van Rooyen, the impeccably sophisticated chairman of the Appeal Board, appeared to pale a little. If the ghost of Verwoerd himself had burst through the wall rattling chains and roaring the impact could not have been more unnerving. You could tell that no one had expected her — or the daughter who accompanied her and who spent most of her energy beaming hard stares at Colman and Krouse.

Perhaps, someone pointed out consolingly, it would have been even rougher on everyone's nerves had the Tsafendas family arrived.

Well, Hendrik Verwoerd's daughter and granddaughter hadn't seen the allegedly scurrilous revue, but they were about to hear it.

Louis Visser, acting on behalf of the Publications Directorate, got down to the gritty by describing an early scene from *Famous Dead Man*: Holland, 1902, Hendrik Verwoerd's mother tries to persuade his father to emigrate to South Africa while engaging him in oral sex. "Were you, Mr Uys, shocked by that scene?" "No," Uys replied, "because it wasn't really about sex." This threw Visser, who exploded "What on earth else could it have meant?" Pieter-Dirk Uys held his palms upwards in a gesture of reasonableness. "She could have been biting a button off his jacket."

Entertainer Des Lindberg, the other witness for the appellants, at least agreed with Visser that what Mr and Mrs Verwoerd senior were doing was fellatio, and interpreted the scene as an "absurd parody of woman's desire to manipulate man".

Lindberg described *Famous Dead Man* as typifying the theatre of the grotesque, "a valid and broad drawing of cartoon theatre."

"We are living in a very warped society and this well-wrought production has a definite social role to play in a country that needs an alternative slant or viewpoint on its society." Lindberg used artists to exemplify his point: "Goya made a valuable contribution when he stopped painting flattering pictures of his proud and powerful subjects and — started showing the pimples on their faces. Likewise Francis Bacon didn't paint to please Francois Oberholzer, he painted to please an art public who would understand and enjoy it."

"Are you comparing," one of the Appeal Board members interjected disbelievingly, "these two (a contemptuous wave in the direction of Colman and Krouse) to *Goya*"?

Lindberg rephrased the point of his point but couldn't resist adding for the indignant member's benefit, "Even Goya had to start somewhere, sir."

Pieter-Dirk Uys emphasised the role of satire as a mirror held up to society as not only a reflection of it, but also as an important outlet for anxiety and a constructive watershed for anger. "Over the years I've had quite a few historical figures in my repertoire. *Famous Dead Man* was a surprisingly well-researched production and there was a tremendous amount that I recognised that helped me lay bare some of the ghosts of Dr Verwoerd."

Counsel for the appellants, Edwin Cameron, continued this theme in his argument, comparing this form of cabaret to that which took place in Berlin just prior to the Second World War, "a form of important social comment when no other was any longer available". 'The historical legacy of white and black South Africans is rooted in a government who constantly refers back to its chief architect of apartheid. His compelling impact on this country may be painful, but it cannot be avoided," Cameron submitted. "Current political debate still centres on what he said and did."

He explained the opening song, which Visser had earlier dismissed as having absolutely no relevance to this theme, as being a depiction of Verwoerd's "notorious intransigence". The refrain, *If you don't want to f . . . , then baby, f . . . off*, reflected Verwoerd's attitude of "if you don't want to do it on my terms, then I don't want anything to do with you".

"Dr Verwoerd was a man of vainglory, of *hubris*, prepared to attain his aim at almost any price. This raises questions of delusion and his assassination must be seen against this background."

Cameron also inverted the accusation of blasphemy to reflect on Hendrik Verwoerd himself rather than on the actor . "When in the show Verwoerd tells God 'you are sitting in my chair', it is not Colman and Krouse who are blaspheming, but clearly the suggestion is that it is Verwoerd and the people who see him as an invincible hero who stand accused of near-blasphemy."

It was about then that Anna Boshoff and her daughter picked up their handbags and, with final glare at the gallery and a bow to Jan van Rooyen, left the room.

Weekly Mail, November 7th, 1986.

BOARD KILLS DEAD MAN

The ban on Robert Colman and Matthew Krouse's *Famous Dead Man* cabaret has been upheld by the Publications Appeal Board.

Curiously, the show's desirability was not dismissed on the strength of its satirical send-up of Dr Hendrik Verwoerd, although his role as a character in *Famous Dead Man* was really what ruffled the wrath of everyone from his daughter to a cabinet minister in the first place.

No, in the end, the Appeal Board decided that the show was both "obscene" and "blasphemous" but did not "bring into ridicule or contempt any section of the Republic".

Chairman of the board, Prof Kobus van Rooyen said in his lengthy judgement that the board remained "unconvinced" that Verwoerd was representative of any section of the population.

Weekly Mail, 21st November 1986.

SUNRISE SAVES IT ALL FOR THE CENSORS

Sunrise City was banned on grounds of obscenity. It gained a kind of reprieve when the appeal board decided to use the Wednesday night performance as an appeal hearing. IVOR POWELL reports

AROUND 9pm there is a bustling in the Warehouse doorway and a perfect cross-section of officialdom comes sloping in — some it later turns out from the appeal board, others from the Publications Control Board scrum.

There's a brown suited one who looks like a kind of see-through Danie Craven and carries a tweedy fisherman's hat; there are a couple of well-preserved female *nuwe*-Afrikaner academic types whose fluffy perms all but hide the puritanical pinch of their mothers' faces in the set of their lips: there's the bearded polo-necked intellectual; a few dark suits which may or may not have people inside them . . .

The audience, there to see *Sunrise City*, breaks into spontaneous hoots and clapping which accompany the guardians of our morals to their reserved seating.

Actually this treatment was more than a little unfair. The appeal board, under JCR van Rooyen, is a relatively *verligte* body. It is made up of putative experts in the relevant field and should not be confused with the Publications Control Board itself, which is an arm of the Civil service, made up of . . . well, one wonders exactly what their qualifications are.

On May 4 the Market Theatre management received a communication from the Publications Control Board in Cape Town banning the City Theatre and Dance Company's (CTDC) production of *Sunrise City*.

After an urgent representation to the appeal board of the PCB in Pretoria it was decided that *Sunrise City* would be performed on Wednesday night after all; a delegation from the Appeal Board would use the performance as an appeal hearing.

Sunrise City is not a good play. It was an ambitious project to stage Brecht and Weill's *Mahagonny* in the first place. Then the rights were withdrawn — for purely technical reasons, the executors of Kurt Weill's estate insisting, among other things, on a full symphony orchestra. Instead of abandoning the project, the CIDC decided to write the play from scratch in a matter of a few weeks.

It shows. Apart from being underwritten, under-directed and under-rehearsed, the play is structurally creaky to the point of falling right over. Among other things it attempts a kind of democratised transposition of Brecht's German workers into the South African context. They come out the mangle as three Boksburg *Joller* types and two black proto-Cosatu unionists — all big chinas, you understand . . .

But tonight a curious thing starts to happen. The presence of the censors has somehow given a focus to the previously nearly dormant satire and moralism. It has forced an interpretation where before, in earlier performances, the actors had been tentative and ambivalent, nervous to the point of drawing the wrong kind of attention to it, about the nudity, the obscenity, the provocation.

Tonight the play becomes intensely moral and the nudity slots with naturalness into an expression of anger and horror at the obscenities the play is condemning, the provocation works because its targets are in the actors' sights as it were.

By the end of the performance, the outcome is more or less foregone. The play may continue its run — with a two to 18 age restriction, pending judgement.

"When you first get one of these things," says Pretorius, referring to the banning order, "You think its a joke. Things have got to the point in this country where it's quite a glamorous thing to get banned. But then you start to think about the logistics . . . *Sunrise City* cost us R35 000 . . . and then it doesn't seem so glamorous any more."

But why did *Sunrise City* receive those banning orders in the first place? As actor Matthew Krouse, veteran of no less than three banning orders in the past year puts it:

"Bare breasts are no longer such a very great delicacy. I don't think it's that. It's just the climate in this country doesn't permit any radical enquiry."

Very true. A few weeks ago Minister Stoffel Botha made a public statement to the effect that a tougher line was going to be taken on subversion in the arts.

But a tougher line with a difference. For the moment at least, the *Sarafinas* and the *District Sixes* are relatively safe. Things have gone too far already for them to be in a position to ban these mega-productions without precipitating an international outcry — and ending up with some very old and smelly egg all over their faces. Anyway the government is seriously lacking in reformist credibility and those productions boost their image as just and open people in the world at large.

But productions like *Sunrise City* are far from safe. At the same time as the government wants to push its image as being reformist, it also wants to appease an increasingly rampant rightwing. What better way to demonstrate that you have not strayed from the *laager* than to uphold a few stern Calvinist values in public?

• At an Appeal Board hearing in Pretoria Wednesday 11th May, Professor van Rooyen, assisted by eight members of his board, decided to reserve judgement yet further. The play may continue its run subject to a 2–18 age restriction, once again pending final judgement.

Weekly Mail, 20th May 1988.

NOTES ON CONTRIBUTORS

Antony Akerman, author of *Somewhere on the Border*, spent seventeen years in exile mostly in Amsterdam. Now returned to South Africa, he recently directed *Substance of Fire* by Jon Robin Baitz at the Alexandra Theatre in Johannesburg for Pact. In 1993, he won the South African Council for Performing Arts Councils (Sacpac) prize for his play about Roy Campbell, *Dark Outsider*.

Christopher Balme, a New Zealander, taught at the University of Würzburg and has recently completed a post-doctoral dissertation on syncretic theatre at the Drama Department of the University of Munich, where he now holds a professorship.

Arnold Blumer teaches in the Department of German at the University of Stellenbosch and has worked as theatre critic for *Vrye Weekblad* and *Theater Heute*.

Brian Crow teaches in the Department of Drama and Theatre Arts at the University of Birmingham, England, and specialises in African theatre. After *Studying Drama* in 1983, he has just written *An Introduction to Postcolonial Theatre* for Cambridge University Press.

Fatima Dike was for long associated with the Space Theatre in Cape Town where her early plays, among them *The Sacrifice of Kreli* and *The First South African*, were performed. After a long period in the United States, she has now returned to Cape Town and recently created *So What's New?* at the Market Laboratory in Johannesburg. In 1994, it was performed at the Nico Malan Theatre, Cape Town.

Mark Fleishman, while still a student at University of Cape Town, created *The Comfortable Concentration Camp* for the Fringe at the 1986 Grahamstown Festival. After devising *Carnival of the Bear* with the Handspring Puppet Theatre Company, he and his wife Jenny Reznek formed a circus company to tour South Africa. Their latest collaboration is the play *The show's not over 'til the fat lady sings*.

Peter Horn, Professor of German at the University of Cape Town, is a performance poet and critic. Among his best-known works are *Voices from the Gallows Tree* (1969), *The Civil War Cantos* (1987), and *Poems 1964–1989* (1991). He founded the literary review *Ophir* in 1967.

William Kentridge, probably best-known for his charcoal drawings and short video films, began a parallel theatre career with Junction Avenue Theatre company while still a student at Wits. After *Will of a Rebel*, *The Fantastical History of a Useless Man* and *Security*, he created the decor for *Sophiatown*. In 1992 he collaborated with the Handspring Puppet Theatre Company on a multi-media adaptation of Büchner entitled *Woyzeck on the Highveld* which was invited to the World Theatre Season in Munich. His latest project is *Faust in Africa*.

Matthew Krouse is the author of several plays including *Famous Dead Man*, *Noise and Smoke*, and *Sunrise City*. Also an actor, he has recently played in Genet's *The Maids* at the Market Theatre, Johannesburg. He worked for the publishing division of COSAW for whom he edited *The Invisible Ghetto: Lesbian and Gay Writing from South Africa*.

Ramolao Makhene began his work in the theatre with Workshop '71 before joining Junction Avenue Theatre Company where he has been active in both the devising and performing of such recent productions as *Sophiatown* and *Tooth and Nail*. He was elected first chairperson of the Performing Arts Workers Equity and serves on the Joint Working Group (JWG) of the Grahamstown Festival.

Maishe Maponya teaches in the Department of Drama at the University of the Witwatersrand. A number of his plays, *The Hungry Earth, Gangsters* and *UMongikazi* were created by the Bahumutsi Theatre Group and toured overseas. He is himself a noted performer and cultural activist.

Doreen Mazibuko has worked with Junction Avenue Theatre Company and as a field worker with the Market Laboratory. She was employed by the Matla Trust to develop a theatre-in-education project related to the first democratic elections in South Africa in 1994.

Robert McLaren was the founder of Workshop '71 and edited one of the first collections of plays by black South Africans: *South African People's Plays*. He is the author of *Theatre and Cultural Struggle* and now teaches in the Drama Department of the University of Zimbabwe in Harare. He recently returned to Wits University as a visiting lecturer and produced *Samora Continua* with students there.

Zakes Mda is a well-known playwright, poet and painter. Author of *We shall sing for the Fatherland, The Hill* and *The Road* he founded the Maratholi Travelling Theatre while teaching at the National University of Lesotho. His most recent publication is a study of theatre for development entitled *When People play people*. He was a fellow at the Southern African Research Program at Yale before moving to the University of Vermont and has recently returned to South Africa.

Jerry Mofokeng graduated from Columbia University, New York, in theatre directing and management and on his return to South Africa took up a post in the Drama Department at the University of the Witwatersrand. He was appointed resident director at the Market Theatre where he directed a notable production of Fugard's *Boesman and Lena*.

Martin Orkin teaches in the English Department at the University of the Witwatersrand and among his publications are *Shakespeare against Apartheid* and *Drama and the State in South Africa*.

Malcolm Purkey teaches in the Drama Department at the University of the Witwatersrand. Well-known for his work with Junction Avenue Theatre Company both as co-director and co-author of such plays as *Marabi, Sophiatown* and *Tooth and Nail*, he has also directed plays at the Market Theatre and Wits Theatre. He spent the academic year 1992–1993 on a British Council scholarship studying television script-writing at the London Film School in the United Kingdom.

Barney Simon has been artistic director of the Market Theatre since its foundation. Author of short stories and film scripts he is best known for his workshopped productions such as *Black Dog, Cincinnati, Born in the RSA* and *Starbrites*. He collaborated with Percy Mtwa and Mbongeni Ngema on *Woza Albert!* and more recently has been instrumental in setting up the Market Laboratory.

Ari Sitas teaches in the Sociology Department at the University of Natal in Durban. He was a co-founder of Junction Avenue Theatre Company and has been deeply involved in the development of workers' theatre in Natal. He also published a collection of poetry entitled *Tropical Scars* and a novel, *William Zungu: A Christmas Story*.

Carol Steinberg teaches in the Drama Department at the University of the Witwatersrand. She is working on a doctorate on the rôle of the Performing Arts Councils in South Africa and prepared PAWE's report to the ANC on this subject.

INDEX OF PROPER NAMES

INDEX OF TITLES

(Unless otherwise indicated, titles are those of plays.)

SUBJECT INDEX

Other titles in the Contemporary Theatre Studies series:

Volume 11
Edward Bond Letters: Volume II
Selected and edited by Ian Stuart

Volume 12
Theatre and Change in South Africa
Edited by Geoffrey V. Davis and Anne Fuchs

Volume 13
Anthropocosmic Theatre
Nicolás Núñez, translated by Ronan Fitzsimons and edited, with a foreword, by Deborah Middleton

Volume 14
Edward Bond Letters: Volume III
Selected and edited by Ian Stuart

Volume 15
Pulp and Other Plays by Tasha Fairbanks
Edited by Gabriele Griffin and Elaine Aston